# MOSHE DAYAN

# Moshe Dayan

## *Israel's Controversial Hero*

——◆◂◆▸◆——

MORDECHAI BAR-ON

Yale
UNIVERSITY
PRESS

New Haven and London

Yale University Press books may be purchased in quantity for educational, business, or promotional use. For information, please e-mail sales.press@yale.edu (U.S. office) or sales@yaleup.co.uk (U.K. office).

Set in Janson Oldstyle type by Tseng Information Systems, Inc.

Printed in the United States of America.

*Library of Congress Cataloging-in-Publication Data*
Bar-On, Mordechai, 1928–
Moshe Dayan : Israel's controversial hero / Mordechai Bar-On. — 1st ed.
p. cm.
Includes bibliographical references and index.
ISBN 978-0-300-14941-8 (alk. paper)
1. Dayan, Mosheh, 1931–1979. 2. Generals—Israel—Biography. 3. Statesmen—Israel—Biography. 4. Arab-Israeli conflict—Biography. I. Title.
DS126.6.D3B37 2012
956.9405092—dc23
[B]
2012000595

A catalogue record for this book is available from the British Library.

This paper meets the requirements of ANSI/NISO Z39.48-1992 (Permanence of Paper).

10 9 8 7 6 5 4 3 2 1

Frontispiece: Moshe Dayan as minister of agriculture participating in a ceremonial planting of trees. Courtesy Yad Ben-Zvi, Jerusalem.

# CONTENTS

THE STORY OF MOSHE DAYAN is the story of the State of Israel.

His life is best understood within the context of four crucial periods during which Israel evolved from an aspiration to an accomplishment. Under the British Mandate of Palestine (1922–48), Dayan worked in Nahalal, a cooperative agricultural village, contributing to the Zionist efforts to establish a productive Jewish community in Palestine comprised of immigrants from around the globe. During these years, while Jews were establishing communities and building infrastructure, opposition from Arabs who feared that the Zionist enterprise threatened their national existence grew. From an early age, Dayan actively battled this opposition and proved himself a fearless fighter. In 1948, the State of Israel was born in a war against the Arabs of Palestine and surrounding states. At the war's conclusion, Jerusalem was divided between Israel and Jordan. Dayan was appointed commander of the Jewish-controlled section of Jerusalem.

During the second pivotal period, from 1948 through 1967, the State of Israel created the economic and communal infrastructure necessary to absorb millions of Jewish immigrants, mainly from Europe and the Arab world. Dayan held key government and security positions throughout these formative years. The Arab states, unwilling to accept their defeat in 1948, constantly threatened war. Dayan, as chief of General Staff of the Israel Defense Forces (IDF), commanded military missions that foiled the Arabs' attempts to weaken or destroy Israel. On the eve of the Six Day War in 1967, Prime Minister Levi Eshkol appointed Dayan minister of defense, and he led Israel to a sweeping victory over the armies of Egypt, Jordan, and Syria. The war ended with Israel's conquest of land that amounted to several times the country's original size, including the Sinai Peninsula, Jordanian territory west of the Jordan River, and the Golan Heights.

From 1967 to 1974, as minister of defense, Dayan was in charge of protecting the new borders and governing the many Palestinians within them. He tried to frustrate guerrilla strikes by Egyptian, Syrian, and Palestinian forces while facilitating prosperity for the Palestinian people in the territories under Israeli rule. He failed in both attempts. The Palestinian Liberation Organization (PLO), founded in 1964 to advocate for an "armed struggle" to liberate Palestine, grew, and many quickly recognized it as the representative body of Palestinian national aspirations. During these violent years, the Yom Kippur War erupted in 1973; despite dramatic operations by Israeli forces, the war ended with Egypt dislodging the IDF from the banks of the Suez Canal. Among the many casualties of that war, Golda Meir's government dissolved and Dayan's career as defense minister ended.

Dayan devoted the last years of his life to forging a peace agreement with Egypt, the largest and most important Arab state. As Israel's foreign minister, he played a major role in its accomplishment. His conception of solving the conflict with the Palestinians, however, remained unchanged: he believed that Israel should accord the Palestinians broad autonomy but retain control of the West Bank and the Gaza Strip, thus denying them self-determination there. To his dying day, he opposed recognizing national rights for Palestinians, and in this respect he reached the end of his life disappointed and frustrated.

Moshe Dayan is etched in Israel's national memory as the man who reconstructed the Israel Defense Forces in the 1950s and honed it into an efficient fighting unit. He led the IDF to victory in the 1956 Sinai campaign and helped guide the army's stunning successes in the Six Day War. But he is also widely remembered as the minister who shirked responsibility for the fiasco of the Yom Kippur War, a claim that continues to trail him, tainting even the memory of his central role in Israel's peace treaty with Egypt.

Despite common perceptions, Dayan was not the sabra par excellence, but a complex personality with an inquisitive mind, a man who sought solitude and reflection in order to conceive practical solutions to intricate problems. His Achilles' heel was his insensitivity to historical undercurrents and his inability to see the larger picture, shortcomings that ultimately led to his political and military decline.

Moshe Dayan's life story has attracted many biographers. In addition to his two autobiographies, his parents; his first wife, Ruth; his daughter, Yaël; his secretary Neora Matalon-Barnoach; and others who worked at his side all illuminated chapters of his life. The historian Shabtai Teveth wrote an excellent biography (published in 1971), but it covers Dayan's life only up to the beginning of his tenure as minister of defense after the end of the Six Day War.

For this book, I made ample use of Teveth's well-researched study; I have also taken advantage of the thousands of documents available on Dayan, especially those archived by the IDF, the State of Israel, and the press, which gave him broad coverage. Having served as his bureau chief in the Sinai campaign in 1956–57, I, like so many, was captivated by his charm and, like only a few, was privileged to know him personally. I spent many hours in his company, followed him into battle, and attended all his meetings with Prime Minister David Ben-Gurion. I also acted as the secretary of the top-secret meetings held in Paris in preparation for the Suez War and wrote the only existing records of them. In the 1970s, however, our political paths diverged, and both my fascination with and my criticism of Dayan's course after the Six Day War find expression in this book.

## ACKNOWLEDGMENTS

MANY PEOPLE HELPED in the preparation of this book, and I am grateful to them all: Professor Moti Golani read the manuscript and made valuable comments. Aaron Kaplowitz's editorial insight was much appreciated. Simcha Nir and my wife, Erela, helped edit it. Yael Dinovitch, secretary of the Ben-Zvi Institute, patiently helped me unravel the mysteries of the Internet. Evelyn Abel helped with the English. I especially thank Neora Matalon-Barnoach, who placed at my disposal the pre-publication manuscript of her book *Makom Tov BaTzad* (A Good Spot on the Side) and enlightened me about various episodes in which she had been involved. I would like to express my appreciation to General Shlomo Gazit, who worked with Dayan for many years, and to Ruth and Rachel Dayan, his first and second wives, who were good enough to shed light on lesser-known aspects of his personal life. Other people who kindly provided testimony, and the sources I used, are cited in the notes. The appraisals and criticism throughout the book are entirely my own.

Special thanks go to Professor Anita Shapira, who persuaded me to write the book and warmly followed its development from start to end, and to Dr. Zvi Zameret, director of the Ben-Zvi Institute, which in recent years has been my academic sanctum for this and other works.

# I

## Wild Grass: Childhood and Teens

THE SIGHT OF A BAREBACK MULE trudging into the farmyard on November 22, 1913, filled the Deganya residents with
foreboding. Only hours before, a member of the community,
Moshe Barsky, had set out on the mule to fetch medicine for his
friend Shmuel Dayan. A tiny, four-year-old *kevutza* — an early
collective settlement that was more intimate than a kibbutz —
Deganya was situated where the Sea of Galilee spills into the
Jordan River, a few miles upriver from Barsky's destination.
As the young man's absence continued into nightfall, a small
search party was dispatched. The group came upon Moshe
Barsky's mangled body near the river before dawn, the apparent victim of brigands coveting his money and his mule. But as
his friends well knew, Barsky was not merely a robbery victim;
he was a casualty of the growing Arab hostility to the Zionist
homeland that he and his fellow pioneers were developing in
the midst of the Arab community in Palestine.[1]

A year and a half later, on May 20, 1915, when Shmuel and Devorah Dayan welcomed their firstborn into the world, they had no doubt what to call the child: Moshe, after Barsky, Shmuel's serious, straightforward, and dependable friend.

Shmuel Dayan was born in 1890 in a small town near the Ukrainian capital of Kiev to a poor but devout family. Influenced by peripatetic Zionist propagandists, he sailed from Odessa to Palestine in early 1908 with his brother and sister. When their boat docked at the port city of Jaffa, they were greeted with "cries and commotion; a strange, alien Arabic; donkeys and camels, cheerless lanes, women with covered faces, and a stench rising from it all."[2]

Initially, Shmuel roamed the *moshavot*, farming colonies built at the end of the nineteenth century by the first wave of Zionist immigrants. He knew the language of worship from his Jewish upbringing and could soon speak the vernacular Hebrew adopted by Palestine's Jews. In 1910, he joined a commune establishing its own farming village, which members named Deganya for the grain — *dagan* in Hebrew — they hoped to grow. Though founded as a kevutza, Deganya is considered the first kibbutz in Palestine. "The transition from poor, decadent town life in eastern Europe to a life of physical labor practiced by Hebrew-speaking farmhands creating a new culture and new way of life was a real revolution," Moshe Dayan wrote about this period in his father's life.[3]

Devorah Dayan was also born in Ukraine, in a small village along the Dnieper River where the only Jews were her Russian-speaking family. At the university in Kiev, she discovered the great Russian literature and revolutionary ideals of the generation. "She loved her country, Russia, with all her soul, breathed the [Russian] language and agonized over the plight of Russia's poor,"[4] Moshe wrote of his mother's early years. She returned to her Jewish roots only after encountering antisemitism as a twenty-one-year-old volunteer nurse in the Balkan War. "My life was founded on a mistake," she wrote. "Those to whom I wished to devote my energies were not my people. . . . I had to start all over again."[5] In January 1913, she, too, sailed for Palestine, carrying a letter of introduction to a member of the Deganya community—her destination.

Her welcome was hardly warm. "She was met with skepticism and suspicion . . . stemming from an affluent family, a university graduate with budding literary ambitions," Moshe wrote. "What could she want with farmwork in the Jordan Valley?" Devorah remained torn: "Mother left the banks of the Dnieper but not the cultural lode. The beauty of Tolstoy's work, the warmth of Chekhov's writings, Pushkin's brilliant verses, Gogol's gentle wisdom . . . were stamped on her soul. Her attachment to them impeded her fitting in with Deganya's members, jealous fanatics of Hebrew culture. Here, too, in her early days, she felt like an outsider."[6]

But Shmuel Dayan fit right in. He was a hardworking laborer and self-proclaimed ideologist. He could wield a plow steadily and ride a horse with weapon in hand—the valued skills of the pioneer. He would also engage in passionate discourses on the future of Zionism and the path to Jewish settlement. The members of the small Deganya kevutza soon found themselves at loggerheads. Shmuel contended that pioneers should develop new core groups to form more agricultural settlements, whereas most members felt it was time to settle down and build their own homes. Communal life exposed another ideological rift. The kevutza founders preached collectivism and equal ownership, provisions for basic and social necessities, and shared childrearing responsibilities. The nuclear family was secondary. Although Shmuel and his group agreed with the founders on shared ownership of land and other means of production, they felt that the community had to be rooted in the family and that each family had the right to develop its farm to its choosing and according to its ability; marketing and costly equipment beyond the individual family's means would be shared expenses. They proposed the idea of a *moshav ovdim*—a cooperative workers' settlement—which allowed more freedom for private life and personal initiative.

The eye that Moshe Dayan would lose in battle years later was nearly lost in childhood to a severe case of trachoma, rife among the Arab peasants. To ward off blindness, he and his mother visited clinics and hospitals from Tiberias to Jaffa. Finally, in the summer of 1918 (the year the British seized the country from the Ottoman Turks), a Jerusalem eye specialist succeeded in improving his condition.

He would remember his early years in Deganya with the acerbity of a sickly child. "Clouds of dust filled my eyes and made it hard to breathe. . . . The . . . struggle . . . from morning against heat, thirst, and unsavory water; in the afternoon, a hot, dry, stifling wind; and the nights—hot and sweaty, dust, mosquitoes, flies, carrying disease for man and beast."[7] He had far sweeter memories of Tsemah, a small Arab town on the Sea of Galilee's southern littoral, which he often visited with his father. Tsemah had a train station and a bustling market, Arab farmers and peddlers going about their business. And yet one of his earliest memories related to the growing Arab-Jewish tensions following World War I.

In the Jordan Valley, Arabs massed to attack the British military base at Tsemah, as well as a nearby Jewish settlement. Shmuel had already moved his family to a new kevutza, a mile south of Deganya, where he was in charge of security. Known as Deganya Bet, the settlement was built around a large wooden shack and collection of tents. Without fortifications, it was an easy target, and the women and children were evacuated to Deganya, where they took refuge behind the fenced perimeter. When the assault began, Shmuel realized that the hundreds of Arab attackers would easily overrun the few men in his charge, and he decided to retreat. He torched the main shack, and five-year-old Moshe watched from Deganya as the flames dazzled in the night sky. The rising inferno ignited the boy's awareness of the violent expressions Arab nationalism could take, a stark contrast to his perception of the peaceful Arab vendors making a living at Tsemah's market. The dichotomy between these two scenes spawned Dayan's acute, lifelong ambivalence toward treatment of the Palestinians.[8]

After failing to convince the bulk of Deganya's members to found new settlements, Shmuel moved his family to Deganya Bet before Moshe's sixth birthday. In the summer of 1921, he helped inaugurate Nahalal, the country's first cooperative settlement, with the family unit at its foundation. These trailblazers called their new form of settlement a *moshav*.[9] It was established on the lands of Mahloul, a small Arab village whose name, the pioneers believed, was a garbled interpretation of Nahalal, the biblical city mentioned in the book of Joshua. In his memoirs, Shmuel cited the Bible, Talmud, and writings of Josephus as if these were Jewish title deeds to the land.[10]

Nahalal's first tents were erected on a hill at the edge of Lower Galilee. These makeshift abodes were pitched on the same earth that would eventually serve a more permanent function: the Nahalal cemetery, where Devorah, Shmuel, and later Moshe would be laid to rest. The moshav was built on the plain below, about a mile to the south, on fertile soil allocated to the settlers by the Jewish National Fund, the Zionist land-purchasing agency. Before cultivating the land, the settlers first had to drain the surrounding malarial swamps. Many settlers contracted the disease, but they simply downed quinine and went on working.

Mosquitoes and renewed Arab violence temporarily drove the mothers and children to the nearby Arab city of Nazareth. There, Devorah gave birth to Aviva, and Moshe started school. Shmuel rarely visited. Though Nahalal was only an hour away, he worked long hours in the swamps and fields. On most evenings he was too exhausted to make the uphill trek. Instead, he wrote Moshe long letters, which the child was not yet able to read. They brimmed with the romantic ideology and historicism spouted by the pioneers. "Walking behind the plow this morning," he wrote, "I was aware that, for the first time, the soil was being tilled with a European plow, which made the plowing hard." Shmuel finished the letter with a flowery discourse on the history of the Jewish people in Exile, the emergence of the Zionist movement, and the Zionists' aspirations to redeem the land from the wilderness.[11]

In the spring of 1922, the violence subsided and the families returned to Nahalal and moved into shacks at the settlement's permanent site on the edge of the Jezreel Valley. In the early years moshav life was arduous. In addition to battling malaria, the settlers worked from dawn into the night, often on insufficient food. But for Moshe it was paradise, filled with rivulets, fruit gardens, lush vegetation, geese, and cattle. By the time he was ten, he could milk cows, drive mule carts to bring in the harvest, and till the vegetable garden next to the house. Soon he was also handling the mule plow while Shmuel walked behind him scattering seeds. The labor left its mark—Moshe attained the calloused hands of a veteran farmer.

While her husband and eldest son worked the land, Devorah, often ill, spent weeks in the hospital and sanatoriums. Still, she managed to give birth to her youngest son, Zohar, four years Aviva's junior. While the Dayan family grew, Shmuel had become a key figure in the burgeoning moshav movement and would travel overseas to recruit young people for Zionist settlement. The responsibility for the farm fell on Moshe, who took the chores in stride.

"I was left alone to celebrate my eleventh birthday," he wrote. "I took the cows out to the public pasture, watered the seedlings, saw to the urgent chores. I kept a diary, composed verse, and read a lot. The fact that I was alone did not bother me. I was at 'home': the plowed fields, the young plantation, the anticipation of rain, looking after the hatcheries until egg time, the night sound of crickets and frogs, and the cows in the barn."[12]

Shmuel and Devorah added a tiny room to their modest home. Hardly big enough for a bed and small desk, this became Moshe's private place, in which he grew accustomed to reading and thinking in solitude.

That same year, Meshulam Halevi, a young teacher, arrived at Nahalal. He was allotted a large tent but chose to teach the older children in a flimsy shack that shivered in the winter wind and baked in the summer sun. He called it Noah's Ark.[13] Halevi emphasized the environment and Bible studies and enriched his classroom lessons with nature walks, teaching his young pupils to recognize the flora and fauna close to home. His curriculum encouraged independent thought, and he had his students keep diaries, publish a school newspaper, and correspond with one another. Halevi's approach to education exploited Moshe's strengths in writing and drawing, and the school newspaper provided Moshe with a practical medium to showcase those talents.

Meshulam Halevi left a lasting impression on Dayan, who years later would write *Living with the Bible*, a personal narrative juxtaposing his life with events of antiquity, and he credited his first teacher with transforming the ancient Bible into a living text for him. "Our actual surroundings served to further bridge the distance of time, returning us to the days of antiquity, our patriarchs and nation's heroes," he wrote. "The language we spoke—the only language we knew—was Hebrew, the language of the Bible."[14]

In the fields around Nahalal, Moshe encountered Bedouins, a nomadic people who seemed to emerge straight from the Bible's passages. He learned to chat in Arabic and befriended one of the Bedouins, Wahsh (Wolf), who would visit Moshe and Shmuel in the fields and share in their meals. Occasionally, Wahsh would lead the mule while Moshe held the plow.[15] Later, when Nahalal's young men quarreled over field rights with Wahsh's tribe, Dayan was knocked unconscious by his friend. Understanding the young Bedouin's motives, Moshe held no grudge. Early on, he empathized with the Arabs, while also maintaining the resolve to repulse their attempts to thwart the Zionist cause.

Moshe's appetite for knowledge was insatiable. He devoured books and newspapers, and became a reliable source of information for the other children. Still, he lagged behind his classmates and struggled to obtain his teacher's affection. His peers viewed his reclusive personality as conceited, and his sharp tongue occasionally offended.

But when he offended, he did so in Hebrew. As devoted Zionists, Shmuel and Devorah insisted on speaking only Hebrew in the home, effectively refusing Moshe access to the language that had molded their own cultural world. Halevi, his cherished teacher, was fluent in Russian, Yiddish, and Hebrew but appreciated the importance of English as the language of the British regime. Throughout his life, Moshe struggled to learn English, the key to Western culture.

After elementary school, Moshe's continuing education was in doubt. He would not have time to fulfill his agrarian responsibilities if he left the village to attend the closest school. But in 1926 one of Nahalal's founders, Dr. Hannah Maisel, established an agricultural boarding school for girls in Nahalal. Moshe, then fourteen, along with his male peers joined the girls' classes for general studies. They devoted two hours a day to learning and the rest to practical labor. The girls worked on the school training farm, the boys on their family farms.

At school, the girls were older than Moshe, and it was not until his second year that he dared pursue Haya, the youngest girl in the school, who was a year older than he. It was a puritan era, and young Moshe was bashful and fearful of rejection—a hesitance for which he would more than compensate later in life. He began his courtship by suggesting that they do homework together. They walked in the fields, discussed books, and exchanged flirtatious letters. On Sabbath eves, he excelled at couples' folk dance at the youth clubhouse that the moshav had provided. The first kiss would follow.

Much like their son among most of his peers, Shmuel and Devorah were not particularly popular in the community. As recognized national leaders, they had a reputation for arrogance and pride. Shmuel, especially, drew fire for preaching the virtues of manual labor while pursuing public positions off the farm. Moshe's own relationship with his parents was uneven: "I didn't especially respect my father. In fact I didn't respect him at all. My mother—I respected highly."[16] As an adult, Moshe's aversion to party hacks and partisan politics may well have stemmed from this period, when he saw party politics distance his father from home, making his mother unhappy and causing the family hardship. Moreover, he disliked the way his father saturated everything with ideology and rhetoric. Moshe later acknowledged that "as a child I saw my father as a man of high but empty words, like his party comrades. When a child realizes that his father is talking nonsense, he loses respect."[17]

For all their disdain, Moshe's peers came to appreciate his courage. Before his thirteenth birthday, his uncle, who was in charge of the moshav security detail, assigned Moshe to the mounted guard. On horseback, the ragtag outfit was tasked with driving the Bedouins and their herds off Nahalal's harvested fields. In 1929 tensions resurfaced, and Arab rioters killed 133 Jews in communities across Palestine. Nahalal increased its vigilance, inducting more youngsters into its fledgling force. The local blacksmith fashioned primitive spears for fourteen- and fifteen-year-olds who patrolled the homes and farmyards at night, with Moshe extending his watch a couple of miles beyond the private Nahalal properties. He was an excellent horseman, a deadeye stone thrower, and usually the first to reach a fracas. Though his elders may have reprimanded him for pursuing danger, he earned a reputation for fearlessness. The scuffles highlighted his leadership qualities.

"We felt good setting out with Moshe to fight," one friend recalled. "He was very daring. He never looked twice, always ran ahead. We saw that he was uninhibited by any fear for his own safety . . . [and] merciless."[18]

When clashes between farmers and shepherds escalated to an armed struggle between Zionism and an awakening Arab nationalism, Dayan's courage and leadership qualities would naturally set him on the path to military command.

# 2

## On the Path of Command

Starting in the early 1930s, the Zionists in Palestine faced increasing opposition and organized violence from Arab nationalists. On the night of December 22, 1932, the violence reached Nahalal when an Arab hurled a bomb at a home, killing the Jewish owner and his eight-year-old son. In response, many Nahalal residents decided to join the Haganah, the clandestine Zionist paramilitary organization in Palestine. The Haganah High Command began to supply the moshav with weapons, which were hidden in public caches, and instructors arrived to train the people to use them properly. The Haganah conscripted the moshav's young men, including Dayan, whose reputation for fearlessness compensated for his youth. He was already familiar with firearms, having cleaned and fired his father's carbine for target practice from age ten; he would also ride through the fields with his uncle's hunting gun. In the Haganah, he learned the basic rules of military field conduct, but he would not divulge the details of his instruction, allowing instead the aura of secrecy to intrigue the girls at school.

In the fall of 1934, after the harvest was in on the farm, Dayan and two friends set out along the Jordan River for the southern Negev Desert. Hiking was a popular pastime for Nahalal's youth, who would trek north to Mount Hermon on the Syrian border and south to Beit She'an along the Transjordanian border, but no farther. At the time, there were no Jewish settlements in the entire Jordan Valley down to the northern tip of the Dead Sea. Inhabited mainly by Bedouins, it was a dangerous expanse for Jewish excursions. Moshe Dayan, at nineteen, pushed the boundaries: the three friends walked roughly forty-five miles along the Jordan River from Beit She'an to Jericho, arriving two days later at the Dead Sea potash works. There, the local Haganah commander stopped the trio and rerouted them toward Jerusalem. Passing Jerusalem, they visited Hebron, where Arabs had massacred the Jewish community only five years earlier. The following day, Dayan and his friends continued their journey via taxi to Beersheba and walked the rest of the way to Gaza. Upon arrival, they were detained by an Arab policeman. The young idealists from Nahalal insisted on speaking Hebrew, one of the three official languages under the British mandate, and demanded to see an officer who understood the language. It took the intervention of a British policeman to resolve the dispute and send the travelers packing on an Arab bus to Jaffa. From there, they walked to Tel Aviv.

Already having a good idea of the value of publicity, Dayan deemed the bold adventure worthy of public attention. The three presented themselves at the Tel Aviv office of *Davar*, the popular workers' newspaper, and related their exploits to the editor. The next day, the paper carried an item about the courage and Zionist pride of the young men who had stood up for their right to speak Hebrew. By the time they returned home, their saga was widely known: *Davar* could be found in every home in Nahalal. For Dayan, the trip had helped shape his identity and understanding of homeland and driven home the importance of belonging.

Moshe Dayan's fame would soon soar. At the end of 1934, a territorial dispute with Nahalal's Bedouin neighbors came to a head. The first winter rains sprouted a cover of green over a wadi at the edge of Nahalal, and the Bedouins, as usual, brought their sheep to graze. In its founding years, the members of the moshav had tilled the land intermittently, but for two years the fields had lain fallow. Now, however, the members decided to reassert their ownership and sow wheat and barley. Nahalal's youth were recruited to finish the job quickly. The Bedouins responded with a barrage of stones. Dayan sauntered along the fresh furrows with a seed sack, sowing with a wave of the hand, seemingly impervious to the steady volley of rocks. When he reached the Bedouins at the head of the wadi, he was greeted with a crushing blow to the head from a heavy club, apparently delivered by his childhood friend Wahsh. Dayan was rushed home, unconscious, with a cracked skull.

Dayan's intrepidity and injury were the talk of the day. The daily press fanned patriotic passion as Arab "wildness" and "wickedness" were widely condemned, a choice of words to which Dayan was not party. To him the incident was characteristic of the rivalry between farmers and shepherds dating back to Cain and Abel. "It was clear that we and they wanted the same thing," he later wrote. "This did not make them worse [than us]."[1]

Seated at Moshe's bedside after the fracas, his schoolmate Ruth Schwartz looked down at Moshe, bruised and bloodied. "It was my first sense of helplessness in the face of injury," she later observed, though it would not be her last.[2] Her parents, Zvi and Rachel, belonged to Jerusalem's Jewish elite. Zvi, a jurist, filled various positions in the Zionist establishment, and

Rachel, a trained educator, was known for her charitable works. Their home was a salon and meeting place for top British administrators, Zionist leaders, Jewish writers and artists, and members of the Arab aristocracy. Their daughter had spent her early years in London, where she learned English. In 1934, Ruth, a member of the Labor youth movement, entered the Nahalal agricultural school. Compared with Moshe, she was sophisticated and cultured; her friends described her as "wonderful, beautiful, charming, graceful, vivacious, sociable, amiable, energetic, and smart."[3] Moshe was captivated, and the two became a couple soon after she agreed to teach him English.

On July 12, 1935, Ruth, eighteen, and Moshe, twenty, were married in the Dayan farmyard at Nahalal beneath the lush walnut tree the family had planted fifteen years earlier. The guests included Zionist leaders, the entire Nahalal moshav, and members of the Bedouin tribe that was responsible for Moshe's cracked skull the year before. They had been hesitant to attend, but Moshe sent a personal invitation through one of his friends, and the tribal council approved the request. To them, Mussa, as they called him, was a hero. In the best Bedouin tradition, they danced debkas, played flutes, drummed on darbukas, and fired bullets into the air from galloping horses. Moshe shook Wahsh's hand in reconciliation.

Ruth's parents felt that their rustic son-in-law could benefit from some polishing and as a wedding gift presented the young couple with boat fare to England. Ruth and Moshe sailed third class to Marseilles, spent a few days in Paris, and disembarked in London. The plan was for Moshe to study agriculture, but World Zionist Organization (WZO) president Chaim Weizmann had persuaded Professor Harold Laski to accept Moshe at the London School of Economics. In those early days, according to Ruth, "we must have given the impression of a mad couple. We both insisted on wearing sandals irrespective of the European winter. Moshe refused to wear a tie and I refused to wear the dresses that Mother had bought me at Jerusalem's fancy stores."[4]

New opportunities for the young couple were ostensibly imminent, but they did not materialize as hoped. "Moshe hated London from the very first," Ruth wrote. "He wanted to go home." He struggled with English, suffered from the London smog, and felt alien in the cosmopolitan milieu. Moreover, letters from home troubled him. The farm was not in good shape, and rioting had erupted across the country. Worry and longing gnawed at him, and, after six months, he packed up. The trip, he acknowledged, had been a failure. "Being abroad oppressed me," he recalled. "The English I learned allowed me to chat. The LSE classes did not especially interest me. Since my stay in London served no purpose I returned to the farm. I would have liked to study, but it did not work out."[5]

They returned to a farm that was not the same as the one they had left. At the end of 1935, while the Dayans were abroad, the youth of Nahalal's second generation had split from their parents' moshav and founded a new kibbutz. Though the moshav movement had made impressive strides since Nahalal's founding, the heart of the early Zionist ethos was the total collectivism actualized by the kibbutz. The young people set up temporary quarters at Givat Shimron, where their parents had first assembled their tents fifteen years earlier. Ruth was enthusiastic, having dreamt of kibbutz life since her early teens, Moshe less so: "Absolute collectivism, group life, and equality did not suit my nature and disposition."[6] Nevertheless, upon returning from London, they joined the group at Givat Shimron, only to be met with skepticism from Moshe's childhood friends. They deemed him unsuited for collective life, though they agreed to accept him on a trial basis. He was offended, feeling that they knew him well enough to waive the trial period, but for Ruth's sake he consented. There at the hill site their daughter, Yaël, was born, but Moshe still remained alienated from the kibbutz members. His life's path would not remain on the kibbutz after all.

In the spring of 1936, Arab-Jewish relations grew more violent and politicized with the outbreak of the Arab Revolt. In April, bloody riots broke out on the Tel Aviv–Jaffa border. An enraged mob murdered Jews entering Jaffa on business, and Jewish residents living on the border of the two towns became refugees. The violence quickly spread throughout the country and lasted three years, from 1936 to 1939, targeting both Jews and the British regime. Some eight hundred Jews and several thousand Arabs were killed in armed clashes. Ultimately, the British Army suppressed the revolt. The Arabs, however, had scored a political victory: London decided first to restrict, and then to stop, the immigration of Jews to Palestine and limit the purchase of land by Jews for settlement. Dayan's military leanings, meanwhile, led him to join the armed forces, where he quickly climbed the ladder of command.

Originally, the Arab Revolt had fostered cooperation between the British Mandatory Government and the Haganah. With few troops in Palestine, the British allowed the Jewish community to establish the Jewish Settlement Police (JSP), a volunteer force to protect settlements, and equipped its members with rifles, machine guns, and small patrol vans. The Settlement Police received a modest salary from His Majesty's government and donned uniforms replete with Australian slouch hats. Though formally under British command, the JSP was in fact run by the Haganah.

Military units arriving from Britain required trackers to guide them through the unknown and sometimes hostile territory. The regime turned to the Haganah, and Dayan was one of the first scouts the Haganah entrusted to the British. He served as an adviser to the battalion commander and as a scout for soldiers of an itinerant Scottish company based in Afula, not far from the battlefield described in the book of Judges where Devorah and the Israelites defeated Sisera's chariot-mounted army. Like most of his generation, Dayan saw himself as the descendant of biblical heroes. Inducted into the JSP, he shared a tent with Scottish soldiers his age, wore a policeman's uniform, and earned a paltry supplement to his Haganah salary. He visited his family sparingly in Givat Shimron.

In the spring of 1937, Dayan earned his sergeant's stripes and took command of a Nahalal-area JSP mobile patrol consisting of a van and six policemen. As Arab violence escalated, he sided with a cadre of Haganah commanders who advocated going on the offensive, attacking Arab villages and the roads leading to them. The initiatives were steered by Yitzhak Sadeh, a senior Haganah figure who had fought with the Bolsheviks in the Russian Revolution. He had preached a strategy that favored assaults in the countryside to repel Arab fighters and force them back to their villages before they neared Jewish homes. Dayan applauded the approach. He ran his patrol unit aggressively and nimbly, scurrying up and down the western Jezreel Valley to confront Arab violence. At night they set up ambushes near Arab villages and surprised the fighters emerging from their bases.

As part of his training, Dayan attended a sergeants' course for JSP commanders delivered by the British Army. In addition to conduct, discipline, and drills, the instructors emphasized attention to detail—polished weapons, spruce uniforms, and shiny shoes—all aspects of soldiering that the casual Dayan detested. But he appreciated the importance of military order and made sure to drill his policemen on the parade field.

The sergeants' course brought Dayan face to face with Yigal Allon for the first time. Allon, also from Galilee, stood out as a talented young commander in the Haganah ranks. He, too, commanded a mobile JSP patrol, in eastern Galilee. In 1948 he would tell Arnan Azaryahu, his aide-de-camp, that he had disliked Dayan from the start. "I enjoyed the course . . . except for one thing," he told his friend; "there was an insufferable fellow there who spoiled the whole course for me. His name is Moshe Dayan."[7] Allon and Dayan were studies in contrast. Allon was handsome, affable, and social, always surrounded by friends and admirers. Dayan was introverted and aloof, preferring solitude. The two would frequently cross paths, often clashing, over the next forty years.

At the end of 1937, after several months of calm, the Arab Revolt flared up again. Arab guerrillas were more organized now, controlling extensive areas in Samaria and Galilee. The British implemented tougher measures and expanded their cooperation with the Haganah. By the start of 1938, Capt. Charles Orde Wingate, a Scottish intelligence officer stationed in Jerusalem and sympathetic to the Zionist cause, concluded that the British needed a more aggressive approach to quell the attacks. In June he received permission to establish a new force—the Special Night Squads. Dayan, though not officially a member, frequently participated in their operations.

A devout Christian, Wingate took the fight to the Arabs on their own turf, at night. Wingate's methods impressed Dayan, who also admired the Scotsman's free and easy manner. Like Dayan, Wingate loathed pageantry and roll call but insisted on clean weapons and audacity in battle. Whenever he was in the vicinity of Nahalal, he would visit the Dayans, and the two military men would talk for hours. Dayan considered him "a genius, a trailblazer defying convention."[8]

The Arab Revolt targeted Zionist efforts to settle the land. The WZO responded with a concerted effort to create new communities. In late 1936, Palestine's Jews devised the tower-and-stockade method, erecting a new settlement within hours and fortifying it against certain attack. Such frantic efforts required a band of recruits to load a convoy of trucks with resources early in the morning and assemble sheds, tents, and a watchtower soon afterward. They then surrounded the structures with stockade of gravel-filled double panels to protect against gunfire. By dusk, the new settlement would be ready.

One of these hastily constructed outposts, Hanita, would go down in Zionist lore. Established on March 21, 1938, on the Lebanese border, Hanita was surrounded by hostile Arab villages and far from other Jewish settlements. Expecting Arab opposition, the JSP, under Yitzhak Sadeh's command, secured the operation, and both Dayan and Allon participated in the patrols. Sadeh was photographed with the two young men, his arms on their shoulders. His copy of the photograph contained the scribbled words "l'état major," a prophecy that these two warriors would constitute the General Staff of the Jewish State's army one day. Allon never did serve on the General Staff, though in the 1948 war he was the IDF's most celebrated field commander. Dayan, however, validated Sadeh's prescience by becoming the IDF chief of General Staff decades later.

As the Arab Revolt abated, contention between the British regime and Palestine's Jews intensified. Following the publication of the White Paper of 1939, a government-issued document that marked a sharp turn from previous policy, the British severely limited Jewish immigration and ceased cooperation with the Haganah in order to conciliate the Arab world.

In the summer of 1939, the Haganah organized a covert platoon officers' course with both Dayan and Allon as instructors. The soldiers trained in a remote village in Lower Galilee, but on October 4 two British officers paid a surprise visit and discovered illegal weapons. They noted the violation and left. The Haganah volunteers, fearing repercussions, decided to relocate the course. They departed late at night, and the hike was arduous. When dawn broke they were still deep in hostile, predominantly Arab territory. A British border police unit on patrol spotted them. The Haganah group took cover in the gullies, but an Arab peasant directed the British patrol to them. The patrol apprehended the young Jewish nationalists and brought them to the old Acre Port prison for investigation.

Acre prison served as a main British facility, holding mostly criminals. Among the sordid collection of pimps, crooks, rapists, and murderers detained behind the thick walls of the old, moldy Crusader fortress, Arab guerrillas mixed with members of the Haganah and the Irgun, a Haganah offshoot. The prisoners took walks in the central courtyard and were able to enjoy the fresh breezes from the Mediterranean, but the gallows within the walls served as harsh reminders of the fate that awaited some of the prisoners.

Dayan and the forty-two other Haganah prisoners assumed that the Zionist leadership would intervene and soon have them released, but they were disappointed. The British made a show trial of them, and because there was no question about the events that had occurred, Haganah attorneys focused on motives rather than actions. They claimed that the young men had been training for war against the Nazis, the common enemy. The military judges were not convinced and according to the emergency regulations implemented by the British during the Arab Revolt, the illegal possession of arms merited a death penalty. The judges instead handed down a ten-year prison sentence, still a severe penalty that stunned the defendants, their families, and the Jewish community of Palestine. The British wanted to show the Arab world that they made no exceptions for Jews. Dayan's young wife, Ruth, was devastated.

"Ten years, meaning 1949," she wrote to Dayan in prison. "All the expectations, the hopes, the beautiful dreams, all destroyed. Impossible to absorb. . . . No one said a word. Only a deep hatred of the English took root in our hearts. Can words express the great pain and despair?"[9]

Dayan, always the pessimist, had not deluded himself. He had prepared for a harsh sentence even before hearing the verdict: the day before sentencing, he wrote a letter to Ruth asking her to send an English-Hebrew dictionary, an English grammar, and English reading material. "Some of the reading material should be in large letters," he added, "for in the evening it is already dark in the room, especially in winter." He remained level-headed: "Anyone able to say 'A' should be able to say 'B' and accept the punishment."[10] Though he could not fight his imprisonment, he took full command of improving conditions within the prison. His fellow inmates elected a committee and put him in charge of liaising with the British.

While Dayan devoted his energies to the day-to-day prison grind, the Zionist leadership worked on reducing the prisoners' sentence. Their efforts paid off, and the British High Commissioner lowered the penalty to five years. For Dayan, even with the punishment cut in half, the confinement left him in despair. "Memories of the past played a more important part than plans for the future," he recalled in one of his many letters to Ruth; "the date of release became a matter of faith, severed from objective political logic."[11]

As his letters to Ruth revealed, Dayan, a low-ranking Haganah commander at the time, did not see himself as anything more than the leader of a group of prisoners and a simple farmer from a small house in Nahalal. His letters described the humdrum routine of prison life but also unveiled his intimate and affectionate side, which was hidden from the public during his lifetime. "I wake up almost every night remembering you both," he wrote to Ruth and their baby, Yaël. "If I could relay to you a thousandth of what I feel for you those nights, you would perhaps sense what you both mean to me."[12] No doubt, of all the prison hardships, Dayan was most devastated by his separation from his wife and daughter, the destruction of his family life.

While the Zionists struggled for statehood in Palestine, World War II raged. In early 1941, the British forces in the Middle East suffered a setback. General Erwin Rommel, the distinguished field marshal who led the German and Italian forces in North Africa, transferred the Afrikakorps to Libya. With French Vichy forces controlling Syria and Lebanon—and permitting German air force bases there—the British were once again inclined to utilize the military capabilities of Palestine's Jewish community. As a result, on February 17, 1941, the British released the forty-three Haganah prisoners, only a year and a half after their arrest. Ruth brought Moshe new clothes and drove him home to Nahalal. She hoped that he would rest and settle into a quiet family life on the farm. That dream was short-lived.

In the spring of 1941, the Haganah created a national standing army to defend the Jewish community against the possible Axis conquest of Palestine. In the north, Yitzhak Sadeh led two companies with Yigal Allon and Moshe Dayan serving under him as company commanders. The young officers were neck and neck on the road to advancement. The newly established fighting division soon expanded and became the Plugot Machatz—strike force—better known by its Hebrew acronym, the Palmach. This unit became the Haganah's elite force in the Jewish people's struggle for independence in their biblical homeland.

Just as Allon and Dayan began forming their companies, the British requested Haganah scouts and sappers to bolster their army's invasion of Lebanon to drive out the Vichy forces. Allon's company was attached to troops on the eastern front, near the Syrian border, and Dayan's to the Australian 7th Division on the western front, along the Mediterranean coast. Dayan assembled some thirty poorly trained but eager fighters at Hanita and enlisted the help of an Arab scout, Rashid, a leader in the Arab Revolt, to help the Jewish fighters navigate the unfamiliar terrain beyond the northern border. Dayan and his men gained valuable fighting experience during their reconnaissance missions deep behind French lines.

The invasion began on June 8, 1941. The night before, Dayan and four of his men, including his friend Zalman Mart, joined three Australian officers and seven soldiers to secure two adjacent bridges crossing the Litani River, twelve and a half miles north of the border, until the main force arrived the next day. Dayan gave expression to the pride he had felt marching with his men, leading the invasion to Syria. "At long last we go to war against the Axis," he wrote in a report years later. "Our boys are at the head, without uniforms, poorly equipped. Nevertheless, here are the border stones; we are in Syria not as sneakers, not as smugglers—we are conquerors." He did not forget to mention that ahead of them an Arab scouted the way.[13]

The multi-ethnic unit reached the bridges shortly after midnight. With no enemies or booby traps in sight, the men waited for the reinforcements to arrive. Dayan stretched out beneath one of the bridges to nap, a habit he would maintain during breaks in battle. His rest was brief. As night turned to dawn, concern grew over their comrades' delay. Only later would they learn that the French had blown up a number of smaller water crossings and mined the road closer to the border, impeding the troops' advance. With no sign of approaching Allied forces, and without the cover of darkness, the unit was left exposed at the bridges. They decided to walk a few miles south to capture the local police station, unaware that the Vichy forces had seized the building and transformed it into their headquarters.

As the Australian and Jewish fighters approached the station, they were greeted by heavy gunfire from surrounding orchards and roadside positions. Bullet bursts from a machine gun on the roof of the police station spurred Dayan to action, and the brawny farmer from Nahalal became a fearless Haganah legend. Dayan hurled a grenade twenty-five yards, silencing the gun, and without waiting for orders from his Australian counterpart, he stormed the rooftop. There he organized the Haganah men.

The roof was not fortified, and the low railing offered little protection. While Dayan peered at the battle below through a pair of binoculars he had found, a bullet struck the left lens and shattered it into his eye. Zalman Mart dressed the wound, and Dayan was transferred on an improvised stretcher to a sheltered spot on the ground floor. "Moshe, what do you say?" Mart asked his wounded friend. "I lost an eye, but if I get to a hospital quickly, I'll live," Dayan responded, maintaining his composure throughout. For six hours Dayan lay wounded "like a sack . . . making no sound," Mart later testified. "I admired him."[14] Dayan offered his own matter-of-fact description: "I took a bullet in the eye. I did not pass out. I received first aid at once. But from then on, all I could do was hear what was happening around me."[15]

When the Australian vanguard finally arrived in the early afternoon, Dayan was evacuated to a hospital in Haifa. Throughout the ordeal, Rashid, the Arab scout, held Dayan's hand, and he accompanied him to the hospital. "It doesn't matter," Dayan told Mart before being taken in for treatment, "I lived with two eyes for twenty-six years. It's not terrible. You can live with one eye, too." *Davar*'s editorial board, already familiar with Dayan's exploits during his trek throughout much of Palestine years earlier, published a brief article titled "Disaster for Moshe Dayan," which explained that "Dayan was wounded while performing a heroic feat." His Australian comrades were equally impressed. One of the officers, upon meeting

Ruth at Moshe's bedside, noted with some exaggeration that "if there's anything military that your husband doesn't know, it's not worth knowing."[16]

After rushing Dayan to the hospital in one of their army ambulances, the British recorded his injury on a field medical card: "Moshe Dayan. Palestinian civilian, accidentally wounded, 8.6.1941."[17]

# 3

## *Back to Military Work*

IF HE HAD NOT BEEN WOUNDED, Dayan would have returned from Lebanon crowned with laurels, a rising Haganah star. But the bullet had smashed the bones around the eye cavity and the bridge of the nose, requiring close medical attention in place of a hero's welcome. He remained out of combat for seven years. After the initial injury healed, he moved his small family to his in-laws' home near a Jerusalem treatment center. He underwent further surgery to allow a glass eye to be fitted, but the operation failed, and Dayan had to wear an eye patch for the rest of his life.

He was despondent about his future as "an invalid with no line of work and no financial base."[1] When Ruth announced that she was pregnant with their second child, he burst out, "Who will hire a one-eyed man? I can't support my family."[2] As the Haganah military organization took shape without him, Dayan felt "finished" and "washed up."[3] His appearance only aggravated matters. He worried that with his black eye patch he resembled a pirate and frightened children.

But ever since Germany had invaded Russia, on June 22, 1941, it had posed a real danger to the Middle East, and Dayan's services were still needed. The British and the Haganah feared that German forces in the Caucasus would descend from the north while Rommel's troops—already at the gates of Alexandria—would rise from the south. Reuven Zaslani, who lived in the apartment underneath the Dayans' in Jerusalem and took turns with Ruth and her mother driving Moshe to treatment, was in charge of Special Affairs at the Jewish Agency's Political Department, liaising with British military intelligence. Only three months after Dayan's injury, Zaslani (later Shiloah), who is credited with founding the Mossad, Israel's renowned secret service, asked Moshe to set up an espionage ring to penetrate the German camp in the event of Axis forces overtaking Palestine. The few who knew about the group called it "Dayan's network." Its mission was to establish and operate clandestine transmission stations to inform the British of developments within German-occupied territory.

But with Rommel's defeat at El Alamein in northern Egypt in the fall of 1942, the immediate German threat was avoided and the network dismantled. The Palmach absorbed Dayan's men, leaving him unemployed once again. He decided to return to Nahalal to develop the new farm he had purchased.

Moshe devoted the next five years to the farm. For Ruth, these were golden days: "Those were wonderful years . . . of family unity and the kind of life I loved," she remembered. "We were together that entire period, working together for a common goal and living together just like anybody else."[4] There they had two more children, Ehud and Assaf, who came to be better known by their nicknames Udi and Assi.

It is difficult to imagine Dayan at peace on a farm during those particularly turbulent times. As World War II ended, the

Jews and the British halted their cooperation, the latter again choosing to impede the Zionists. The British closed Palestine's ports to arriving Jews, forcing increased undercover Jewish immigration. When the United Kingdom turned against the Zionist cause, incidents against the British regime intensified. In October 1945, Yitzhak Rabin led a Palmach raid on the Atlist prison and liberated 208 Jewish prisoners, and a month later the group sabotaged railway lines at more than 150 locations. On June 17, 1946, the Haganah carried out its largest and most impressive operation: Palmach units blew up 10 bridges connecting Palestine to its neighbor countries.

Although Dayan played no part in any of these operations, the Haganah command still regarded him as a senior officer and occasionally recruited him. In early 1945, he was assigned a thankless mission deemed necessary to stunt the developments brought on the previous year by the Irgun Zvai Leumi (IZL; National Military Organization). On February 1, 1944, Menachem Begin, head of the IZL, had called for a revolt against the British regime. The IZL, which would respond to Arab attacks with violence, had split from the Haganah in April 1937 after refusing to acknowledge the authority of the Jewish Agency, regarded by most of Palestine's Jewish population as its pre-state authority. By 1945, the Jewish Agency and the Haganah command had concluded that ongoing cooperation with the British regime was important and the IZL's actions were therefore dangerous. They decided to dissolve the IZL. A special Haganah unit launched the *saison* (hunting season)—pitting brother against brother. The Haganah, with Dayan involved, detained numerous IZL members and even turned some over to the British.

The regrettable in-fighting exposed raw nerves and generated a bitterness that lingered. Dayan rarely spoke of his key role in rounding up IZL members. When he met up with the leaders of the dissenting underground group, he chatted at length with Begin. "Dayan offered heartwarming, encouraging words," Begin wrote; "he admired our actions . . . they showed Jewish youth that the British could be beaten."[5] Dayan acknowledged his praise for their operations and dedication, but he remained committed to David Ben-Gurion, chairman of the Jewish Agency at the time, and opposed any break from national authority.

Dayan's work for the Jewish Agency and his role in the saison propelled him toward the political ranks of the ruling Mapai Party.[6] In 1944, the party split. A minority formed the Labor Unity Party, which advocated activism and opposed the land's partition, attracting many young people. Most Palmach commanders backed the Labor Unity, which, in return, supported the Palmach. Ben-Gurion, in response, tried to woo young leaders to Mapai. Dayan joined Mapai's young guard, where he met Shimon Peres, eight years his junior. Peres, who had immigrated to Tel Aviv from Poland in 1934, would eventually serve as Israel's prime minister and president, and the two men would work together for years.

In the winter of 1946, Dayan and Peres were sent to Switzerland to observe the Twenty-second Zionist Congress, the eminent WZO forum. Ruth accompanied Moshe since a Parisian doctor had agreed to attempt a bone transplant around his eye. The operation failed, however, and he was hospitalized for a month, restless and in the care of nuns.

"For four days . . . Moshe lay with high temperature, unable to eat," Ruth later described. "I was at his bedside day and night. . . . As he recovered, he grew angry and fidgety, insisting on my presence. 'What am I to do with all these nuns?' he demanded. 'I don't even speak French.'"[7]

He returned from Paris with no glass eye and the same aggravating eye patch. "I was prepared to endure anything to be rid of it," Dayan wrote. "It drew attention. . . . I preferred to stay at home."[8] While the distress would remain, over time his black eye patch would become a greatly admired icon.

In 1947, the United Nations was on the verge of deciding to partition Palestine into two states, one Jewish, one Arab. Palestine's Jewish population, the Yishuv, braced for attacks from neighboring Arab states. Three groups made up the fledgling Jewish army's officers—seasoned Haganah fighters, Palmach commanders, and World War II veterans of the British Army. Dayan was not included in the urgent process of building a conventional military.

On November 29, 1947, the United Nations General Assembly adopted Resolution 181 calling for the partition of the territory of Palestine into two independent states, free of British rule. The Jewish leadership accepted the resolution, while the Arabs rejected it and almost immediately initiated attacks on the Jewish communities in Palestine. Soon after, the Arab League established the Arab Liberation Army, which included a Druze battalion headed by an officer from the Syrian army. In early April, the Druze battalion attacked Kibbutz Ramat Yohanan, near Nahalal. It took the Haganah forces four days to repel the Druze. When the fighting concluded and the damage could be assessed, Moshe's younger brother Zohar was among the casualties.

Dayan and his brother-in-law, Israel Gefen, set out to identify the body. "There was mourning at home," Dayan later noted tersely. "The raging war and high daily toll of sons dulled outward expressions of individual grief." His mother's bereavement gave him pause. "Mother was closer to [Zohar] than to Aviva and myself to some extent because he was the youngest, mostly because of his personality. . . . He had an incredible vitality, an abundant, radiant cheerfulness. He had burst upon life as if there were no stops." His mother was devastated. "This wound would not heal," Moshe wrote. "The light went out of her life."[9]

Beginning in mid-April, the Haganah went on the offensive. Many of Dayan's old colleagues were now battalion and brigade commanders, and he was eager to enter the fray. In early May, his friend and mentor Yitzhak Sadeh suggested that Dayan set up a commando battalion within Sadeh's new armored brigade. Dayan jumped at the chance. On Friday, May 14, 1948, with the British Mandate set to expire the following day, the Jewish leaders convened and proclaimed an independent Jewish state. They deliberated over its name and decided not to call it Zion, which would have made it the last country to vote in the alphabetized system of the United Nations. With the Sabbath fast approaching, they agreed on Israel. The next day, five Arab armies invaded the newly established Jewish state. The Syrian army attacked the area south of the Sea of Galilee and approached Deganya, Dayan's birthplace. Multiple Jewish forces were operating in the area and the Haganah General Staff (HGS) sent Dayan to coordinate the efforts. By the time he arrived on May 19, the Syrians had already taken Tsemah and readied to attack Deganya. For Dayan, retreat was not to be considered.

His authority had not been properly defined, and he sidestepped formal channels to operate as he saw fit. He appointed a Nahalal friend as commander of Deganya Bet, the site Shmuel Dayan had torched thirty years earlier. In the nine-hour attack on both Deganya Aleph and Deganya Bet, two Syrian tanks breached the fences but were stopped by a flurry of Molotov cocktails. As the stalemate continued into the afternoon, Dayan decided to introduce a battery of old field cannons into the battle. Though they were missing their sights, accuracy was not the priority; the Syrian soldiers were spread out. The cannons, the first used by the Jewish army, served their purpose and surprised the Syrians, who scattered in every direction.

By nightfall, the front was quiet, and Dayan assumed that the Syrians had retreated from Tsemah. Escorted by a handful of former colleagues, he headed for the battered police station and found it "empty, silent and abandoned." All around, bodies of Syrian and Jewish soldiers killed in the first retreat were strewn about. He was overcome with shock and grief.

"A hard battle, tragic and depressing," he recalled. "Much young blood spilt. Not the blood of war-seasoned soldiers. Young blood, meeting death open-eyed. Casualties abandoned to moan at the roadside. Their friends, pursued by fire, unable to attend to them or gather them up. Defenders fighting with pathetic weapons against Syrian tanks, cannon, and armored cars. . . . It was a valiant . . . desperate battle of no retreat, this battle for the Deganyas."[10]

In June 1948, the United Nations declared a monthlong truce. Dayan was preoccupied with building his army unit, known as the Raiders Battalion No. 89. The unit deployed jeeps, machine guns, and half-tracks purchased on the U.S. junk market.

On June 20, Sadeh called upon Dayan to handle a particularly sensitive situation. A ship carrying arms and nine hundred Jewish immigrants had reached the central coastline. The *Altalena*, purchased and outfitted in France by the Irgun, had dropped anchor at a deserted beach and had unloaded its cargo. Ben-Gurion viewed the operation as a blatant breach of the Haganah agreement with the Irgun at the end of April, whereby the latter was to dissolve after the establishment of the Israel Defense Forces and to forfeit its firearms. Sadeh ordered Dayan to confiscate the weapons brought by the *Altalena*.

Hurrying to the site with his company from the Jezreel Valley, Dayan found a small cache of weapons on the beach, surrounded by Irgun members threatening anyone who approached. Dayan issued an ultimatum, which was answered with gunfire that killed two of his men and wounded six others. He ordered his men to shell the beach with mortar fire. The Irgun surrendered, but the ship turned around and sailed for Tel Aviv. A battle ensued and the *Altalena* was set on fire, exploded, and sank. This was not an episode that Dayan relished, but his allegiance to Ben-Gurion remained unshakable.

Following the *Altalena* tragedy, Dayan was summoned to General Headquarters, where he was instructed to accompany Col. David Marcus's body to West Point for burial. Col. Marcus, an American Jewish officer who had volunteered his services in the war against the Arabs, had been accidentally killed by friendly fire. Marcus's lack of Hebrew cost him his life when he was unable to communicate with a Palmach fighter to stop him firing on his position. Dayan and Yossi Harel, captain of the SS *Exodus*, escorted the coffin back to the United States. Upon his return to Israel, ignoring an order to report immediately to Ben-Gurion, Dayan rushed to rejoin his battalion for a major offensive against Jordan's Arab Legion stationed in the Arab towns of Lod and Ramle near Tel Aviv. Four brigades were organized under Allon, whose rank was now comparable to general.[11] Dayan, a major, was one of a dozen battalion commanders in the campaign, but his battalion, inspired by his daring and fighting spirit, stood out.

On the day that Dayan returned, his companies moved on two fortified villages on the Samarian slopes. One village opened fire on the company of half-tracks leading the battalion, and the company halted. Dayan ordered the commander to attack head-on while he took charge of the second company and stormed the other village. It was the battalion's first engagement, and a successful one. The men were heartened, enabling Dayan to act even more daringly.

After his battalion completed its initial mission in the Arab villages north of Lod, Dayan presented himself to Ben-

Gurion. Ben-Gurion, now prime minister, offered Dayan the challenging position of commander of Jerusalem, a considerable advancement. But Dayan asked for a postponement.

"I was appointed battalion commander only recently," he reasoned. "I haven't seen any fighting yet. This morning we started our first battle. I really don't want to leave my battalion and my job. In Jerusalem I'll have to instruct others to fight; here I myself fight."[12]

Ben-Gurion was impressed with Dayan's grit and agreed to allow the young commander to return to his unit. Night fell as Dayan made his way back to the lines, and, worried that he would trigger a mine in the dark, he decided to catch some sleep in a sorghum field and wait for dawn. "Now, too, after joining the 'cavalry' and fighting from a jeep, there was nothing closer or more calming to me than the ground," Dayan later wrote. "Its radiating warmth, the loose sand and earth, the shelter and mystery it enfolded were family. No barriers, no betrayals. It could be counted on in battle, and one could lay one's head on its shoulders for a night's rest."[13]

Reunited with his battalion, Dayan led his men into an important battle, part of a wider IDF offensive to take Lod and Ramle, pivotal Arab-controlled towns on the road from Tel Aviv to Jerusalem. Arab Legion and Palestinian irregular forces had taken positions in these towns to fire on Jewish travelers even before the war's start. These Arab militias succeeded in disrupting transportation along the main road leading up the Jerusalem hills. The Haganah launched the offensive, "Operation Danny"—named in honor of Danny Mass, the late commander of a Haganah unit that lost thirty-five men in an effort to resupply the Gush Etzion communities south of Jerusalem in January 1948—to remove the Arab stranglehold on the travel arteries to Jerusalem.

In the course of capturing a Jordanian armored car fitted

with a two-pound cannon, Dayan's battalion came under fire. Despite its exposure to enemy forces, the battalion managed to take the hills overlooking Lod, northeast of the Arab town, the side considered more vulnerable. While Dayan evaluated his soldiers' position, a Palmach commander whose men were under heavy fire on the southeast edge of town sent for help. Dayan arrayed his battalion along the road behind the captured Jordanian armored car and took his place in the second half-track of the advance company, totaling some two hundred soldiers.

The stage was set for one of the most celebrated battles of Israel's War of Independence. Though the Dayan-led attack drew criticism for its undue risk, generations of IDF soldiers would be raised on the drama that unfolded. The key to the troops' success was firepower and speed. In only forty-seven minutes of fighting, Dayan's battalion breached Lod's defense lines, crossed the village to the outskirts of the neighboring Arab town of Ramle, and returned under a downpour of fire from Arab Legion fighters holding two fortified positions on the main road. The battalion lost nine men and seven wounded; every car was hit including Dayan's half-track, which had to be pushed and pulled the entire way. As Dayan's men emerged from the fierce battle on the north side of the village, they sighted Palmach fighters sprinting into town.[14]

The battalion's raid undoubtedly helped topple the town's defenses and paved the way for the infantry's victory. Dayan, like all the other Haganah battalion commanders, had no previous experience or training in leading large corps into battle. Guided by his temperament, he acted on instinct. Tactically his actions lacked sophistication, and he narrowly avoided disaster. But success speaks for itself, and his daring exploits warranted the glory he received when he returned with his battalion to their base on July 19. Ben-Gurion could wait no longer and four days later promoted Dayan to colonel and appointed him the commander of Jerusalem.

The glory earned in the trenches was mostly unattainable to the commander of Jerusalem. While leadership in battle required personal courage and direct contact with subordinates, Dayan's new position relied on delegating other commanders to lead. Here he learned to develop his strengths in diplomacy.

Aside from minor daily skirmishes, there were only two major clashes during Dayan's tenure as commander of Jerusalem, both of which ended in failure for the Israelis. In early August, Arab irregulars violated the demilitarized zone surrounding the United Nations headquarters (previously the British Government House) on the Hill of Evil Counsel south of Jerusalem's Old City walls, and seized a few hilltop positions. The Israelis decided to dislodge the Arabs from these positions. The mission fell to a battalion in Dayan's brigade that was instructed not to harm the U.N. personnel or enter the U.N. compound. This restriction led to a failed campaign, leaving the hilltop in Jordanian hands. Eleven IDF soldiers were killed, five taken captive, and twenty wounded. Battalion and brigade commanders assigned blame to one another.

The IDF initiated the second major incident under Dayan's command of Jerusalem. With an ongoing IDF offensive in the south, Dayan directed his brigade's attempt to take the Beit Jala ridge overlooking Bethlehem on the night of October 21. At first the campaign went well as the brigade took control of points north of the Tel Aviv–Jerusalem railway line. But while ascending the steep slope to the next target, the advance units encountered heavy opposition. Dawn soon broke, and the forward battalion was recalled to the northern side of the railway track, rendering this operation a failure as well.

The two unsuccessful operations notwithstanding, Dayan's leadership and decisiveness were effective in his new command,

and they were on particular display following the murder of Count Folke Bernadotte, a Swedish U.N. mediator, on September 17 by the Stern Gang, a small splinter paramilitary group also known as LEHI (Israel Freedom Fighters). The Stern Gang, along with the IZL, had retained a quasi-independent status in Jerusalem. Following the murder of Bernadotte, this above-the-law privilege would end. The IZL surrendered their arms peacefully, but Dayan's men had to surround their camp before the Stern Gang did so. Afterward, Dayan assumed control of all the Jewish armed forces in the city.

When Dayan was appointed commander, he relocated his family to Jerusalem, leaving the Nahalal farm to hired workers. They moved into a posh apartment that had previously been owned by Abucarius Bey, an Arab attorney who had fled the city during the fighting. Foreign diplomats, U.N. officials, journalists, senior Israeli government officials, and members of the local Jewish elite all found their way to the Dayan salon.

Moshe Dayan had become part of Israel's political and social aristocracy, causing a drastic change in the family's lifestyle. His children, accustomed to Nahalal's open fields, struggled to adjust to the city life and resorted to mischief. Moshe, now a regular in the headlines, often found himself "embroiled in argument" and he gained weight. A changed way of thinking accompanied the new life: Dayan began to understand the art of diplomacy.[15]

As one of his first diplomatic achievements, Dayan established good relations with Jerusalem's Jordanian commander, Abdullah al-Tal. The two men trusted each other and would meet at the solitary cross-point of the divided city controlled by the United Nations. Al-Tal told Ruth, who occasionally came along, that it was "a pleasure to meet with an enemy such as your husband."[16]

On November 28, 1948, Dayan and al-Tal decided to sign an

"Absolute and Sincere Ceasefire." They had set up a direct "red line" of communication to avert potential clashes in the fragile arrangement. Problems, however, often cropped up about the exact demarcation of forces. Using a chinagraph pencil, the two commanders would draw the lines on maps unfurled on a stone-strewed dirt floor. The bumpy stone would occasionally cause the pencil to stray into the wrong neighborhood or street, inviting argument.

Still, the Absolute and Sincere Ceasefire in Jerusalem encouraged diplomatic efforts to resolve outstanding issues in other areas. Dayan and Reuven Shiloah, the neighbor who had founded the Mossad, were in direct touch with Prime Minister Ben-Gurion, who entrusted them with representing him in talks on territorial exchange to allow free movement to Arabs between Bethlehem and Jerusalem, and to Jews between Tel Aviv and Jerusalem as well as to the Western Wall. Jurists drafted official authorizations, which were duly exchanged, but the gaps between the sides were too wide to bridge.

Though Dayan believed the IDF was strong enough to expand its control all the way to the Jordan River, he pledged his allegiance and unquestioning trust to Ben-Gurion and his peaceful state-building approach. The talks with al-Tal proved fruitless, and soon Jordan's King Abdullah invited the Israeli representatives to meet with him at his winter palace in the town of Shuneh, east of the Jordan Valley.

The first meeting took place on January 16, 1949. Dayan and Eliahu Sasson, the senior expert on Arab affairs at Israel's Foreign Ministry, represented Israel. The issues raised with King Abdullah related to Jerusalem and the West Bank, both occupied by Jordan. Israel demanded a boundary change on the western slopes of the Samaria Hills, including the annexation of several large Arab villages near the central mountain range. The Israelis also wanted control of Wadi Ara—"Nahal Iron" in

Hebrew—a strategic road connecting the coastal lowlands and Galilee.

The meetings with the king followed the finest Bedouin tradition: a chess match that would end in victory for the king and a recital of verses he had composed, followed by a banquet late in the evening. King Abdullah enlivened the discussions on territory with erudite Eastern proverbs and epigrams. After several such discussions, it became clear that the cautious king preferred armistice talks over peace talks, and in March 1949 formal negotiations between Jordan and Israel began at the Hotel des Roses in Rhodes. Dayan and Shiloah again represented Israel, and Ralph Bunche, Count Bernadotte's replacement as U.N. mediator, oversaw the talks.

Dayan took in the scenery, admiring Rhodes's antiquities and the famed Valley of Butterflies, at its most vivid during that season. But he was aggravated that Jordan's delegates had no authority to conclude matters. To overcome the deadlock, he flew back to Jerusalem to join the Israeli diplomats negotiating directly with King Abdullah. In another meeting with the king, he presented Israel's demands amiably and courteously but refused to negotiate. It took an additional meeting for the Jordanians to let down their guard and consider Israel's proposal. This meeting was also attended by Yigael Yadin, the chief operations officer of the IDF, and Yehoshafat Harkavi, a senior intelligence figure. Dayan addressed the king: "The three military members of our delegation, Yadin, Harkavi, and myself, each lost a younger brother in this war—a war that we did not want and that would not have erupted had the Arab states, including Jordan, not attacked us. The time to have talked about concessions and compromise was before the war, so as to prevent it. Now it is necessary to bear the consequences and end it."[17]

At the end of the discussion, the king fetched a bouquet of roses and gave each Israeli a flower. "Tonight we ended the war," he said; "we brought peace."[18] The next day, Dayan returned to Rhodes. All that remained was to sign the agreement. But the talks dragged on for another two years and ended only in July 1951 when a Palestinian nationalist assassinated Abdullah as he was leaving the al-Aqsa Mosque on Jerusalem's Temple Mount. Dayan's main accomplishment—taking advantage of the positive climate created in the talks—amounted to minor territorial exchanges that netted Israel an important gain: complete, unfettered control of the railway line to Jerusalem. Deserving of the credit and praise that Ben-Gurion heaped on him, Dayan had earned the renown and respect that positioned him for more senior roles.

Among the IDF's senior officers, Dayan had become the leading expert on Armistice Agreement issues. On July 19, 1949, he was put in charge of armistice affairs, a responsibility that placed him in close contact with Foreign Ministry officials and, in particular, Foreign Minister Moshe Sharett, who managed diplomatic efforts with the United Nations. Dayan's comments reflected a hawkish stance. At a conference of ambassadors and diplomats convened by Sharett in July 1950, he astounded participants by questioning whether Israel's "present borders suffice . . . and will remain as they are in the future." According to the conference minutes, "Dayan believes that the first campaign in the process of Israel's establishment as an independent state is not yet over since we have not yet specified whether its spatial identity today is the final one. . . . He believes that the period we are living in is still open to change."[19]

Dayan did not accept the borders determined by the result of the War of Independence as final, nor did he abandon his ambition to expand them. Historians are fond of citing Dayan's words at Sharett's conference as evidence that the farmer from Nahalal sought to conquer the West Bank and establish Israel's border along the Jordan River. In the 1950s, occasional proposals to conquer parts of the West Bank emerged, but they always stemmed from the fear that Jordan's Hashemite regime was about to fall and that hostile elements would replace it. Dayan's proposals to change the state borders, however, were aimed at the Egyptian front. For the time being, he accepted Ben-Gurion's policy of supporting Jordan's control of the West Bank.

When Dayan retired from the IDF years later, Ben-Gurion sent him a warm letter that included a list of his many military accomplishments. Referring to his stint of service in Jerusalem, he wrote: "You have been endowed not only with first-rate military ability but also with extraordinary political acumen and statesmanship."[20]

# 4

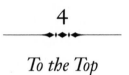

## *To the Top*

ON OCTOBER 9, 1949, Moshe Dayan was appointed officer commanding (O. C.) of Israel's southern front and promoted to the rank of major-general. In his new capacity, he oversaw a region that bordered Egyptian territory in the Gaza Strip and Sinai Peninsula, and Jordanian territory in the Hebron Hills and along the Arava, a desert plain that stretches from the Dead Sea to Eilat. The War of Independence had left the borders of this expanse unresolved, and disputes flared up. One such altercation escalated into a serious exchange of fire and gave Dayan the opportunity to demonstrate his leadership abilities.

After taking Eilat on the Red Sea without a fight in March 1949, the IDF had built a dirt road through the Arava, which Jordan claimed infringed on its sovereign territory. The Jordanian army blocked the road with boulders and fences, and Dayan rushed to the site to demand that the corridor be reopened. Jordan refused, and Dayan ordered a battalion of half-tracks to break through the blockade. When the Jordanians opened fire, Dayan called in mortar fire in return, forcing the Jordanians to abandon their posts. Some days later, U.N. observers determined that Jordan's grievance was legitimate. Dayan respected the finding and authorized a bypass road. This episode characterized Dayan the leader: firm, sharp, and quick to protect Israeli interests, but also able to admit when he was wrong and remedy the situation.

As O.C. Southern Command, Dayan directed most of his attention to civilian affairs. From 1949 to 1952, large-scale immigration to Israel doubled the country's Jewish population. The government adopted a countrywide policy of population dispersal, settling many immigrants in new rural communities. Dayan's jurisdiction contained small kibbutzim built under the British Mandate. Most of the territory was desolate, and he understood that true security was not only a military matter but also a matter of filling the land with thriving communities.

There were some six thousand families distributed among the fifteen transit camps in his jurisdiction, tent cities exposed to debilitating heat in the summer and raging storms in the winter. The army helped the immigrants in every way possible. The Engineering Corps paved roads and drained rainwater; the Women's Corps provided hundreds of soldiers as teachers; the army brought food and supplies where roads were impassable; and, at some camps, officers assumed full management responsibilities.

Most of the new immigrants were not inclined toward a collective way of life. Dayan suggested that the cooperative moshavim of his youth might be more suitable, and he pressed the settlement institutions to create immigrant moshavim along the border with the Gaza Strip and Jordan. In 1950, mere months after moving to Israel, immigrants from Kurdistan developed the moshav of Mivtachim opposite the Gaza Strip. It suffered from infiltration by Arab guerrillas, the occasional shelling, and mining of the dirt roads, and Dayan placed all the resources he commanded at its disposal. Today, Mivtachim is a prosperous community, exporting flowers and vegetables to Europe.

The Southern Command also offered fine hunting grounds, much to Dayan's delight. He stalked partridges and pigeons, returning from his patrols with a dozen birds, from which he prepared delicacies. The sport inadvertently introduced him to a new passion: archaeology. On one expedition with his older son, Udi, the two passed Tell es-Safi at the edge of the Hebron Hills. Rain had exposed antiquities in the biblical town's ruins, and pottery peeped out of the steep wall of the grooved wadi, requiring little digging to extract a few jugs. Consulting with an archaeologist, Moshe learned that these were from the Kingdom of Judea in the ninth or tenth century BCE. The following Saturday, he excitedly returned to the tell with a spade and uncovered more vessels. It was a defining moment, bringing Dayan his "first intimate encounter with ancient Israel . . . life from three thousand years ago."[1]

His brush with the past sparked an uncontrollable obsession. Israel is filled with archaeological mounds, and after his original discovery Dayan spent hours unearthing artifacts and piecing together shards in his garden. "For me, born in the Land of Israel, love of homeland was not abstract," he explained. "The lily of the Sharon and Mount Carmel were as real as could be; a flower is fragrant, a mountain has paths trodden by my feet. And yet the Israel that I saw with my eyes and touched with my hands was not enough for me; I wanted to make ancient Israel concrete too. Much as my parents who hailed from the Diaspora wished to make the spiritual Israel of books a physical homeland, I wished to lend my physical homeland the depth of spirit and history, to breathe the soul of the past into ruins and tells, to bring alive the Israel of the Patriarchs, Judges, and Kings."[2]

His digs were flagrantly illegal and widely condemned, but he either could not resist or did not care to. Archaeological excavation would become a lifelong passion, and he would exploit his public stature, his personal relationship with archaeologists, and ambiguous laws to amass a rich, valuable collection.

In early 1952, the IDF sent Dayan to England to attend a course for senior officers. He formed instant friendships with some of the other foreign officers, although his relations with the British were less warm. Some of them had served in Palestine during the Jewish struggle against the Mandate and had unpleasant memories of their run-ins with Jews. But Dayan's sense of humor and casual manners quickly thawed the British chill. His English had improved considerably, and his recollections of the discomfort he had experienced in London six years earlier had faded. Undoubtedly his spirits were also improved by having a personal valet assigned to him, as was customary in the British Army. He was brought tea in bed every morning, and every evening his shoes were polished. The instructors' comments in his notebooks speak of Dayan's diligence and indicate their respect for his battle experience and command.[3]

On June 1, back in Israel, Dayan was appointed O.C. Northern Command, moving him up another rung on the IDF ladder. The senior generals, some ten years Dayan's senior, were wrapping up their military careers, and Dayan, the outstanding officer of his generation, would not have long to wait to take their place. He moved his family north, though not back to Nahalal. The army allotted him a spacious flat in Tivon, a small town located between Nahalal and Haifa. His farming days were over.

Dayan knew the region of the Northern Command very well. His headquarters were in Nazareth, the town of his childhood school. He was now in charge of a much more populated area than the Southern Command, including roughly a hundred villages and three urban centers with some hundred thousand Arabs who had remained in Galilee after the 1948 war. Only a few years had passed since these Arabs had fought the Jews, and their allegiance to the State of Israel was questionable. Their lives were managed by army officers and heavily restricted under a military government that they despised.

Dayan's worries in the North also included Syria. The armistice agreements had left matters open to contrary interpretations. The two sides disagreed over the right of Syrian civilians to fish in the Sea of Galilee, of Israelis to carry out development work in areas declared demilitarized, and of the utilization of the Jordan River's waters. These issues caused friction between Israel and Syria for years. Through personal contact with the Syrians, Dayan tried to settle the discrepancies, but his charisma failed him and he could not convince them to yield.

At the end of that year, the top command of the IDF was embroiled in a crisis when Prime Minister David Ben-Gurion cut the defense budget to maximize resources for immigrant absorption. The chief of General Staff (CGS), Yigael Yadin, deemed the cuts too drastic and resigned. His second-in-command, Mordechai Makleff, consented to serve as CGS for one year. Dayan was offered the position of his second-in-command but turned it down, saying it was not in his nature to be anyone's second. He had no problem accepting authority, he added, even if he disagreed with his superiors, but as a deputy he would not be able to express his own opinions or dispute those of the chief if he thought them wrong. He agreed instead to head the General Headquarters (GHQ) branch in charge of operations, training, strategic planning, and intelligence—an appointment that raised eyebrows. Dayan was considered unpredictable, a maverick who was not afraid to change his mind and often surprised those around him with apparent inconsistencies. "Only asses don't change their minds," he would say, smiling, hardly relieving the unease of both subordinates and superiors. A lone wolf, he had no army coterie or party support. Ben-Gurion alone believed in him and continued to promote him.

On December 7, Dayan reported to the General Head-quarters near Tel Aviv. For all his aloofness, there he formed warm friendships. He was especially close to three co-workers: Shlomo Gazit, his senior assistant and formally his bureau chief; Neora Matalon, a lieutenant who served as his secretary and in fact ran the bureau; and Noam, his dependable driver. He kept no secrets from them, not even in intimate matters. He instructed his secretary to open every letter, including those marked "personal."

"I will not start keeping private files," he would tell his aides.

Dayan was very fond of Neora Matalon.[4] For her compulsory military service, Matalon was assigned to his bureau at the age of nineteen, having already completed the officers' course and attained the rank of second lieutenant. A woman of integrity, she was fiercely loyal to Dayan, though she did not spare him criticism when necessary. She later carved out a career in medical services and raised a family of her own, yet she stood by him at important junctures of his life and in his last years. Her fascinating memoir, *A Good Spot on the Side*, provides some of the most vivid descriptions of Dayan. She opens with her impression when she first stepped into his office: "The office looked like the headquarters of a tent camp. Makeshift tables and folding chairs. The commander acted like a field officer who may have arrived in the morning in a clean, pressed uniform, but by midday looked like he had been through a series of drills: dusty shoes, trousers baggy at the knees, sleeves carelessly rolled up."[5]

Shlomo Gazit, Dayan's first bureau chief, would also be found at Dayan's side in subsequent chapters of his career, and

Dayan would continue to consult him even after retiring. In those early days at GHQ, Dayan deliberately tried to create a casual and playful atmosphere. He ate his meals in the officers' mess, not in his office, as his predecessor had done. He held staff meetings on the outdoor stairway so they could all bask in the sun. He pilfered oranges from orchards he drove by and shared them with his passengers—once, entering the headquarters carrying two fruits, Dayan tossed them at the guard, whose arm was raised in salute. "Catch!" he yelled.[6]

The years preceding Dayan's arrival at GHQ marked a low point in IDF combat performance. The generation that had fought the great war—the War of Independence—was discharged from active duty in 1949 and replaced by immigrants whose military prowess left much to be desired. The IDF suffered a number of defeats in the first three years after the war, including the failure of an entire infantry battalion to overwhelm a small local band of militia in the Arab village of Falama in the winter of 1952.

Dayan knew that the IDF needed to take drastic measures to transform itself from a ceremonial army into a fighting force. He began by changing the atmosphere from the top down. Instead of emphasizing lectures and exhortations, he encouraged personal examples and gestures to signal the change that would cascade down through the ranks. He designed his office to look like the workplace of a field commander rather than that of a bank director. He refused to hire a personal adjutant, chiefly a ceremonial position, and chose a rugged jeep over a fancy limousine at the start of his term. Bored by long, drawn-out discussions in air-conditioned offices, he delegated authority to various GHQ division heads and spent most of his time on field inspections and visits to different units.

Dayan did not believe that a full-scale war was imminent and accordingly concentrated on the IDF's long-term fighting capability rather than on daily maintenance and alert. He preferred the acquisition of modern weaponry over the improvement of soldiers' living quarters, a cost-benefit analysis expressed succinctly by a popular IDF song: "A cannon instead of socks, a tank instead of shoes." He instilled combat tenacity in his officers, driving home the point that failing to perform a mission was not acceptable "unless 50 percent of the [officer's] men are wounded." An article he wrote for the official military magazine, *Ba'Mahaneh* (In the Camp), noted: "The commander is not the unit's most important member, to be protected. The unit's most important member is the enemy, to be quashed." He breathed new life into the exclamation that IDF officers continue to shout today: "After me!"[7]

In 1953 murders and robberies committed by Arab refugees proliferated. The hundreds of Jewish immigrant settlements that had sprung up along Israel's borders were vulnerable, and some were abandoned. Defensive measures failed to prevent recurring sabotage, and Dayan believed that the only way to reduce the violence was to persuade the surrounding Middle East regimes to clamp down on Arab infiltrators on their side of the border. Dayan's "persuasion" took the form of reprisal, on the theory that if the IDF tormented the Arab marauders, it would provoke the desired reaction: more supervision on the other side of the border. "We cannot safeguard every water pipe against explosives or every tree against uprooting," Dayan wrote. "We cannot prevent the murder of orchard workers or a sleeping family. But we can exact a high price for our blood, a price that an Arab community, Arab army, Arab regimes will not consider worth paying."[8]

The IDF command entertained the idea of creating a commando unit to carry out these reprisals, a concept that Dayan opposed at first. He thought all combat units should develop a fighting spirit rather than "subcontract" the missions to a special forces unit. But there was too much at stake for the reprisal operations to risk failure by inexperienced soldiers, and

Unit 101, which would become legendary in the IDF, was created. Maj. Ariel Sharon, a young former intelligence officer under Dayan in the Northern Command, established the volunteer unit, which consisted of Palmach veterans and daring young recruits. Among these young men eager for adventure was Meir Har-Tzion, from a Jezreel Valley kibbutz. Dayan met him under unusual circumstances when in September 1953 Unit 101 was sent to drive the Azazma Bedouin tribe back across the border. Dayan recalled their introduction: "Two dead camels lay in a wadi as birds of prey pecked at the entrails. I aimed . . . at a bird, prepared to press the trigger, when someone deflected my hand in reproach: 'What are you doing? That's an eagle!' I turned around. Before me was the patrol commander, Meir Har-Tzion, a tall, lean young man with a childlike face, his locks falling onto his forehead. The light never left his face, even when he was angry. For a corporal to grab a general's rifle was hardly an everyday occurrence; Har-Tzion explained that only thirty pairs of eagles remained in the country."[9] Dayan would encounter Har-Tzion again in a much tenser situation and come away regarding him as the best soldier the IDF ever had.

In 1953 violent and sometimes lethal Palestinian provocations from the Jordan-occupied West Bank intensified, as Arab infiltrators planted mines along the border roads, blew up bridges, stole cattle, sniped at Israeli patrols across the border and killed many Israeli soldiers and civilians. The attacks came to a head on October 12, when Palestinians hurled a grenade into a home near the Lod Airport, killing a mother and two children and wounding a third.[10] The deadly blast spurred the IDF to respond, and it approved a large-scale operation in Kibiya, a village garrisoned by an Arab Legion platoon. With Sharon in command, Unit 101, totaling only forty soldiers, merged with a paratroop battalion. In conveying the

GHQ order, Sharon rephrased it so that rather than being instructed to blow up homes *after* "putting inhabitants to flight" the orders read that the solders were to inflict "maximal damage to life and property." (This would not be the last time that Sharon tampered with GHQ intentions and escalated Israeli aggression.) The soldiers swarmed through Kibiya and blew up forty-five houses with the residents inside, killing some seventy civilians, mainly women and children. The brutal operation provoked worldwide anger. Many countries protested, including the United States. Dayan flew to New York to bolster the Foreign Ministry delegation at the United Nations and attempt to defend Israel's position. But he failed to ward off condemnation by the U.N. Security Council. Although many Israelis outside the military establishment protested the attack, the IDF took no disciplinary action against Sharon.

While Dayan was abroad, his daughter, Yaël, caused a minor scandal. Not yet fifteen, she was bright, talented, and mature for her age, due to graduate from high school two years early. She had befriended Uri Avneri, the editor of a popular weekly newspaper that often criticized the government and the IDF, and around this time Avneri published confidential information on military activity that strengthened his articles excoriating the IDF reprisals. Security personnel suspected that Yaël had provided Avneri with some of the confidential files. They searched her room, combed through her diary and school notebooks, and questioned her. Although it was assumed that Yaël was the source of the leak, no clear-cut evidence definitively implicated her.

Ruth was stunned. She, too, had been questioned. She sent three frantic telegrams to Moshe demanding that he return from New York. Furious, he rushed home and waited for Yaël in her bedroom. "My diary, which he had obviously just read, was open on the desk," Yaël wrote in her memoirs. "He kissed me warmly as we hadn't seen each other for a long while, and then he slapped my face, so hard I was almost thrown across the room. . . . I cried from the pain." Yaël would have liked to discuss the matter further, but her father was embarrassed by the entire affair and anxious to end the conversation. "As far as I'm concerned, the matter is closed," he said. He suggested that she come upstairs to see the dresses he had bought her in America. "I love you very much," he added, "but don't take advantage of it."[11]

At the end of 1953, Lt. Gen. Mordechai Makleff's term as IDF chief of staff drew to a close around the same time that Prime Minister David Ben-Gurion decided to retire from politics. Ben-Gurion moved to Kibbutz Sde Boker in the Negev to work and settle the land in hopes of reigniting the pioneering spirit that had swept across the region in the first half of the twentieth century. His Mapai Party appointed Foreign Minister Moshe Sharett to replace him and become Israel's second prime minister, while Pinchas Lavon, a man known for his wit, eloquence, and moderation on the Arab-Israeli conflict, succeeded Ben-Gurion as minister of defense. Hours before leaving office, Ben-Gurion appointed Dayan the IDF chief of staff, much to Sharett's chagrin. "I said . . . that Moshe Dayan is a soldier only in wartime, but in times of peace, he is a politician," Sharett wrote in his diary. "He has no interest in managing the military organization. The appointment spells the GHQ's politicization. The new chief of staff's remarkable talent for intrigue will be a hotbed of complications."[12]

Sharett was right about Dayan being a politician with no interest in military organization per se; the charge of intrigue, however, stemmed from Dayan's overblown image at the Foreign Ministry. Senior Israeli diplomats noted Dayan's disrespect toward them, his belittlement of their concerns, and his open disparagement of Sharett with whom he was at odds both by temperament and by policy on the Arab-Israeli conflict. Their mutual wariness certainly created "a hotbed of complications," and their relations continued to sour.

Despite his rocky relationship with the prime minister, Dayan, now with complete authority as the chief of staff, devoted himself to improving the Israel Defense Forces. In June and July 1954, Dayan, Yitzhak Rabin (then head of IDF training), and several officers took an extensive tour of the United States Army. Dayan was especially interested in the commando units and the training that the combat commanders endured. On the delegation's return, he decided that every combat officer would have to pass a paratroopers course.

Dayan, of course, led by example. Along with a group of GHQ officers that included the chief military rabbi, he learned to jump out of an airplane. On his sixth and final jump to complete the course, he sprained his ankle, but he showed up at the ceremony to receive his "jump wings" badge with a bandaged leg. The badge was pinned on his uniform by the commander of the paratroop battalion that had absorbed Unit 101, Ariel Sharon. The event was widely covered and came to symbolize the fighting spirit instilled by the new chief of staff. By the end of 1954, after one year in office, the atmosphere in the IDF had entirely changed.

Dayan was aware that he would now play a key role in the history of the State of Israel. Just as he had kept a childhood diary, he began to record every event in which he was involved. At the beginning of his term as IDF chief of staff, Dayan's secretary, Neora Matalon, set aside an hour at the end of each day for him to chronicle his thoughts and experiences in his journal. But he quickly lost patience and delegated the diary's management to Matalon and Shlomo Gazit, his bureau chief. One or the other was usually at his side and able to report directly on meetings and trips. In time Dayan would use the bureau diary as the basis of two memoirs about that period of his life.[13]

Dayan would begin his workday with two hours allotted to reading intelligence reports from the previous day. He would arrive at his office at eight in the morning—no meetings were ever scheduled before ten—and pore over the raw intelligence material. Though detailed documents bored him, he did not trust summaries or expert assessments. Instead, he insisted on reading decoded enemy telegrams and full reports from his intelligence agents so that he could reach his own conclusions. He also scanned the daily press and Foreign Ministry telegrams to stay current on the diplomatic front.

During the two years of Sharett's premiership, suspicion and tension characterized the relationship between the prime minister and the IDF chief of staff. Sharett believed that Dayan overstepped his authority, evaded his instructions, and withheld information. Dayan did not hide his opposition to Sharett's stance on security issues, which the military man regarded as dangerous to vital state interests. While Sharett understood that there was no chance of reaching peace with the Arabs in the foreseeable future, he believed that a moderate Israeli policy might eventually soften their opposition to a Jewish state in the Middle East. Sharett felt that Israel should be careful not to stoke resentment among the Arabs by using disproportionate force against Arab incursions. But Dayan, like Ben-Gurion, was sure that another war loomed in which the Arabs would try to make up for their defeat in 1948 by destroying the despised Zionist state. Bolstering his belief, the neighboring Arab countries, not yet ready for full-scale war, constantly tried to weaken Israel. They interfered with the development of water sources, blocked the Suez Canal, economically boycotted states trading with Israel, and denied access to Israeli and foreign ships bound for the Eilat seaport. Israel countered these attempts at sabotage with force when necessary. If such action was the slippery slope that would lead to an all-out war, Dayan held, Israel nonetheless had to take the necessary measures to protect its citizens.

A number of incidents involving IDF officers, particularly paratroop commanders, exacerbated Sharett's distrust of Dayan. Though in none of these had the officers acted with the chief of staff's approval, Sharett blamed Dayan, suspecting him of complicity and casting doubt on his explanations. The worst case concerned Meir Har-Tzion. On December 23, 1954, Bedouins raped and murdered Har-Tzion's sister Shoshana, at the Dead Sea, not far from the Jordanian border. Har-Tzion, who had been discharged a short time earlier because his father was ill, set out with friends on a personal vendetta. Supposedly with Sharon's knowledge, they killed several Bedouins opposite the border point where Shoshana was killed.

When the matter became public, Dayan put Har-Tzion and his accomplices on trial, but they hired a shrewd lawyer who threatened to turn the affair into a political issue, something nobody wanted. The defendants were released. Sharett objected to the trial's cancelation and suspected Dayan of deliberately covering up the episode. In his diary, Sharett attributed the atmosphere that precipitated the crime to Ben-Gurion and Dayan's reprisal policy.

"We heedlessly jettisoned the emotional, moral brakes on the instinct of vengeance that is stamped on man's soul to do evil," he wrote, "and thereby enabled a paratroop battalion to elevate vengeance to the level of moral principle."[14] Sharett's anger over the incident illustrated the gulf separating him and Dayan, who regarded the paratroop battalion as the army's finest unit.

Dayan remained close to Ben-Gurion, visiting him often at Sde Boker to report and consult even when Ben-Gurion was no longer in office. He offered to help Ben-Gurion advance his program to help new immigrants who had no farming experience and faced a dangerous life on the frontier. Ben-Gurion sought to inspire a volunteer movement of young native Israelis to assist the immigrants, but his efforts were unsuccessful. Dayan interceded and mobilized childhood acquaintances — young people from the established moshav farming communities. Several hundred went to live on the new moshavim for months and taught agriculture to the newcomers, aided in social integration and medical services, and tutored children in school and adults in Hebrew.

Dayan supported the project enthusiastically, and his office became a quasi-headquarters for moshav volunteers needing advice. He harnessed IDF resources to bolster Ben-Gurion's project and toured the moshavim to boost their inhabitants' morale. The successful project helped the immigrants acclimatize to their new surroundings, and later, when Dayan entered politics, the young people of these moshavim were his most loyal public supporters.

While Dayan was away during June and July 1954 on his official study visit to the U.S. Army, a minor, foolhardy episode escalated into a major national scandal that cast a lingering shadow over Israel's political leaders. Years earlier, IDF intelligence had established a ten-person spy cell in Egypt. Now Col. Benjamin Gibli, the head of IDF intelligence, activated the sleeper cell to conduct an operation, code-named Operation Susannah, to instill fear and instability in the country in order to delay Britain's withdrawal from the Suez Canal. Young Egyptian Jews detonated small firebombs, damaging several U.S. and British cultural institutions in Cairo and Alexandria. One bomb, however, ignited inadvertently in the pocket of a Jewish spy, Philip Natanson; there were no casualties, but it compromised the operation and led to the arrest and trial of all ten members of the cell. Two senior Jewish Egyptian agents were executed, an Israeli agent committed suicide in jail, and seven received long jail sentences, among them Marcelle Ninio, who was tortured in prison. The incident garnered worldwide attention. Israel denied any connection to the cell, yet information leaked, albeit after passing through tight military censorship. Enigmatically called *HaEsek HaBish* — "the unfortunate business" — it left most Israelis in the dark about the affair.

Behind the scenes, fingers were being pointed. Who gave the order for the operation? Gibli, the spymaster, blamed Defense Minister Lavon, who, in turn, adamantly denied the charges. Prime Minister Sharett appointed a commission to investigate, but it failed to determine the source of the operation. Despite the lack of clarity, the fallout was severe: Lavon resigned and Gibli was relieved of his command.

On January 21, 1955, following Lavon's resignation, David Ben-Gurion left Sde Boker and assumed the post of defense minister. His return to politics deflected attention from the amateur episode in Egypt and restored stability — for the time being.

# 5

## *Gathering Clouds*

DAVID BEN-GURION'S RETURN to government in January 1955 enhanced the Defense Ministry's operation, prompting Dayan to note that "things are becoming increasingly clearer and the alternatives more and more apparent."[1] After the Kibiya massacre, Jordan's Arab Legion had attempted to keep the border calm. Conversely, Egypt's new president, Gamal Abdul Nasser, embarked on an aggressive pan-Arab policy in which incidents of sabotage and murder were escalated along the Gaza Strip. Two days after Ben-Gurion's return, an Egyptian intelligence unit infiltrated Israel and came within twenty-five miles of Tel Aviv, vandalizing water installations and killing a passerby en route. Israel, already incensed over the execution of its two Cairo spies, retaliated with a paratroop attack on an Egyptian military base north of Gaza City on the night of February 28. Egyptian reinforcements ran into an Israeli ambush, but the paratroopers also met with fierce resistance at the

Egyptian base. When the smoke cleared, thirty-eight Egyptians were dead and thirty-one wounded, while Israel lost eight elite paratroopers.

Egypt's reaction to the attack contrasted starkly with Jordan's prudent response to Kibiya. Nasser created a special Gaza unit of fedayeen, fanatical suicide fighters committed to a holy war. Dayan's reprisal policy, which had partially succeeded on the Jordanian border, had utterly failed on the Egyptian border. He developed the idea that extreme Israeli reprisals were necessary, even at the risk of full-scale war. When he broached the idea to Ben-Gurion, the defense minister asked him whether he sought war. "I am not for initiating war," Dayan said. "But I am against concessions in any area, and if that's the reason the Arabs seek war—I am not against it. Their threat should not impede our actions."[2]

Another factor crystallized his strategic thinking: Egypt had a dangerous advantage if it chose to initiate war. Egyptian troops in the Gaza Strip were less than forty-five miles from Tel Aviv, and "the only force they would encounter on the way would be a couple of lovers picking oranges in an orchard."[3]

Dayan believed that the IDF had to seize the opportunity to drive Egypt out of Gaza and take control of the Rafah Junction on the Sinai border. He wanted the boundaries that had been established at the armistice to be moved to provide the Israelis with defensible positions. These considerations led him to push for tougher responses to the Egyptian provocations that began in the spring of 1955. On March 24, infiltrators from Gaza reached Moshav Patish near Beersheba and during a wedding celebration sprayed the Kurdistan immigrants and their guests with gunfire and grenades, wounding twenty people and killing moshav volunteer Varda Friedman, who had answered Ben-Gurion's call to help the new immigrants. Outraged, Ben-Gurion the next day urged the government to conquer the Gaza Strip, but Prime Minister Sharett rejected the proposal.

Tensions with Egypt rose when the Egyptian government further restricted Israel's sea route to Eilat that summer. Passage through the Suez Canal had been blocked to Israeli ships since the 1948 war, and now Egypt claimed sovereignty over the Straits of Aqaba and asserted the right to prevent ships from sailing to Eilat. The IDF began to consider a military solution, but Eilat did not have an operable port, which meant that the IDF Marines would be unable to participate in the battle. The insufficient port also meant that ships were unable to sail to and from Eilat to test the blockade and perhaps break it.

Later that summer, friction intensified along the Gaza border as well. Israel had demarcated the fenceless border by plowing a deep furrow the entire length of Gaza, flanked by a dirt road for daily IDF patrols to protect Israeli farmers. Dayan encouraged the settlements along the Strip to cultivate their fields right up to the border even if it exposed the farmers to gunfire from the Egyptian posts. Occasionally, Arab shepherds crossed the line to graze their herds on the manicured kibbutz fields and were driven off by Israeli patrols. The Arabs laced the patrol road with mines, and Dayan ordered IDF units to stand firm and respond with force to any provocation. He allowed the border units to launch mortars without waiting for approval and instructed them to blow up Egyptian posts that endangered the Israeli patrols.[4]

The events that unfolded on August 22 marked a turning point in the border skirmishes between Israel and Egypt. Nasser's forces fired on an Israeli unit patrolling alongside the Gaza Strip, and the commanding IDF officer, acting on what he considered Dayan's basic reprisal philosophy, crossed the border and captured and destroyed the Egyptian military post. In response, Nasser days later deployed his suicide squad, and for the first time fedayeen roamed Israeli territory and struck inland targets, raising the anxiety level in the South. During the final week of August alone, fedayeen squads killed sixteen Israelis.

Assuming that Sharett's government would not approve a large-scale retaliation, Dayan proposed pinpoint actions, such as blowing up bridges on the Gaza-Rafah road and laying ambushes. Sharett limited the operation to four small units, and Dayan submitted, giving Ariel Sharon's commando battalion the green light. Dayan traveled to Mafalsim, a border kibbutz serving as Sharon's frontline headquarters, to observe developments. After midnight, as Sharon's commandos neared their targets, Ben-Gurion's military secretary arrived at the southern headquarters and instructed Dayan to recall the units. Elmore Jackson, a representative of the American Society of Friends (Quakers), had arrived on an Israeli-Egyptian peacemaking mission, and Sharett did not wish to impede Jackson's efforts by instituting any acts of Israeli aggression.

Dayan returned to Tel Aviv and handed Ben-Gurion his resignation. "The contradiction between the government's defense policy and that which I consider vital makes it impossible for me to bear the responsibility demanded of the CGS."[5] Under normal circumstances, the resignation might have been construed as illegitimate pressure by the military on the government and been accepted. But with Ben-Gurion poised to return to the premiership and threatening to resign in support of Dayan, Sharett capitulated. He approved a broad IDF reprisal for the following day. On August 31, paratroopers stormed the large Khan Yunis police station and razed it to the ground, killing some seventy Egyptian soldiers and wounding more than forty. One Israeli paratrooper was killed.

War appeared imminent. Daily shootings and mortar shelling gave the border area the semblance of an active front. On September 1, the Israeli Air Force downed two Egyptian Vampire aircraft in a dogfight, and the IDF mobilized a large infantry force to occupy the Gaza Strip. But on September 4, calm was restored. The fedayeen returned to base, and both sides agreed to the call for a ceasefire issued by the head of the U.N. Truce Supervision Organization, Gen. E. L. M. Burns.

Amid the hostilities, Ben-Gurion appointed Gen. Chaim Laskov as the deputy chief of General Staff. Dayan and Laskov could not have been more different. Laskov had commanded a company in the British Army's Jewish Brigade that fought on the Italian front during World War II. He brought his British Army knowledge and experience to the IDF: strict formal discipline, efficient organization, and exemplary order. Unlike Dayan, he was convivial, warm, and sensitive beneath his tough exterior. Dayan was unhappy with the appointment and tried to convince Ben-Gurion to leave Meir Amit, head of the GHQ branch, at his side. But Laskov, in Ben-Gurion's eyes, epitomized the consummate soldier. At the defense minister's insistence, Dayan accepted the appointment. For the year that the two men headed the military structure, Dayan's relationship with Laskov was professional, though never warm. In retrospect, their division of labor was efficient and effective. Dayan preferred to focus on policy and strategy, glad that Laskov freed him of the responsibilities that he regarded as chores: coordinating GHQ work, dealing with administrative matters, and developing the military organization. Laskov performed his duties skillfully and helped Dayan prepare the army for what awaited.

On September 27, 1955, a new development radically changed the Middle East. President Nasser announced that Egypt had signed an arms deal with Czechoslovakia, a Soviet-bloc country. In effect, Egypt, considered a Western ally, had opened the Middle East to the Soviets. Dismayed, Britain and the United States rallied to find ways to contain the political damage and retain relations with Nasser.

From Israel's perspective, the arms deal was earth-shattering, tectonically shifting the balance of power in the Middle East. Egypt had suddenly obtained an abundance of warplanes, bombers, tanks, cannons, destroyers, and torpedo boats that left Israel at a grave disadvantage. The quality of the weaponry and machinery also left Israel with no adequate technological response. Soviet warplanes were much faster than Israel's old British aircraft, and the range of Soviet tank cannons was three times that of Israel's outdated tanks.

In the days following the arms deal, the extent of Egypt's windfall remained unclear. The day after Egypt's announcement, at Ben-Gurion's weekly Defense Ministry gathering of the Senior Forum—himself, CGS Dayan, and the ministry's director general, Shimon Peres—the three discussed the deal without knowing the specifics. They nevertheless decided that Peres should leave immediately for Paris to expedite an arms deal that was under discussion with the French. Dayan was scheduled to leave on a four-week trip with his wife, and Ben-Gurion did not consider it necessary to stop him. "You deserve a vacation," he said.[6]

The Dayans sailed with another couple to Genoa and from there traveled through Italy and continued to Switzerland and France. Ruth had fond memories of the trip, recalling that their friends were interested in art and did not skip a single museum. Moshe, for his part, was a good sport. He did not have "much patience" for museums, "but he would not miss anything," Ruth later said.[7] He was cut off from news in Israel and glad for the breathing room after his incessant worries about upholding Israel's defense in recent months. Two weeks into the trip, he arrived in Paris and met Peres, who updated him on events at home. Reality disrupted his blissful vacation. Ben-Gurion was suffering from an ear ailment that caused dizziness and required lengthy bed rest. The country was swept by a wave of pandemonium over the Czech-Egyptian arms deal, and various quarters clamored for preemptive attacks on Egypt before Nasser could integrate the menacing Soviet-supplied arsenal into his army.

Dayan did not see the trip through to the end. On October 21, Ben-Gurion's military secretary wired him, "This morning the Old Man rose from bed for the first time. His first wish was to meet with you."[8] Dayan boarded an airplane to Israel, a routine flight that he would later describe as "the most important event of my personal life." He found himself sitting next to a pretty woman, elegant and gentle, well-set-up and refined. Rachel Rabinovich, who was married to a Jerusalem attorney, had boarded Dayan's plane in Rome. "I don't know if it was love at first sight," Dayan recalled, "but from the moment I met Rachel, there was nobody else that I so wanted to be with or share joy and sorrow with."[9]

Rachel, who would later become his second wife, remembered being impressed that "Moshe was relaxed and pleasant." In a 2009 interview, she recounted their first conversation. "At some stage, he told me that I have lovely hands and asked me if I ever make salad. I said yes and he added: 'You cut onions as well?' Just before landing, he asked me if he could invite me for a cup of coffee one day. I said I would gladly invite him to my home. And he asked: 'Will you lay a tablecloth on the table?' It was strange, but I gave him my phone number."[10]

Rachel's upper-middle-class elegance apparently captivated him and starkly contrasted with Ruth's simple lifestyle. Dayan had been with many women in his life, but he had only two loves: Ruth, his first love, and Rachel, the irresistible product of a chance encounter.

On October 23, Dayan and Ben-Gurion met privately. No minutes were taken, but on his return to the IDF headquarters, Dayan summoned Laskov and Yehoshafat Harkavi, the head of intelligence, and reported the details of the meeting to them, conveying the defense minister's instructions. Ben-Gurion was opposed to a preemptive war, believing that the global community would not accept such a move. Nevertheless, he agreed with Dayan that Israel had to protect its interests assertively. According to Dayan, Ben-Gurion instructed him to prepare his soldiers to conquer the Gaza Strip if IDF reprisal operations provoked a forceful reaction from Egypt. The reprisals Ben-Gurion wanted taken would be a response to Egypt's blockade of the Straits of Tiran, which broke international law and justified Israeli military measures. Ben-Gurion also ordered Dayan to organize an IDF campaign to capture Sharm el-Sheikh, a small port located at the southern tip of the Sinai where the Straits of Tiran begin, and to end the blockade of Eilat.

Dayan understood Ben-Gurion's guidelines as a sweeping authorization for a strategy of "escalation," with the goal of forcing Egypt into battle by stepping up provocation. Dayan convened the GHQ and gave orders to prepare for war. The forces mobilized at a frenetic pace as the IDF began to flex its military muscle. Dayan knew Ben-Gurion well and was aware that though the "Old Man" showed grit and addressed the Knesset confidently, he had his doubts about entering a full-scale war. A few days after receiving the order to prepare for the Sharm el-Sheikh campaign, Dayan remarked to Ben-Gurion's secretary that "he doesn't really want it."[11]

Nonetheless, Dayan embraced the policy of escalating reprisals. On November 2, the day Ben-Gurion once more became Israel's prime minister, the IDF attacked Egyptian positions in the demilitarized border zone near Nitzana Junction, where Egypt had infiltrated hundreds of yards into Israeli territory. The operation was the largest the IDF had undertaken since the War of Independence. An entire brigade was involved, and Dayan hoped that the large force's actions would lure Egypt into responding with might. He asked Ben-Gurion to keep the Israeli troops in position until the next morning.

Ben-Gurion, wary of acts that could be interpreted as unjustified aggression, refused. He ordered the troops back to Israel. At dawn, the Egyptians launched a counterattack on the posts that Israel had conquered, only to find them empty.

Less than two weeks after Ben-Gurion's instructions to prepare for war, Dayan knew for certain that the prime minister was filled with doubt. Sharett, now the foreign minister, was leading the Ministry of Foreign Affairs on a major diplomatic effort to acquire arms to cancel Egypt's military edge. Israel's ambassador to the United States, Abba Eban, worked his lines to the State Department and the White House, trying to persuade Washington to lift the de facto embargo on Israel imposed by Secretary of State John Foster Dulles. President Dwight Eisenhower had dropped a few encouraging hints, and Sharett believed that aggressive military action by Israel would undermine these diplomatic endeavors.

To reinvigorate Ben-Gurion's fighting spirit, Dayan sent him a memo on November 10 stating that action was necessary. But three days later, his fears were realized: Ben-Gurion hesitantly informed him that the Sharm el-Sheikh campaign would be postponed to mid-January. Dayan returned to his office and sent Ben-Gurion another letter. "In my opinion," Dayan wrote, "we have to bring about a large-scale confrontation with the Egyptian army soon in order to gain three objectives: to deal the Egyptian air force a hard blow; to take the junctions of Rafah and Nitzana; to conquer the Straits of Eilat (Sharm el-Sheikh)."[12]

Dayan was unrelenting. He directly addressed Ben-Gurion's reservations at another meeting and stated that he did not think that Israel's hopes for an arms deal with the United States would bear fruit—and even if they did, "we prefer to fight now, without American weapons, rather than later, with American weapons."[13] The two leaders held opposite positions. At the weekly Senior Forum meeting on November 17, Ben-

Gurion again explained that if Israel initiated an offensive, all its sources of weapons would dry up, and the country would find itself isolated. "It's not a case of being able to shoot and end it," he said. "Afterward, are we to flee? Where to?"[14] Ben-Gurion at this point had adopted Sharett's logic. On December 4, before flying to the United States, Sharett managed to persuade the government to vote to avoid offensive initiatives in principle. Ben-Gurion voted in favor of the proposal.

Less than a week after the government's decision, Dayan made one last-ditch effort to revive the escalation policy. The Syrians over the years had shot at Israeli fishermen on the Sea of Galilee from positions on the northeastern shore, although there had been no recent dramatic incidents to justify retaliatory action. Yet it occurred to Dayan that given the defense pact between Syria and Egypt, this area might provide the catalyst he had been seeking to goad Nasser into a large operation. Dayan surmised that a comprehensive attack on the Syrian army at the Sea of Galilee might induce Egypt to respond on the Sinai front.

Although his reasons remain unclear, Ben-Gurion approved Dayan's proposal to attack Syrian positions, even though it clearly defied the government decision. Without question, he had not properly assessed the national and international outcry that would follow the incursion at the Sea of Galilee.

On the night of December 11, Sharon led his brigade against the Syrian military installations. By the time the sun broke over the horizon on Galilee's eastern shore, his soldiers had destroyed every post, killed thirty-seven Syrian soldiers and twelve civilians, and taken more than thirty prisoners. Six Israelis were killed during the clash. Dayan greeted the soldiers as they returned with weapons and vehicles, a sizable booty for one melee. In the IDF's brief history, this was one of the most daring, brilliant, and successful operations. But within hours, that success had instigated a political fiasco. Sharett's scheduled meeting the following day with Secretary of State Dulles—who before he learned of Israel's attack had intimated that he was prepared to release a quantity of weapons—was canceled. Sharett was overcome by feelings of shock and betrayal. "Universal darkness, the weapons matter undone," he recorded in his diary. "Horrific."[15] In a telegram to his bureau director, he wrote: "Never has there been such abomination in Israel."[16]

The Israeli press was harsh in its censure, and the cabinet ministers were in an uproar. Not only did the action defy their policy, but Ben-Gurion had not consulted any of them before giving Dayan the green light. They decided that every future act of reprisal would require cabinet approval. Although Ben-Gurion had suggested this new system of checks and balances to conciliate his colleagues, their decision was a slap in the face.

Nobody understood Ben-Gurion's motives, and many believed that Dayan alone had decided on the operation. The prime minister denied the charge and openly defended Dayan and the army. Yet he, too, had obviously been surprised by the size of the IDF operation. The day after the incident, Dayan took Sharon to see Ben-Gurion in Jerusalem to describe the battle. Dayan noticed that Ben-Gurion was displeased because the mission "had been too successful." Two days later, Ben-Gurion was asked what the army should do now. "From now on, the army must be ready for an Egyptian attack," he replied, "which may come in the next few months."[17]

With those words, Ben-Gurion dismantled the strategy that Dayan had been constructing since Ben-Gurion's return to the Defense Ministry. Instead of training for an Israeli-initiated attack, the army now had to prepare for defense against an enemy attack. The defensive stance clashed with Dayan's approach to combat. He was disappointed and hinted that he might resign at the end of his three-year term as the IDF chief of General Staff. Conveying his dismay, Dayan mentioned to Ben-Gurion that he felt he must travel to Japan to acquire weapons. Asked by Ben-Gurion whether there was nothing he could do in Israel, Dayan replied, "The things I need to do, I don't feel like doing."[18] Ben-Gurion rejected Dayan's insinuation that he would retire, and Dayan relented, and in January 1956 he reorganized the army for its new task: defense.

Ben-Gurion had highlighted the urgency—and futility—of Dayan's modified undertaking a month earlier, when he had appeared before the IDF High Command to explain why he had canceled the offensive initiative. There was a basic asymmetry between Israel and the Arabs, he explained. Whereas the Arabs could destroy Israel if they defeated it, no Israeli victory could bring an end to the conflict. "After every war from which we emerge as victors, we will face the same problem, just as we do today," Ben-Gurion warned. "We will face the fear of a third, fourth, and fifth round, ad infinitum. Even a war from which Israel emerges triumphant—if it is the initiator, it will suffer moral defeat because the world will not accept its initiative, and Israel will find itself isolated. In the eyes of the entire world, we will remain sullied."

Dayan did not argue. He merely asked the prime minister from the audience, "When should the army be ready for war?" Ben-Gurion did not go on record with a specific timetable, but the prevalent view was that preparations should be made for an Egyptian offensive in the summer.[19]

# 6

On the Edge of the International Storm

CONVINCED THAT THE GOVERNMENT'S decision to take a defensive rather than offensive posture toward Egypt was wrong, Dayan nonetheless remained firm in his allegiance to Prime Minister Ben-Gurion, and he set about reorganizing the army for defense. Ben-Gurion was well aware of Dayan's frustration but trusted him to toe the government line, even pressing him to continue briefing newspaper editors, as he had done before.

Inwardly and before his senior commanders, however, Dayan continued to develop his tactical thinking. On January 15, 1956, he convened all IDF officers with the rank of colonel or higher and delivered an address that filled twenty sheets of paper—his complete doctrine of state and security. He had closeted himself in his office for three days to compose the treatise, and the result was worthy of a defense minister, not simply a chief of staff. His calculations were measured and cautious, supported by clear analysis and a rational prognosis. I had just become his new bureau chief and was surprised when he asked me to comment on his draft. I had no comment to make.

On the most pressing issue facing Israel, he postulated that "as a result of the Czech deal and the absence of a countervailing Israeli deal . . . Egypt might start war." Sooner or later, Egypt had to confront Israel if it wished to assume leadership of the Arab world. Nevertheless, he argued, the superior munitions of the Egyptian army "do not rule out an IDF victory. They do, however, demand supreme effort, stamina, and endurance." Referring to the IDF infantry's short-range weapons, capable of hitting Egyptian tanks from a distance of about 100–150 yards, he added drolly, "This is not an ideal range, but compared with all the troubles the Jews have suffered down the generations, it is no cause for despair."[1]

The Czech-Egyptian arms deal in September 1955 had engendered anxiety among the Israelis and inspired an outpouring of donations to the Defense Fund, a state account reserved for the purchase of arms. Women from all levels of society donated necklaces and rings, children smashed their piggy banks, those without available funds borrowed from friends, unions imposed employee levies, and businessmen opened their pockets. The Israeli public organized mass rallies and distributed hundreds of thousands of flyers, and youth groups paraded through the streets chanting, "Arms for Israel—our answer to those plotting against us." In high demand to appear at the rallies, Dayan, with his distinctive eye patch, became an Israeli icon.

In January, the government again called upon the public to exhibit its volunteering spirit. Israel's defense rested not only on the army but also on border settlements, particularly those strategically established after the 1948 war that needed to be fortified with firing positions, barbed-wire fences, and bomb shelters. The needs exceeded the IDF's limited budget, but workers, students, and professionals alike responded to the call and volunteered to fill sandbags, twist wires, and haul re-inforced concrete to fortify the settlements.

The GHQ code-named the campaign "Wall" and launched it with great fanfare. On March 8, GHQ officers and soldiers set out for Mivtachim, the moshav settled by Kurdistan immigrants near the Gaza border during Dayan's term as O.C. Southern Command six years earlier. For the cameras, Dayan dug diligently as generals worked shoulder to shoulder with military clerks, drivers, and cooks. Even the seventy-year-old prime minister showed up to knot barbed wire. The publicity achieved its goal: dozens of journalists and photographers documented their leaders performing laborers' work, and all the dailies carried snapshots of Dayan and Laskov digging trenches, and Ben-Gurion and the head of the Women's Corps bending barbed wire. The world got the message that Israelis were both worried and determined to defend themselves.

Tensions on the border subsided in early 1956. Despite the broader strategic threats facing Israel, Dayan acknowledged in a meeting with senior army commanders that "in terms of day-to-day security, Israel has never had so quiet a period."[2] Attempting to settle matters and reconstitute the armistice agreements between Israel and Egypt, U.N. Secretary-General Dag Hammarskjöld asked both sides to retreat from their forward positions, a situation viewed by each side as a provocation. Much to Dayan's displeasure, the Foreign Ministry, with Ben-Gurion's backing, handled contacts with the United Nations.

The situation again deteriorated, however, as the first blossoming signs of spring brought Palestinian shepherds across the "furrow line" that had been plowed the length of the Gaza Strip. In early April 1956, IDF patrols and Egyptian military posts exchanged fire, and Ben-Gurion authorized an artillery operation if it were deemed necessary. Dayan's guidelines adhered to his philosophy: "There is no need for provocation, but if battle ensues we must not lose."[3] Matters came to a head on April 4 when an IDF patrol aiming to drive Arab shepherds off kibbutz fields ran into an Egyptian ambush, and three Israeli soldiers were killed. Next Egypt shelled border kibbutzim with mortars. Israel responded with cannon fire, and the Egyptians, in turn, intensified their attacks with a heavy barrage of mortars on Kibbutz Nahal Oz. Dayan now diverted the IDF fire to Gaza City, where shells landed in the main marketplace, hitting homes and the municipal hospital. Though he was acting with Ben-Gurion's authorization, it is doubtful that the prime minister had intended such extreme measures. When Dayan reported to him with an update, Ben-Gurion ordered the chief of staff to halt the firing on Gaza. The roughly fifty dead and one hundred Egyptians wounded consisted primarily of civilians, including women and children. Nasser was bound to retaliate.

Dayan headed for the kibbutzim. Nahal Oz alone had sustained about a hundred shells. There Dayan encountered Ro'i Rothberg, the charming and composed commander of the heavily shelled zone adjacent to Gaza. Rothberg left an indelible mark on Dayan, an impression that later inspired one of Dayan's most important speeches. The next day, much to Dayan's annoyance, Ben-Gurion submitted to Hammarskjöld's demands and drew the IDF back about five hundred yards from the border. But it was too late.

On April 8, Nasser unleashed dozens of fedayeen, who assaulted Israel's south. They blew up water pipelines and bridges, hurled grenades at homes, and attacked cars on the roads. The IDF and the police mounted an extensive search-and-destroy mission and ordered hundreds of ambushes set on the fedayeen retreat routes. Israeli forces killed fourteen infiltrators and took four captive in response to the brazen guerrilla attacks that left three Israeli civilians dead and nineteen wounded. Tensions ebbed and flowed. On April 11, Nasser agreed to Hammarskjöld's request to halt the infiltrations and exchanges of border fire. But that same night, the fedayeen sprang to action. They had apparently been in the field and not received word that hostilities had been halted. Striking near Tel Aviv, they attacked a bus, the gate of a large army base, and, worst of all, a synagogue at Kfar Chabad, where the community's children were convened for prayer and Torah study. The Egyptian suicide squad murdered five children and wounded many more, as well as the rabbi.

The GHQ believed that Nasser was paying lip service to Hammarskjöld while continuing his aggression toward an all-out war. After the Kfar Chabad murders, Ben-Gurion instructed the IDF to brace for war. Dayan drew up battle plans to attack Egyptian positions deep inside Sinai, including air force bases near the Suez Canal. He ordered a covert call-up of the reserves, the arming of airplanes, and the mustering of forces in the Negev. Intelligence sources, however, reported that fedayeen actions had completely stopped. On April 13, the government decided to wait, and the crisis passed. Dayan gritted his teeth and accepted the verdict once again as the IDF returned to routine duties.

Only weeks later, Israel received a tragic reminder that the U.N.-brokered lull in violence remained tenuous. On the morning of April 29, Ro'i Rothberg, the commander who had earned Dayan's admiration, set out from Nahal Oz on horseback to drive Arab shepherds off the kibbutz fields. A few hours later, his bullet-riddled body was returned, mutilated.

Dayan was distraught. He delivered a eulogy at the open grave, expressing his grief and bitterness over the agreement contrived by the Foreign Ministry and the United Nations, and perhaps, too, over Ben-Gurion's wavering. Dayan, unlike many chiefs of staff, wrote his own speeches, and his eulogy became a major text in the historical record of Israel; it is often quoted. In it, he summarized his view of the Arab-Israeli conflict.

Yesterday morning Ro'i was murdered. The morning stillness so dazzled him that he did not see those lying in wait for him on the furrow line. Let us not cast blame on his murderers today. It is pointless to mention their deep-seated hatred of us. For eight years they have been sitting in Gaza refugee camps while before their eyes we have been making the land and villages where they and their forefathers had lived our own.

It is not from the Arabs in Gaza that we should demand Ro'i's blood, but from ourselves. How we shut our eyes to a sober observation of our fate, to the sight of our generation's mission in all its cruelty. Have we forgotten that this group of young men living at Nahal Oz carries the heavy gates of Gaza on their shoulders, gates behind which hundreds of thousands of eyes and hands pray that we will weaken so that they may tear us to pieces—have we forgotten that? Yes, we know that if hope of our destruction is to cease, we must be strong, morning and evening, armed and ready. We are the generation of settlers, and without the steel helmet and the cannon maw we will be unable to plant a tree or build a home. Our children will have no life if we do not dig shelters, and without barbed wire and a machine gun we will not be able to pave roads or drill for water. Millions of Jews who were annihilated without having had a country look to us from the ashes of Israeli history, commanding us to settle and build a land for our people. But beyond the furrow border, a sea of hatred and vengeance swells, waiting for the day that calm will dull our vigilance, the day that we listen to the ambassadors of scheming hypocrisy who call on us to lay down our arms.

Ro'i's blood cries out to us from his rent body. A thousand times we vowed that our blood would not be spilled in vain, and yesterday, again, we gave in to temptation; we listened; we believed. Our account with ourselves we will settle today. Let us not be deterred from seeing the abiding hatred that fills the lives of hundreds of thousands of Arabs living all around us and waiting for the moment that they will manage to shed our blood. Let us not avert our eyes lest our arms slacken. This is the decree of our generation. This is the choice of our lives—to be prepared and armed, strong and resolute or to let the sword fall from our fist and our lives be cut down. Ro'i Rothberg, the blond, slender young man who left Tel Aviv to build his home at the gates of Gaza and serve as our bulwark, Ro'i—the light in his heart blinded him to the gleam of the knife. The longing for peace deafened him to the sound of lurking murder, the gates of Gaza were too heavy for him and they overwhelmed him.[4]

The eulogy was broadcast on the radio and the words impressed Ben-Gurion. But he asked Dayan to omit the line about "ambassadors of scheming hypocrisy" from the press version for the following day: Hammarskjöld was in Israel and Ben-Gurion thought the allusion too blunt.

At the same time that the government was retreating from full-scale war the previous December it had been making a concerted effort to procure heavy munitions. The Foreign Ministry came up empty in Washington, but Peres was exploring informal channels in France. He counted on the loose structure of France's republican government to enable him to bypass the French Foreign Ministry (familiarly known as the Quai d'Orsay), with its pro-Arab veteran diplomats, and instead form direct contacts with the Defense Ministry, the military, and even the arms industry.

The French Socialist Party under Guy Mollet had formed a coalition government in early 1956, with Christian Pineau as foreign minister and Maurice Bourgès-Maunoury, the republican representative, as defense minister. Peres had long felt at home in the French Defense Ministry, and there had been talks of purchasing sixty Mystère fighter-bomber aircraft, Vautour jet bombers, and hundreds of tanks and mobile cannons.

But Peres carefully studied France's political interests and realized that the deal could be still more lucrative for Israel. The new French government, busy suppressing the Algerian rebellion that began in 1954, had learned that Nasser had ties with rebel leaders who had sought asylum in Cairo. It occurred to Peres that here was an opportunity for strategic convergence between France and Israel. Returning from Paris on April 30, Peres relayed to Dayan the remark by Republican representative Bourgès-Maunoury in their meeting: "The tidal waves of the Mediterranean waters lap the shores of France and Israel with equal frequency."[5] The metaphor was clear: France and Israel shared an interest in weakening Nasser. Peres and Bourgès-Maunoury began to devise ways to smuggle tanks and cannons into Israel by sea, a scheme dubbed "The French Invasion." But they still had to figure out how to circumvent the Quai d'Orsay.

The solution came from an unexpected quarter. Israeli intelligence intercepted broadcasts from Cairo to Rome and Switzerland transmitting the movement of Algeria's rebel leaders. Yehoshafat Harkavi, the head of Israeli intelligence, assumed that the French might find this information interesting and met in Paris with Robert Lacoste, the minister in charge of Algerian affairs. Lacoste pounced on it. Working within French law, the prime minister possessed the authority to form intelligence contacts with foreign states without advising the Foreign Ministry. Mollet brought France's Secret Service into the picture and convened a clandestine meeting led by Pierre Boursicot, the head of French intelligence. Foreign Minister Pineau was briefed confidentially, but the rest of his ministry was kept in the dark.

On June 22, an Israeli Air Force transport plane with French markings departed from a semi-abandoned airfield carrying Dayan, Peres, and Harkavi. Landing at a military airport near Paris, the Israelis were whisked off to Veimars, a town in which a Jewish businessman had placed his mansion at the disposal of the Secret Service. Boursicot chaired the meeting with the participation of Deputy Chief of Staff Gen. Maurice Challe, at this time one of Israel's strongest supporters in the French establishment.[6]

The two-day Veimars Conference resulted in agreements on munitions and intelligence. France would supply Israel with seventy-two additional Mystère jets and numerous tanks. In return, Israel would gather information for French intelligence on the Algerian rebellion and help hinder rebel operations and, specifically, Nasser's assistance to the rebels. Ben-Gurion demanded joint responsibility from France and Britain. Dayan described the Paris talks as "a special experience" that boosted his personal confidence. It was the first time that he had acted as "Israel's main representative" in an international forum, "articulating [Israel's] wishes and motivations."[7] Dayan and Peres reported to Ben-Gurion, who approved the agreements. "It's a somewhat precarious adventure," the prime minister said, "but what of it? So is our entire existence!"[8] Sharett's resignation before the Veimars Conference made it easier for Ben-Gurion to negotiate with the full, unreserved support of the new foreign minister, Golda Meir.

The Veimars Conference greatly increased Israel's military capability, allowed the IDF to alter its defense plans, and forestalled the immediate need to strike Egypt. It was now preferable to postpone any confrontation so as to buy the IDF enough time to incorporate the new munitions into its arsenal and train the units to operate them, to build hangars and broader runways for the air force, and, most time-consuming, to train pilots: three months later, when the Sinai campaign began, the IDF had forty-eight Mystère planes but enough pilots for only one flight squadron.

On July 7, Dayan froze all defense expenditures and ordered a revised budget proposal that would provide for the new acquisitions. On July 9, when Ben-Gurion proposed a series of minor reprisals after two Israeli workers were murdered on the road to Eilat, Dayan found himself opposing any IDF response to avoid arousing the Egyptians.[9] The IDF was also dealing with personnel changes. Ben-Gurion suggested that Chief of Operations Chaim Laskov take charge of the Armored Corps and Dayan agreed. Meir Amit, whom Dayan had originally wanted as his deputy, replaced Laskov.

The French had assembled a small fleet of landing craft in early July to make three trips to Israel. The first, *Chelif*, named after a picturesque valley in Algiers, arrived on the evening of July 25 transporting thirty tanks, ammunition, and spare parts. Dayan and Ben-Gurion joined Peres, the chief architect of the arms deal, on the deserted beach in Haifa Bay to watch the unloading. Thirty Israeli drivers steered the tanks from the ship's belly to shore and then to the nearby railway track. Ben-Gurion, Dayan, and Peres boarded the ship and went to the captain's cabin, where the Frenchman popped a bottle of champagne to toast the operation, the crew, and the ship. At eleven o'clock, less than two hours after docking, the ship lifted anchor and sailed back across the bay, vanishing into the night.

The following day, at a mass rally at Alexandria's Liberation Square, Nasser announced the nationalization of the Suez Canal Company, which had been owned by the Egyptian and British governments, as well as private French investors. A day later, the French army's chief of staff and his English counterpart met to start planning a military campaign to protect their economic, political, and military interests, which had been hurt by the nationalization of the canal. Before that meeting, the French had asked the IDF for details on the readiness of the Egyptian army. They followed up with a request for information on Israel's ports and airfields, apparently weighing their value in a war against Nasser. "We must treat the French as our brothers," Ben-Gurion noted in his diary. "Their assistance and help to us and our cooperation with them is immeasurably vital and we must cooperate wholeheartedly."[10] The British, however, soon demanded that France keep Israel out of the entire affair lest the Arab states regard the Europeans as cooperating with the "loathsome Zionist" enemies against their revered leader, Nasser. Dayan was pleased. He did not consider the IDF ready.

Throughout these developments, Dayan's mother, Devorah, was lying on her deathbed, cared for devotedly by her husband, Shmuel. Dayan visited her as often as he could. On one visit, according to Shmuel, she said to her son, "You are brave; the brave can do everything. Can't you spare me suffering and agony?"[11]

Devorah passed away on July 28 and was buried beside her son Zohar at Givat Shimron, the first foothold of Nahalal's settlers. With her death Dayan lost the person closest to him, the one he held in the highest esteem. Yet she remained with him until his own death. "Whenever I saw a woman bent over a vegetable patch, I saw my mother's image, weeding between the beet and cauliflower seedlings," he wrote.[12] But he had no time for private mourning, nor was he one to show his feelings. After the funeral he hurried back to a meeting with Ben-Gurion.

Despite Dayan's wish to avoid unnecessary tension, more violence flared up in September, mostly on the Jordanian border. Months earlier, Gen. John Bagot Glubb and most of the British officers had been ousted from command of the Arab Legion, leaving discipline lax. The violence peaked on September 11, when Arab villagers attacked an Israeli unit training at the border near Hebron, killing six soldiers.

In response, Dayan proposed a plan to conquer the nearby Arab village, evacuate its residents, and raze their homes to the ground. Most of the ministers, fearing a recurrence of the Kibiya episode, decided to strike at a military target instead—

the police station south of Hebron. As usual, Sharon's paratroopers carried out the operation. They blew up the station
and destroyed Jordanian reinforcements, killing twenty Jordanian soldiers. But for Dayan, waiting at Sharon's command
post, success came at a steep price. Meir Har-Tzion, who had
returned to service after the IDF dismissed his trial concerning the retaliation for his sister's brutal murder, led the attack
and was critically wounded. The unit doctor saved his life by
inserting a tube directly into his windpipe to prevent him from
choking on his own blood. As he was rushed to the hospital in
Beersheba, his stretcher brushed past Dayan.

I noted in the bureau logbook: "I said to Moshe, 'It's Har-
Tzion who's wounded.' Dayan seemed to lose all interest in
everything around him. He got into his car minutes later and
raced behind the ambulance. He waited near the operating the-
ater until the wounded man was brought out and stood at his
bed for a long time. Suddenly, Har-Tzion opened his eyes, a
weak smile alighting on his face before he drifted off again.
I caught an expression on Dayan's face that I had never seen
before. It was impossible not to see his profound pain and his
prayer that Har-Tzion would pull through. He stood there,
alone with himself and his feelings."[13]

Despite the paratroop operation's success, the Jordanian
command seemed to be flaunting its loyalty to the Palestinian
population and seeking further confrontations. Additional assaults in the days that followed hardly appeared incidental;
someone in Amman was pulling the strings, spoiling for a fight.
"The acts of terror from Jordan have exceeded the measure of
restraint we may permit ourselves," Ben-Gurion told his government.[14]

Now the paratroopers deployed two battalions, one against
a police station near Bethlehem, deep inside Jordanian territory, and the other against a Jordanian border stronghold. Despite the operation's success—the IDF took the stronghold, and

killed more than forty Arab Legion fighters—ten paratroopers were killed and sixteen wounded, mainly at the stronghold. Dayan was at the border when Legion cannons fired at Sharon's command post, and his driver, Noam, who had climbed up a nearby water tower, was wounded and evacuated to the hospital. Dayan felt that the conquest of the Jordanian post had been unnecessary and the cost too dear.

In early September 1956, France signaled that Israel might be invited to participate in the campaign against Egypt over the status of the Suez Canal. Before leaving for Paris on September 18, Peres consulted with Dayan, who noted that while Israel would like the Suez Canal to revert to an international waterway, the decision would be left to the world powers. Israel had no interest in reaching the canal, but should war erupt it would strongly encourage changing the borders to allow Israel control of the Straits of Eilat and Rafah. Dayan, echoing Ben-Gurion's apprehension concerning direct confrontations with the English, warned that Britain might be a problem because it had defense pacts with several Arab states. "We must not find ourselves alongside the English on the Egyptian front while clashing with them on the Jordanian front," he said. Dayan also stressed to Peres that Israeli-French relations were being conducted "under the table," which was not right. If France wanted Israel's cooperation in the war in Sinai, "we must free ourselves of the status of a minor member of the tripartite and become an equal ally."[15]

The French feared that Britain's prime minister, Anthony Eden, had lost his resolve, and they began to explore the possibility of a French-Israeli operation. On September 25, the French government formally invited a senior Israeli delegation to Paris to explore the option. Ben-Gurion had his own reservations. "Israel's position depends on the type of partnership offered," he told Dayan. "It must be dignified."[16] Nevertheless, on September 29 a delegation set out with Foreign Minister Golda Meir, Dayan, and Peres. I accompanied the delegation as the mission's secretary. The French had sent an old marine bomber to fly us to a French naval base in Bizerta, Tunisia. We crowded into the flight crew's small compartment for the ten-hour flight along the northern coast of Africa. Only Meir was given a comfortable seat in the cockpit. From Bizerta, we continued in a more spacious aircraft to a military base near Paris. To maintain secrecy, the delegation was hosted outside the city in a palace with cultivated gardens built by Henri IV in the suburb of Saint Germaine en Laye, overlooking the Seine. The gardens were filled with Saturday strollers as sailboats glided on the Seine, but tension marred Dayan's enjoyment of the tranquil scene that was so rare to him. He kept turning different scenarios over in his mind. More than anything he wanted the joint Israeli-French Sinai operation to materialize, and he searched for an argument that would eliminate Ben-Gurion's doubts.

The meetings soon showed that political conditions were not yet ripe for collaboration. Moreover, French forces were already preparing for the Anglo-French operation against Egypt, and it was not at all certain that a campaign could be launched without the British. Another ten days passed before the conditions for Israel's involvement were clarified. Dayan was concerned.

"I did not have a good feeling," he recalled. "The only thing that became clear was that the situation was unclear. . . . Militarily, the uncertainty was obstructive and complicated. Military preparations can't be made without a political decision. And should the decision come . . . we will have very little time at our disposal. How will we manage to do what's necessary?"[17]

The only practical outcome of the meetings was that the French committed to supply Israel with additional equipment, especially materiel for desert warfare. A delegation of officers under General Challe was to leave for Israel immediately to study the proposed Franco-Israeli agreement and Israel's needs for further supplies more closely. For the trip home, the French government furnished the delegation with the much more luxurious DC4 aircraft given by President Truman to President Charles de Gaulle at the end of World War II.

The French officers were impressed by what they saw in Israel, and on his first evening there Challe wired authorization to Paris for the instant provision of more equipment. Dayan, meanwhile, convened the GHQ and issued a war alert, ordering his staff to prepare an update of the plans for the conquest of the Sinai Peninsula: "The plans should be drawn up on the assumption that the fighting in Sinai will be undertaken by the IDF alone, as if we were setting out for war without partners."[18] Within days, the plans were revised and code-named Kadesh, after the biblical settlement of Kadesh Barnea, one of the stations on the route of the Israelite Exodus from Egypt. The countdown to war had begun.

# 7

## On the Front Line

RELATIONS WITH THE BRITISH grew increasingly complicated in October 1956. The rise of pro-Nasser, anti-Western forces in Jordan concerned Amman and London. Britain, which wielded considerable influence in the affairs of the Hashemite kingdoms of both Iraq and Jordan by funding their armies, considered sending the Iraqi army to Jordan. Israel voiced opposition to armed Iraqis on its border and appeared ready to back up the disapproval with force. Israel and Great Britain seemed to be on a collision course.

As the diplomatic discussions continued behind closed doors, in the field Jordanian soldiers continued to harass Jewish settlers across the border. On October 9, Israeli orchard workers were killed in the Sharon Plain, their ears cut off by the perpetrators as proof to show their dispatchers. Still struggling to exercise restraint, Dayan felt that Israel must respond. "We wanted to avoid military action," he wrote in his diary, "but . . . things went too far."[1]

On October 10, Sharon's paratroop brigade attacked and destroyed the police station on the edge of Qalqilya, a town near the murder site. Dayan, determined to prevent civilian casualties and unnecessary IDF losses, ordered Sharon's soldiers to keep out of the town. He rejected Sharon's suggestion that the brigade also capture a Jordanian military post down the road from the town east of Qalqilya. Sharon's paratroopers proceeded with the plans to lay an ambush farther east, deep inside Jordanian territory, and were attacked by Jordanian forces. Sustaining casualties that hampered their retreat, Sharon's soldiers had to break through the military post that Dayan had ordered them to spare, and many more men were hit in the heavy gunfire.

As usual, Dayan spent the night at Sharon's command post, worried. He readied the air force to deploy if infantrymen could not rescue the paratroopers before daybreak. Jordan's King Hussein was also concerned and requested aid from the British, who had an air force base in Cyprus. British Prime Minister Anthony Eden later noted that "we were asked to extend help and our airplanes were about to take off," but at dawn Sharon managed to extract his troops from the entanglement, and the Israeli soldiers returned across the border, so intervention by the Royal Air Force was no longer necessary.[2] Israel lost eighteen paratroopers, leaving the GHQ and paratroop unit dispirited and feeling that the IDF tactics of recent years had caused too many casualties. Ominously, it was clear that a different war was brewing.

After assessing Israel's military capabilities, General Challe returned to France and suggested that Paris should persuade Ben-Gurion to launch an attack on the Egyptian army in Sinai—ostensibly unconnected to the Franco-British operation—to provide a pretext for France and Britain to intervene.

While seemingly protecting the Suez Canal from the expected violence that would ensue, England and France would be in position to capture the canal, invalidate its Egyptian nationalization, and defeat Nasser. Prime Minister Eden welcomed the proposal. An Israeli attack would show cause for intervention in Suez, offering the bona fide justification Britain had been grasping for amid international conferences and growing domestic opposition. But Eden had one condition: the IDF action must not appear prearranged. Ben-Gurion was vexed. According to Peres, he "saw the proposal as British hypocrisy at its worst, smacking more of a desire to do Israel ill than of a resolve to topple Egypt's dictatorship."[3] Ben-Gurion suspected that the British wished to embroil Israel in war in Sinai in order to carry out their scheme to deploy the Iraqi army in Jordan. He spurned the proposed division of roles that would make Israel appear to be the aggressor and permit England and France to seem disinterested.[4] Even Dayan, an advocate for war with Egypt, did not try to assuage Ben-Gurion's anger; he too considered the British condition unacceptable.

Realizing that only a summit might change the Israeli prime minister's mind, Prime Minister Mollet invited Ben-Gurion to Paris on October 16. "If we refuse, we will miss a historic one-time opportunity," Dayan warned Ben-Gurion before they left. "We will have to keep fighting Nasser alone, without the French and British armies and without the French military equipment that they are only providing as part of the joint campaign."[5] Ben-Gurion was unconvinced. Dayan knew that a double task awaited him in Paris: to persuade the French and British to improve the terms of the "partnership," and to persuade Ben-Gurion that a joint operation was feasible without unduly endangering Israel.

The summit, for which I acted as secretary, was held in a modest villa in the garden suburb of Sèvres. The residence belonged to the family of Fernand Bonnier de La Chapelle, a member of the French Resistance who at age twenty had assassinated Adm. François Darlan of the Vichy regime at the end of World War II and been executed by the Vichy police. A bronze bust of his likeness stood on the mantelpiece of the villa. Because of the need for secrecy, Ben-Gurion did not set foot outside the villa for the entire three days lest his distinctive white mane divulge his presence. Dayan and Peres stayed at a hotel in the city and, as a precautionary measure, Dayan exchanged his eye patch for black sunglasses.

The French brought their top ministers to the first meeting: Prime Minister Mollet, Foreign Minister Pineau, Defense Minister Bourges-Maunoury, and a handful of senior officials headed by General Challe. Ben-Gurion began the meeting with a demand for an open agreement that his country would not be left as the scapegoat for a multi-national confrontation. Israel was uncomfortable with the circumscribed role proposed by France and England and wished to be partner to the overall plans for the region's future. The French pointed out that Ben-Gurion's demand was untenable; the British would accept only General Challe's initial proposal of an apparently unrelated Israeli attack in Sinai.[6]

Dayan stepped in to save the summit from failing before it had barely begun. With Ben-Gurion's permission, though without committing the prime minister, Dayan offered a personal suggestion that might satisfy the British. Israel would launch a limited operation near Suez at a time agreed upon in advance, and Britain and France would then demand that Israel and Egypt withdraw their troops from the canal area. Israel would agree to do so and Nasser, presumably, would refuse, paving the way for the British and French to launch their own attack, code-named Operation Musketeer, including air strikes on Egyptian airfields.

Dayan elaborated on the plan to the Israeli caucus in the

afternoon. The campaign would start with a paratroop battalion dropped near the Mitla Pass, a path that snakes between mountain ranges thirty miles east of Suez, and the rest of the brigade would break through from the Israeli border to join them. In the initial hours, the other IDF troops would be stationed at the border awaiting further instructions. The Kadesh campaign would begin only after the British and French started bombing Egypt. If for any reason the British failed to go to war, the paratroopers would withdraw, and Israel would be able to present the operation as a stepped-up reprisal for the constant Egyptian attacks on southern Israel. Ben-Gurion listened to the proposal without reacting.

In the evening, British Foreign Minister Selwyn Lloyd arrived. Though Ben-Gurion had not yet decided whether to accept it himself, he presented Dayan's proposal to the guest. But there was no chemistry between the two leaders. Lloyd failed to grasp the dramatic reversal in Ben-Gurion's position—that, for the first time, he was agreeing to have Israel launch the operation on its own. "Selwyn Lloyd may generally be warm, pleasant and sociable. If so, he did a good job of hiding it," Dayan later wrote. "A more antagonistic exhibition than his is hardly possible. His entire manner conveyed disgust—disgust of the place, of the company, and of the substance of the matter he was compelled to deal with."[7]

Lloyd returned to London late that night and the next morning reported to the cabinet that Israel was not prepared to accept the proposed British plan. The French foreign minister, Christian Pineau, however, did understand the importance of Israel's concession, and he believed that the two positions were bridgeable. He rushed off to London to rectify the situation. At this stage, it was clear to Dayan that his problem was not convincing the British, but rather convincing Ben-Gurion.

The decisive discussion of the Israeli delegation took place on the second afternoon. Addressing Ben-Gurion's doubts,

Dayan underscored the chance of success. He believed that if Israel limited its operation on the first day, the combat would be contained, allowing the option of rescuing the paratroopers and bringing them home. Dayan's words were also a commitment: now, if Ben-Gurion accepted the plan, he had to make sure to stay within these limits. The Old Man was still undecided. He retired to his room for the day.

When he came downstairs the next morning, it was clear to Dayan and Peres that he had reached a decision. He still had myriad technical, organizational, and diplomatic questions, but these were more "guidelines for further handling, no longer spokes in the wheel." Typically, he did not directly state that he had made a decision, he merely announced, "We will have to keep written minutes of the negotiations to be signed by everyone, obligating the parties."[8] With those words, he authorized Dayan's plan.

In London, Pineau obtained Eden's consent to the revised plan, and Sir Patrick Dean, deputy director of the Foreign Office and head of the Intelligence Service Committee, flew to Paris to seal the accord. Sir Patrick, a seasoned diplomat, agreed to Ben-Gurion's suggestion that they follow routine procedure and take minutes of the meeting. Ben-Gurion, Pineau, and Dean, representing Her Majesty's government, each signed the minutes and received a copy. Ben-Gurion folded his copy and put it in his breast pocket. It was compensation for all the insults he had suffered from the British and the best guarantee that Britain would not renege. Still, for years, Eden would try to disclaim knowledge of the events at Sèvres.

On the morning of the decision, Ben-Gurion wrote in his diary: "The action seems to be necessary. It is the only opportunity for two fairly big powers to try to destroy Nasser, for it to be unnecessary that [Israel] confront him alone in the future as he grows stronger and controls the Arab states."[9] There is no overestimating Dayan's role in the decision to go to war in

Sinai. It was entirely Ben-Gurion's decision, but Dayan knew just how to calculate his moves and phrase his proposals to encourage Ben-Gurion to decide affirmatively.

After the British left, the French and Israelis toasted the campaign's success. Dayan's mind was already elsewhere. Zero Hour had been set for the evening of October 29—only five days away. He wired Meir Amit to call up the armored units immediately. On the flight home in the French DC4 he was calm, knowing there was nothing of substance he could do before landing. He passed the time doodling. He sketched a small cartoon with a map of Sinai in the background, depicting the British Lord Bull and the French Marianne reaching out to "Little Israel" and declaring, "After you, sir!" The next day he would be swept up in a whirlwind of war preparations.

Landing in Israel on October 25, Dayan went straight to his office and convened the GHQ Operations staff under Amit. He faced a dilemma: to bring about the conditions agreed to at Sèvres, he had to rework the Kadesh plan with modifications that defied military logic and contradicted the principles he had instilled in the army since becoming chief of staff. In the original Kadesh plan, the paratroop brigade had two major missions: capturing the Egyptian military headquarters at El Arish and then taking Sharm el-Sheikh. Now it was tasked with a less brazen mission of marginal value but vital to ensuring British and French military involvement. Contrary to IDF doctrine and the original Kadesh plan, instead of speeding toward enemy deployments at the start of the action, the Armored Corps would now have to wait thirty-six hours until Britain and France began bombing Egyptian bases.

Dayan could not explain the real reason for the tactical changes nor could he tell the handful who did know of the British-French connection about his promise to Ben-Gurion to limit the scope of the IDF's involvement. He prepared his staff with a disclaimer in general terms.

"Everyone will know only those details necessary to performing their mission even if they do not understand the general scheme," he explained. "Due to political information, orders may be given that seem surprising and defy everything planned to date, sometimes defying even military logic. Nevertheless, the GHQ and combat officers are ordered to comply with the decisions without reservation. Whether in performance or in speech, absolute discipline is necessary."[10] Within a few hours, the GHQ issued orders for Kadesh 2, in line with the new political conditions.

Dayan spent the last few hours before the campaign composing the announcement for the IDF spokesman, which would be publicized two hours after the paratroop drop. Composing the proper statement required close knowledge of the Sèvres agreements and their constraints, and fine maneuvering between contradictory aims: Israel had promised the British that it would create the impression of "a real act of war endangering the canal," but the IDF also had to make the Egyptians believe that the Israeli attack was a limited operation. Only Dayan was capable of finding the necessary balance. When he finished the statement, he brought it for approval to Ben-Gurion, who was bedridden with fever in Tel Aviv. Toward evening, Dayan set out for the war command post near Ramle, not far from the point he had reached at the climax of his battalion's raid in the War of Independence.

Dayan spent most of the campaign on the battlefields. He had no patience with the minutiae of its management and wanted to feel the battles from up close and, if possible, personally observe developments. Dayan usually left for the front early in the morning in a light aircraft, spending hours in the field before returning to GHQ toward evening to receive updates and issue further instructions. He would then visit Ben-Gurion, who was confined to his bed for most of that period.

Five times during the weeklong offensive, Dayan found himself under fire. On the whole, the Sinai campaign proceeded according to plan. Meir Amit directed the war from GHQ, and the countless small decisions that had to be made hardly required Dayan's direct input. He maintained wireless contact during most of the hours that he was away from GHQ, but there were also spells when he could not be reached, a lack of communication for which he drew criticism during the conflict.

"The ongoing management of the campaign is in the trusty hands of staff officers with first-rate knowledge and judgment," he later wrote. "Staff officers claim that my absence from the command disrupts proper working procedures. They may be right, but I am unable or unwilling to act otherwise."[11]

The first operational mishap developed on the second day of the campaign. Late in the morning of October 30, Dayan arrived at the forward command post of O.C. Southern Command Assaf Simhoni. To the chief of staff's astonishment, he learned that against orders the Seventh Armored Brigade was already in action twenty-five miles inside enemy territory. Livid, Dayan berated Simhoni in the presence of the officers and soldiers situated there. This was exactly the sort of development he had sought to avoid. The entry of the armored brigade deep into Sinai could not be regarded by Cairo as a limited operation. The Egyptians were liable to wake up, activate their air force, and hit Israel full blast before the allies intervened. Moreover, Simhoni's action undermined Dayan's promise to Ben-Gurion at Sèvres that the Israeli action would be limited until the British and French took a part, a condition that had been the reason for the prime minister's consent to the entire operation. But though Simhoni knew of the British-French connection, he did not understand its full import, which had led him to act precipitately.

The next morning, Dayan went to see Ben-Gurion before leaving for the front. Telegrams from France advised that

the British, contrary to their promises, had decided to postpone their bombing by twelve hours, putting off sorties by the
Royal Air Force until the evening of the third day. Enraged,
Ben-Gurion suspected that the British were reneging on their
undertaking. Fearing for the safety of the paratroopers, he demanded that they retreat, but Dayan, with the greatest difficulty, managed to persuade him to wait another few hours.
He did not dare tell Ben-Gurion about the Seventh Armored
Brigade's disobedient advance the previous morning. Working patiently he was able to get everything back on track by
evening.

On October 31, the allies began a massive bombardment
of Egypt's air bases and military installations. There was no
longer any reason to curb the operation, and Dayan issued
general instructions to deploy all forces according to plan. He
spent the next twenty-four hours in the northern zone, embedded with Col. Chaim Bar-Lev's armored brigade, which,
following a nighttime raid and with the assistance of the First
Infantry Brigade, had captured all the Egyptian posts around
Rafah. Dayan requisitioned two command cars, one fitted with
communication equipment, the other for his squad, which included myself as bureau chief, a signaler, and a bureau clerk for
technical assistance and to guard the convoy.

At dawn on November 1, the squad crossed the southern
tip of the Gaza Strip straight into a thicket of Egyptian posts
near the Rafah Junction. The sector had not been cleared and
Egyptian soldiers fought on sporadically. At one spot, we came
under machine-gun fire and an anti-tank cannon shell exploded
just yards from our command car, and we all jumped from the
car and took cover in a roadside ditch. The last Egyptian soldiers soon left, and the squad proceeded to the junction, where
a group of officers had briefly stopped to celebrate their gains.
There was hugging all around, and even Dayan permitted him-

self a display of emotion. "We fell into each other's arms like in a Russian war film," he gushed.[12]

From Rafah Junction, the armored brigade headed west along the coastal road and arrived at a chain of dunes about three and a half miles east of El Arish, the Egyptian army's headquarters and logistical nerve center in Sinai. With nightfall approaching and the military vehicles needing to refuel, the attack on El Arish was postponed until morning. Dayan and the squad settled down on the slope of a dune, finishing our combat rations supper and preparing for a short sleep. Suddenly the Egyptians started shelling. The shells landed next to our group, but shattered inside the soft sand, which absorbed some of the shrapnel. Covered with sand and leaves from the eucalyptus tree above our heads, we swiftly rolled down the dune, out of range of the exploding mortars.

At dawn on November 2, the command cars drove into El Arish behind the armored brigade's advance company. As we entered a lavish building alongside the road, our squad was greeted by a burst of automatic gunfire. The bullets killed the bureau clerk and came within inches of Dayan's head, hitting the wall and covering him with dust and plaster fragments. At 11 A.M. we flew off in a light aircraft that had been dispatched to the newly captured airfield of El Arish and asked the pilot to circle above the town. In the distance, Bar-Lev's tanks could be seen gliding westward toward the Egyptian town of Kantara, near the Suez Canal.

Returning to GHQ, Dayan learned of an additional blunder. When Ariel Sharon's paratroop brigade dropped east of the Mitla Pass, Sharon realized that his troops were arrayed along a line of low, exposed hills and sought permission to move them into the pass, protected by steep hills. GHQ firmly opposed Sharon's request, knowing that this advance was not needed for the combat. Defying explicit orders, Sharon placed an entire battalion on the main road, unaware that the night before the Egyptians had advanced two battalions from bases at the Suez Canal and captured fortified positions on the cliffs on both sides of the pass. The paratroopers were trapped and forced to attack the Egyptian positions in broad daylight and under tough conditions. They managed to dislodge the Egyptians from the high ground, but only after a fierce battle that claimed thirty-eight Israeli soldiers. The Mitla Pass battle was the hardest battle of the war—and totally unnecessary.

At the United Nations, pressure mounted for a ceasefire, and Dayan feared that the IDF would be denied the most precious fruit of the entire campaign: the conquest of Sharm el-Sheikh. Expediting matters, he ordered the paratroopers, bruised and battered from Mitla, to descend to the Suez Gulf by dirt roads. One battalion parachuted down over the town of E-Tor on the shore of the Gulf, about ninety-five miles northwest of Sharm el-Sheikh.

On November 5, the seventh and last day of fighting, Dayan returned to the southern front. He flew to E-Tor early in the morning, commandeered an expropriated civilian van from the paratroopers, and, escorted by a squad of soldiers, set out along the coastal road for Sharm el-Sheikh.

The road was filled with armed Egyptian soldiers fleeing Sharm el-Sheikh on foot, and there were occasional random shots. "There was nothing to stop . . . Egyptian soldiers taking cover behind . . . shrubs or in a dip in the ground and making sieves of us with their machine guns," Dayan later recalled.[13] But no one opened fire nor, probably, did anyone recognize the traveler. Dayan reached the paratroopers just as they were preparing to storm the Sharm el-Sheikh compound only to find that it had been captured earlier in the morning by the Ninth Brigade. The paratroopers met up with the soldiers at the pristine gulf. The war was over. The IDF controlled the entire Sinai Peninsula.

Dayan returned to Sharm el-Sheikh the next day, this time in a transport plane filled with senior GHQ officers, for the Ninth Brigade parade celebrating the completion of its mission. As soldiers stood in formation on the local airfield, the CGS, the O.C. Southern Command, and the brigade commander stood side by side on the podium, and Dayan read out a cable from the prime minister. Simhoni looked tense and downcast. Apart from a handshake and a few words of courtesy, he and Dayan did not speak to each other. Simhoni was in a hurry to return to the north for family reasons. The weather was blustery, and the skies darkened by a sandstorm. He took off in a light aircraft, but it lost its way in the haze and crashed into a cliff side across the Jordan. "This death of the O.C. Southern Command after the end of the war rather than in battle has the hallmark of a tragic fate," Dayan later wrote in his memoirs.[14]

Both Simhoni and Sharon's actions clearly breached orders and exhibited a lack of discipline. Simhoni's death painfully spared Dayan the need to judge his conduct. As for Sharon, Meir Amit and other GHQ officers demanded that he be court-martialed, but Dayan took no steps. In response to criticism, he replied, "For all the grievance I felt over the breach of discipline, it is better to fight with galloping horses that need to be reined in than to prod and urge oxen that refuse to budge."[15]

One more small battle awaited Dayan. That evening he and I went to meet the prime minister, now recovered and in his Jerusalem office. Ben-Gurion was in a foul mood, having received a crude, humiliating cable from Soviet Premier Nikolai Bulganin demanding Israel's withdrawal from Sinai. U.S. President Dwight Eisenhower had not spared Ben-Gurion harsh words either.

Late that night, as Dayan and I were leaving Jerusalem for Tel Aviv, our car was stopped by military police, who told us that the fedayeen dispatched by Nasser at the start of the war were operating on the road. Dayan refused to wait for a convoy to be organized. As we set out, a hastily deployed security van took its place in front of us. The two vehicles came under attack from a hand grenade and machine gun just before leaving the Jerusalem hills. The driver, Noam, hit the gas to speed past the danger, but as we started to climb again, renewed fire opened on the van a few hundred yards ahead of our car. This time, Noam braked and we all jumped into a ditch.

"All was still, though we knew that the fedayeen were at the top of the hill," I recorded in my notes shortly after the incident. "The van had disappeared westward. It was cold and wet and I was filled with concern for the CGS. I had long since noticed that one of Dayan's ways to vanquish fear, which, like everyone else, he felt at such moments, was to attack. His gun drawn, he suddenly said to me, 'Come, let's charge at them.' I do not know how I had the presence of mind to tell him at that moment, 'Now I am the commander. If the convoy does not arrive soon, we will make a run for it to the nearby kibbutz.' But there was no need since the convoy showed up within minutes and the terrorists fled."[16]

Dayan often seemed to deliberately challenge death. Years after these events, he intimated as much in an introduction he wrote for a book of poems by the renowned Israeli Nathan Alterman: "Man goes into mortal battle not in order to save others, not in order to sacrifice himself for the future. Man goes into battle because he, personally, does not want to surrender, to be defeated—he wants to fight not for the existence of his life but for the meaning of his life. Death is merely the supreme expression of the courage of his struggle. It is not the death of war, of a historic event, it is a personal death, dynamic, imprinted in the struggle, the fight, not the war."[17]

# 8

## The End of the Military Career

AMID THE INTENSE ACTION and high tension of the military campaign in Egypt, two family developments awaited Moshe Dayan at home. On the day of the paratrooper drop at Mitla, his daughter, Yaël, returned from an extended trip to Europe and the United States. At her request, when war was imminent, her father had cabled her. Yaël was not yet eighteen, and her military conscription was six months away. Nevertheless, she reported for military service upon her return, and Dayan dropped in at her base on her second day of basic training. Yaël appeared before her father, the IDF chief of staff, in a tattered working uniform, wearing a beret and carrying a rifle. "He was too happy to see me to notice how funny I looked," Yaël later wrote. "We kissed and kissed again, and he was obviously delighted to find me just where I was—a soldier in his winning army."[1] Her mother, Ruth, in her own memoir noted without rancor that "Yaël is certainly her father's daughter."[2]

Moshe's relationship with his daughter knew ups and downs, but he always loved her, and he was closer to her than to his two sons, Udi and Assi.

At the same time, Dayan's marriage to Ruth was deteriorating. Moshe had maintained a relationship with Rachel Rabinovich since they had become acquainted on the flight from Rome, seeing her whenever he was in Jerusalem. They met openly at a café in the southern part of town, and news of the affair spread. "We came from totally different worlds but love bloomed," Rachel recounted. "We would talk about everything and anything. A lot about poetry. . . . I never doubted his love for me."[3]

Ruth knew nothing of the romance until a few days after the war, when she was at a Tel Aviv hotel on business and an Italian journalist asked her whether she was planning to get a divorce. "Everyone in the hotel is talking about it," he said; "everyone is waiting for the final word. I would like to be the first to hear it."[4] She refused to believe him, but when she confronted Moshe that evening, he did not deny it. "My world could not be mended," she wrote.[5]

Dayan tried to make it up to her, taking her on a short trip to Italy with the younger children, but the rupture was irreparable. Although Rachel, his new love, had left her husband some time earlier and moved to Tel Aviv, Dayan remained with Ruth for another thirteen years, reluctant to file for divorce. "I married her when she was eighteen and only she can undo that bond,"[6] he explained. His attitude is puzzling, though he may have feared the children's reaction or public censure. In a letter he later wrote Ruth, he said that he held her in profound affection and respect, and hoped that they could continue to live in friendship and understanding, but he would not relinquish Rachel.

"You must know that I do not regret the past nor do I promise or plan to change in the future," he wrote. "If you think that a husband who behaves like this is beneath your dignity or that this sort of family life is intolerable, and you prefer divorce and separation, you have every right to, so choose whenever you wish."[7]

He was prepared to carry on as things were. Ruth, however, could neither come to terms with the situation nor bring herself to initiate divorce proceedings.

When Dayan informed Ben-Gurion that the Sinai campaign was over, the Old Man remarked lightly, "And you can't stand that?" Ben-Gurion was not implying that Dayan liked war, but at that moment he knew that Dayan feared that the prime minister would buckle under the political pressures that would soon bear down on him. On November 7, the day after the Sharm el-Sheikh victory celebration, Ben-Gurion delivered a fiery speech in the Knesset. "The ceasefire agreement with Egypt is dead and buried, and will not be revived," he proclaimed. "Along with that agreement, our armistice lines with Egypt have also expired."[8] He was intimating that Israel would hold on to some of the territories captured in the Sinai campaign. Yet within hours, under growing pressure from the United States, he had to instruct Ambassador Abba Eban to inform the United Nations that in principle Israel accepted the U.N. resolution calling for the withdrawal of its forces.

Ben-Gurion focused his attention over the following months on New York and Washington, not the IDF. He held countless talks with Eban and occasionally postponed his weekly meetings with the chief of staff. The United Nations accepted Israel's demand that the evacuated territories be transferred to a special U.N. force rather than to the Egyptian army and stationed an emergency force under General E. L. M. Burns between the IDF and the Egyptian army; this "emergency" force would remain for a decade.

Dayan, now relegated to the diplomatic sidelines, watched

unhappily as Israel forfeited its war gains. All he could do was slow down the IDF withdrawal, which began on December 2, deliberately drawing back his forces at a rate of about 15 miles a week. The removal of mines laid by the IDF during and immediately after the war provided the excuse for the torpid pace of retreat authorized by Ben-Gurion to gain time for the political struggle at the United Nations. On December 6, Dayan met with General Burns at the El Arish airfield to discuss the deployment in Sinai of the United Nations Emergency Force. Although he held a higher rank, Burns treated Dayan with the awe afforded to a victorious commander. He clearly reveled in the meeting and unabashedly asked to be photographed with Dayan as a memento.

As surely as Dayan knew that the IDF would soon quit most of Sinai, he also knew that it would return one day to fight in this desert. He instructed all units to reconnoiter the length and breadth of Sinai, as he himself spent numerous days doing. On one occasion, he set out for a two-day tour of the new oil fields near the Suez Gulf, the nearby manganese mines, and the old monastery of Santa Katharina at the foot of what is believed to be the biblical Mount Sinai. Near the mines, he headed for a pharaonic shrine dedicated to Hathor, the ancient Egyptian goddess of love and beauty. He ordered the shrine's steles and imposing statue of the goddess to be transported to the Israel Museum and took a statuette of a bird for his own home. At Santa Katharina, the monks made him a gift of a tiny old cannon, which he placed in his garden. The French and British had also looted antiquities when they had occupied Egyptian territory, but those were different times and Dayan may not have been aware of the change in attitudes.

On another tour, he stumbled across a real archaeological find after setting out in a half-track along the shore from Gaza to El Arish. He knew that west of Rafah there had been a Roman-Byzantine town, Antedon, excavated by the British archaeologist Flinders Petrie. As Dayan's company approached from the sea side they spotted a hillock and wooden watchtower erected by the Egyptian army. Dayan was astonished to find that the Egyptians had planted flowerbeds around the tower and marked them off with potsherds—the knobs and necks of ancient amphorae. When Petrie excavated Antedon, which had been built about a mile inland for fear of pirates, he had not, apparently, uncovered the port and the warehouses for marine equipment. These had remained buried in the sandy shore for generations.

As Dayan wandered about the site, he figured out why the Antedon antiquities were being used for such homely tasks. Bedouins digging at the tell would expose the ancient amphorae, cut off the necks and knobs, and use the jugs as a protective cover for palm seedlings, while Egyptian soldiers would take the amphora remains to decorate their flowerbeds. Dayan struck a deal with the Bedouins: amphorae in exchange for coffee, sugar, tea, and rice. Though the IDF remained in the area for only a few weeks, Dayan brought back to Israel a prize of some seventy amphorae.

The Sinai campaign spread Dayan's fame around the world, and his distinctive portrait, the black eye patch with its strap cutting diagonally across his receding hairline, was featured on the covers of major magazines. Journalists flocked to him for interviews, statesmen and celebrities basked in his company. In Israel, his figure overshadowed even Ben-Gurion's. The wife of the editor of the French magazine *L'Express*, visiting Israel in early 1957, asked friends to arrange for her to dance with Dayan at a party. Presumably she wished to brandish a photograph of the encounter before her Parisian salon friends. In early February 1957, the French government made him a chevalier of the Légion d'honneur.

Shortly before retiring from military service in December

1957, Dayan met with Field Marshal Bernard Montgomery, the hero of El Alamein. At Montgomery's invitation, the gathering took place in England, at the home of the acclaimed military commentator Capt. Basil Liddell Hart. Montgomery, serving then as the deputy commander of NATO forces, came from Paris specially to meet with Dayan. It was a meeting of equals. In Liddell Hart's home, Montgomery created an atmosphere in which two extolled generals could sit down and together solve the world's problems. "Dayan is tough, but I like him," Montgomery told Liddell Hart when he was escorting the field marshal to his car.[9] After Montgomery left to return to Paris, Liddell Hart remarked that he had never heard Monty speak so frankly.

Dayan had never aspired to control all of Sinai and was therefore not opposed to withdrawing from El Arish, in northern Sinai, despite the delaying tactics. Nevertheless, when, on January 15, 1957, Israel folded up the flag that had flown from the top of the Mediterranean coastal town's municipal building, Dayan was there to observe, sad and begrudging. Asked by a journalist why he had come to watch, he replied, "IDF commanders must taste all the dishes, both the bitter and the sweet."[10]

By February, it was clear that the United States would insist on Israel's full withdrawal back to the armistice lines, which meant a complete withdrawal from Sinai, including Sharm el-Sheikh and the Gaza Strip. There were threats of U.N. economic sanctions should Israel refuse. The gap between Dayan's views and Ben-Gurion's maneuvering widened. Despite Ben-Gurion's initial belligerent stance, presumably in preparation for a confrontation with Washington, he gradually yielded to the mounting international pressure.

The government afforded Ambassador Eban broad authority to negotiate with the United Nations and U.S. Secretary of State Dulles. Ultimately, this autonomy allowed Eban to agree to the IDF's withdrawal from Gaza as well as Sharm el-Sheikh. Dayan had no influence on these developments. He advised Ben-Gurion that the IDF had enough reserves of munitions, fuel, and food for Israel to endure sanctions for more than half a year. It was always possible to surrender on one's knees, he protested; why do so now? But Ben-Gurion chose to make a gesture of goodwill rather than wait to be coerced.

As when he had ordered the IDF to make the transition to defense in 1955, Ben-Gurion chose to explain his position to the generals in person and invited them to his home on March 1. If the IDF remained at Sharm el-Sheikh in the teeth of world opinion, he argued, maritime transportation would not be allowed to reach the port of Eilat, and the city would never develop.

"There will be no dancing in the streets tomorrow," he said in the meeting. "I imagine that in the army, there will be great regret. But I am sure that six months from now . . . ships and tankers will come, work will start on laying a large pipeline. Then everyone will know that this fateful decision was for the good."[11] The generals were not convinced, but no one wished to express an opinion for or against the prime minister. There was no point—the decision had been made.

On March 4, I noted in the bureau logbook: "Misgivings about withdrawal seem to be weighing on Moshe. It's hard for him to find himself so divided from Ben-Gurion. His attempts to justify and understand Ben-Gurion's measure have been in vain. . . . In Moshe's opinion, Ben-Gurion's consent to withdraw from the Straits and Gaza is the result of weakness, not of farsighted policy."[12]

Developments in the 1960s, however, would prove Ben-Gurion right. "Perhaps we will need to fight again," he told his officers at the March 1 meeting. "But when we do, while the whole U.N. may not stand at our side, some states will, the sort of states that will enable us to do so with a calmer heart."[13] His words were virtually prophetic, reflecting a profounder fore-sight than Dayan had at this stage.

Dayan gritted his teeth and coordinated the details of with-drawal with General Burns. On March 5, he traveled to Gaza "to part with it and its antiquities," he noted in his memoirs. The town was under curfew. Dayan had feared protests by ex-tremists that would compel the IDF to resort to force, but all was calm. He also parted from the soldiers of the military gov-ernment, whose feelings were reflected in the bureau logbook: "Instead of being glad about going home or the leave they have received, the soldiers voice regret about withdrawing and their disengagement from an undertaking that had only just begun, that they had striven for, and which they believed they could sustain to create new political realities for the State of Israel."[14]

Presumably not all the soldiers felt this way, but Dayan cer-tainly did. He truly believed in the possibility of maintaining Israeli rule in Gaza. After Israel's withdrawal, however, he was relieved that he did not have to manage Gaza and its Pales-tinian residents. But then, within days and contrary to expecta-tions, the Egyptian military government returned to its offices in Gaza and there were informal demands among members of the Israeli press and some officials in the Ministry of Foreign Affairs that the IDF recapture Gaza at once. Ben-Gurion dis-missed them immediately. "We do not intend to react militarily to Egypt's entry into Gaza even if its army should follow, pri-marily because I am not convinced that it is worth Israel's while to rule Gaza," he said. "The 'bargain' of 300,000 disgruntled Arab refugees in Israeli territory does not appeal to me."[15]

The U.N. force under General Burns remained stationed on the border as a buffer between the IDF and the Gaza Strip. Egypt ceased its fedayeen raids and kept troops out of the Sinai Peninsula, while the Straits of Eilat stayed open to shipping, allowing it to become an international oil terminal. All this would change in May 1967, but for ten years Israel's border with

Egypt remained calm. A few days after the withdrawal from Gaza, Dayan and the GHQ toured the furrow line on the old border. A picture of border line conditions emerges from the words of the bureau logbook: "Peace and quiet. Shepherds and farmers roam about pleasantly with women and children right near the furrow, not even turning to look when a line of cars drives by. Near the roadblocks, Danes and Norwegians [members of the U.N. force] are busy sprucing up their tents and dwellings."[16] At the sight of the international diversity of the U.N. forces, Dayan quipped, "Who said the Tower of Babel has to rise vertically? It can be laid down horizontally, too, along the border between Israel and Egypt."[17]

In mid-March, a week after the withdrawal from Gaza, Dayan returned to the Gaza border with Ben-Gurion to meet with officers and settlers. Ben-Gurion again tried to explain his motives for leaving Gaza and asked for their opinions. The officers spoke freely, critically, and resentfully. A snapshot taken by a military photographer shows Ben-Gurion talking to the officers on a kibbutz lawn while Dayan is stretched out sleeping at the lawn's edge. In a meeting, some officers asked Dayan why he had not resigned over his differences with the prime minister. "As a citizen and soldier, I would disapprove if the chief of staff tried to use his weight to influence government decisions," he responded. "Anyone who accepts soldiering, including the CGS, accepts the government's defense policy. When the government discusses defense policy, it must assume that the army is an instrument of service and will do as it is told."[18]

Though he did not resign in protest, Dayan had spoken of retiring from the IDF for some time. Having already served for more than three years as chief of staff, longer than anyone before him, he was tired and had been waiting for an opportune time to devote a year or two to study. But Ben-Gurion would not have it, despite their disagreements. He relied on Dayan and his judgment and was unwilling to lose his services.

On November 3, Ben-Gurion suffered a personal tragedy when his military secretary, Nehemiah Argov, who had been at his side since the War of Independence, committed suicide. The reason for his act remains a mystery, but for Ben-Gurion it was a terrible blow. Because of his poor health the doctors had hesitated to tell him the news, and newspapers had printed special editions for him omitting the item. On the day after the funeral, Dayan took on the unhappy task of telling Ben-Gurion the truth. "I spoke and he wept," Dayan told his aides. After he regained his composure, Ben-Gurion took his hand and said, "Moshe, stay in the army," repeating it several times. Argov's death left him feeling alone. He missed the familiar face and could not bear the thought of Dayan, too, leaving.[19]

By mid-November, however, it appeared that Ben-Gurion would no longer stand in Dayan's way and had decided that Chaim Laskov, Dayan's deputy, would become the next IDF chief of staff. (I had left my post as bureau chief in June.) In his final days in the military, a foolish, yet typical, gaffe briefly tarnished Dayan's relationship with Meir Amit, his closest confidant. In the advent of Laskov's appointment, Amit decided to retire as chief of GHQ Operations, and Dayan spoke at his farewell party. He was fond of Amit and respected him, but instead of praising him with the expected military accolades, Dayan spoke of his character, noting that Amit was not a military man at all, that his entire comportment was basically civilian. He meant it as a compliment, wishing to commend Amit's disposition, friendship, informality, and openness. But Amit interpreted the words differently and took offense. Dayan, as soon as he learned of this, dashed off a letter of explanation and apology that mollified Amit, who received it while on tour in the United States. "Working with you inspired and infused me with that spice of life and sense of security that you sowed in the entire army," he responded to Dayan. "I do not know anyone . . . who instilled in me more values than you did:

to stand firm, do one's best, separate the wheat from the chaff, be true to oneself and stick to the goal—all these qualities are often bandied about, but few know how to put them into practice as well as you."[20]

Only Ben-Gurion's warm letter of appreciation to Dayan on his retirement topped Amit's emotional superlatives. Listing Dayan's accomplishments in military service, from his youth in the Haganah to the Sinai campaign, Ben-Gurion wrote:

> From the villages of the homeland where you grew up and your parents' home where you were raised, you imbibed a natural love of homeland and of freedom, the stature of a Jew standing tall, and the belief and confidence in our own strength. From childhood, you harbored a dauntless spirit, tackling difficulties or obstacles head on, and walking—not merely standing—at the front. . . . In the battles of the War of Independence, you showed two basic, seemingly contradictory, qualities that made you one of the most excellent soldiers in the Israel Defense Forces: almost insane daring balanced by profound tactical and strategic judgment.

On Dayan's service as chief of staff and commander of the Sinai campaign, Ben-Gurion wrote: "Your four years of service will remain a highly significant turning point, rich in outcomes for the IDF. . . . The crowning achievement of your efforts— the heroic and glorious Sinai campaign—raised Israel's prestige both internally and around the world. This campaign, in its precise planning and execution, will gleam not only in the history of Israel but in the military history of the entire world as one of the grandest campaigns in the life of all nations."[21]

It was a glowing summation of twenty years of military service, and Dayan was undoubtedly gratified by the words of praise. He included Ben-Gurion's letter in his autobiography as one would hang credentials and testimonials on an office wall.

# 9

## Government and Other Battles

ON JANUARY 30, 1958, Moshe Dayan took a leave of absence from the army to study at Hebrew University in Jerusalem, a pursuit that temporarily spared him from making decisions about his future course. His official military retirement date was set for November 1. He did not speak to David Ben-Gurion about entering politics, nor did the prime minister make any offers. "If they want me, they know where to find me," Moshe told Yaël.[1] He knew that if he had a future in politics it would be within the Mapai Party, Israel's largest, which had been governing since the birth of the state. Mapai was also Ben-Gurion's party, and therefore Dayan's political future depended on the Old Man. He would soon discover that matters were not so simple.

In the interim, the IDF issued him a modest apartment on a small army base in southern Jerusalem, and most days of the week he drove to the Hebrew University campus in a civilian jeep wearing civilian clothes. Ruth, who remained at their home in Tel Aviv, had decided to fight for their marriage, and she was highly concerned about his extreme moods. Yaël described this period as a "very dark" time. "Instead of easing his restlessness and edginess, the study period in Jerusalem had the reverse effect, just as Mother had feared," she wrote. "Lack of responsibility made him more irresponsible and his impatience turned into arrogance."[2]

He found one outlet for his recklessness: women. Though he and Rachel were still close, she lived in Tel Aviv while he was on his own in Jerusalem most of the week. There he formed liaisons that were the talk of Jerusalem society. One evening Yaël was astonished to find a strange woman in his apartment who behaved as though she owned the place. Dayan walked Yaël to the bus stop and explained that the affair was not serious. She was not disturbed by her father's betrayals, but questioned his poor taste in bedmates.

Rachel, too, knew of Dayan's affairs but was confident that she remained his one true love. "He did not love the women," she explained in an interview; "he liked the exercise. I was able to understand it and had no doubt that he really loved only me." She also wondered about her future husband's extramarital tastes. "They were cheap or loose women, and Moshe could not resist the temptation."[3]

One tryst that became notorious involved a young woman at the army base who was married to a childhood friend of Dayan's from Nahalal, also a senior IDF officer. She fell in love with Dayan and was deeply hurt when he ended the relationship, an affair that would return to haunt him. The episode enraged the woman's husband, who wrote to Ben-Gurion demanding that he publicly withdraw his support of Dayan. Ben-Gurion replied by citing King David, remembered as a great king despite impregnating Bathsheba while she was married to Uriah the Hittite. The intimation was clear: personal and pub-

lic affairs were separate matters, and he would continue to endorse Dayan.

Dayan did not wait long before being called to politics.
Less than four months after removing his uniform, he began to
receive invitations for Mapai Party events and political appearances, though he soon vexed the old-timers who ran Mapai.
Following the Sinai campaign, Mapai's young guard, organized
into a quasi-Fabian society, demanded changes to the party
structure that would enable them to win leadership positions.
But they faced opposition from the intermediate generation,
fifty- and sixty-year-olds who deemed them overly hasty.

Dayan gravitated toward the young guard but, typically,
also kept them at a distance. He did not like wheeler-dealers,
old or young. Nevertheless, his personal fame led both the
public and the party to regard him as a prominent representative of the young guard's revolt. His political positions contrasted starkly with the conservatism of party leaders, whom
he seemed to be challenging. Finance Minister Levi Eshkol,
who would succeed Ben-Gurion as prime minister, compared
Dayan to a Cossack hetman charging with sword and whip.[4]

Along the same line as Eshkol's analogy, when Dayan addressed the Tel Aviv student union on May 25, the press likened
his talk to an "artillery bombardment" and "a grenade assault
prior to charging." Lashing out indiscriminately, Dayan criticized the kibbutzim for looking out only for their own narrow
interests and the Histadrut, Israel's trade union, for ignoring
national interests. He also assailed the party apparatus and party
hacks, focusing on the veterans. "The previous generation has
passed the age of revolution," he was quoted the following day
in the newspaper *Ma'ariv*. "All energy burns itself out."[5]

To the public, the kibbutz settlers, and the Histadrut,
Dayan was a revolutionary indeed, defying the values they
had always championed. He believed that from the moment a

sovereign state was established, most tasks should be the government's province. *Pioneering* now meant having a volunteer spirit, giving one's all beyond the line of duty. To party veterans, this was blasphemy. It sounded as if the pioneering frameworks they had created before statehood were being abandoned.

Efficiency was another Dayan concept that differed from the party outlook. The social-democratic Mapai Party was committed to worker interests, whereas Dayan believed the focus should shift to economic efficiency. Histadrut had just recently called a strike at the country's leading textile firm, Ata, and worker demands threatened the company's competitiveness. Dayan's response brimmed with socialistic heresy. "During the Ata strike, I was very sorry that we, the workers, defeated Moller [the owner]," he said. "If the good of the company requires downsizing, cloth can be manufactured using fewer workers."[6]

Ben-Gurion did not endorse Dayan's opinions, but he defended his right to express them. Party veterans took this as a sign that the Old Man was cultivating Dayan for the top position, and they mobilized to thwart the alleged succession. They demanded that because he had not been discharged from the military yet, he should be silent on political matters until he returned to civilian life. They succeeded in barring him from public appearances before his formal discharge on November 1; then the tempest resumed. Elections for the Fourth Knesset were a year away, and internal squabbles posed a threat to the party. Two fruitless meetings were held, attempting to calm the storm. One veteran likened the older party members to frail Eskimo elders being ushered out to die in the snow. Another noted that "not every Moshe [Moses] descending from Mount Sinai brings the Ten Commandments."[7]

Dayan also fueled the fire. In a public speech in Jerusalem, he challenged the audience: "Do young Israelis who over the past fifteen years have crawled through thorns and rocks with rifle in hand . . . understand the needs of nation-building less than those who for twenty years have sat on the fifth floor of the [Histadrut] executive building?"[8]

Some heard a jarring militarism in his words. The cartoonist for the workers' newspaper *Davar* depicted Dayan as a small child flinging stones at that fifth floor, with the caption "The Naughty Boy."[9] Yet the public, especially the young, embraced his anti-establishment spirit. At party rallies, they shouted, "Long live Dayan! Boo to the party!" Ben-Gurion convened senior party figures to put an end to the acrimonious exchanges, and Dayan promised to curb his public remarks. The animosity, however, became a permanent fixture in Israeli politics.

Despite their objections to his political views, Mapai Party leaders could not ignore the electoral value of Dayan's fame and public status. Though he refused to join the party secretariat for fear of being confined in a gilded cage, Dayan agreed to coordinate activity among young voters and recruited Neora Matalon, his secretary from his days as chief of staff, to assist. "I felt like a reserve officer receiving a call-up," she later noted in her memoirs. Matalon would remain at Dayan's side for six years.[10] Among the young guard, he met Yizhar Smilansky, known by his nom de plume S. Yizhar, the greatest Hebrew writer of his generation, who was initially apprehensive about working with Dayan. "He was always considered tough, inconsiderate, volcanic, decisive, brutal, and cruel," Yizhar said in an interview.[11] But he soon witnessed Dayan's sense of humor and abundance of warmth, the characteristics that enabled the two eminent men to become close colleagues.

As part of his campaign, Dayan barnstormed from one party branch to another, satisfying his urge to roam the country. Matalon accompanied him on most trips. "We never arrived at our destination by the main road," she wrote. "Roads that were semi-impassable to cars took us through fruit orchards, ruins of ancient villages, burial caves. Here he was as happy as a child, splitting open a watermelon he found in the fields, picking figs or jujubes from a prickly tree, scooping up a stone arrowhead or fern-embedded limestone. His cries of joy when he called us to see what he had found echoed through the ravine and made us laugh."[12]

With the ordinary people Dayan's encounters were not always easy or pleasant. "There was a crush of people in the auditorium, tired, sweating, with a bellyful of complaints and tumultuous," Dayan described to Yizhar in an interview. "Now and then, they interrupted me with catcalls; they shouted at me, and I shouted at them. They did not reach me—I heard only a general echo—and I don't know if I reached them."[13]

While there is no way of gauging Dayan's personal contribution to the party's success in the election, his celebrity status no doubt brought in supportive votes. With 370,585 votes—nearly three times as many as the next party—Mapai won 47 of the 120 parliament seats, 7 more than in the previous Knesset.

The Fourth Knesset had many new faces that would become mainstays in Israeli politics for decades to come. Among the new generation filling the Mapai Party benches were Dayan; Shimon Peres, Ben-Gurion's right-hand man at the Ministry of Defense; and Abba Eban, the former ambassador to the United States. Ben-Gurion, fearing the wrath of party veterans, offered Dayan the position of minister of agriculture, which was not considered a senior post. Peres was appointed deputy minister of defense, and Eban joined the cabinet as minister without a portfolio though he was soon appointed minister of education. The senior posts remained with the veterans: Levi Eshkol was still the minister of finance and Golda Meir the foreign minister.

Party relations ostensibly calmed down, and Dayan's political standing seemed assured, though scars remained. Ben-

Gurion's chief rival now was Pinchas Lavon, secretary-general of the Histadrut. In 1960 it emerged that during the Cairo Affair of 1954, in which Operation Susannah, the Egyptian sleeper cell of Israeli spies, was uncovered, the head of the Intelligence Branch had forged documents and suborned an officer to commit perjury before the committee of inquiry. Lavon, who had been accused by the head of Intelligence as having ordered the activation of the cell in Cairo, now demanded that Ben-Gurion declare him innocent of the Cairo mishap, but the prime minister refused, arguing that it was a matter for the courts and he was not a judge. Lavon, furious, went public with dramatic recriminations—the opening volley of a struggle that became known as the Lavon Affair. The Mapai Party leadership had split over the issue and some of Ben-Gurion's loyal lieutenants turned against him. Repercussions from the affair rocked Israel's political establishment for years, severely damaging the party's public status and ultimately leading to Ben-Gurion's resignation. One result was that Dayan gradually distanced himself from Ben-Gurion and devoted himself to the Agriculture Ministry, where he served from December 1959 to November 1964. "Wheat fields, fruit orchards, vegetable seedlings, and cattle barns were stamped on my blood more than tanks and cannon," he later wrote.[14] Dayan, after all, had been a farmer, and he was familiar with the problems of agriculture and found them absorbing.

Though he was now on the party steering committee, the meetings bored him and he stopped attending. Instead, he scrambled about archaeological sites and lurked around development and construction areas to uncover the earth's belly, always carrying a spade and change of clothes in the car. One urban neighborhood turned out to be sitting on a Canaanite town. A resident, Leah Morris, who was a young girl at the time, later described her childhood memory of Moshe Dayan, the dilettante archaeologist: "One day, Dayan arrived at our yard in khaki shorts with a spade and began digging at the edge of the tell, without asking anyone's permission. I was curious and for days left off all play and stayed near him. I sat on the mango tree, watching him for hours as he pulled old objects and broken vessels from the kurkar (coastal sand-dune rock), one after another. I would pick him a juicy mango and feed him from my hand because his own hands were dirty from digging. Ultimately, my father politely banished him from the yard."[15]

Israeli agriculture found itself in crisis at the end of the 1950s, owing, paradoxically, to its dizzying success: surplus production had caused prices to plummet. Dayan's first task was to introduce supervision of farm produce and re-regulate production, and he particularly wished to bolster immigrant moshavim, which barely eked out a living. As minister, he controlled three chief appropriations: land allocation and water and production quotas. He decided to remove urban dairy farms from the center of the country, a proceeding that drew the ire of dairy farmers. Dayan also discovered that the new settlements of the 1950s were being shortchanged in water and production quotas, so he altered these, angering the members of the older kibbutzim and moshavim. The change primarily benefited some four hundred immigrant moshavim at the expense of older farming communities.

Dayan learned a valuable lesson in the realities of his position from the unlikeliest source: tomatoes. No matter how sensible and strategic his reasoning, Dayan could not target all civilian agricultural projects. The popular large juicy Israeli strain of tomato had a short shelf life, a fact that made it unsuitable for export. Learning that the British preferred a strain known as Moneymaker, with a considerably longer shelf life, Dayan banned the Israeli tomato in early 1960 and encouraged the cultivation of the Moneymaker. But the affair blew up in his face. Housewives were outraged, and Moneymaker prices plunged through lack of demand, while those of the juicy Israeli tomatoes skyrocketed. Dubbed "General Moneymaker," Dayan carried a belligerent message to the Knesset: "I am prepared to defend the Moneymaker to the last drop of Opposition blood."[16] Nevertheless, he had to compensate the farmers for their losses and lift the ban on the Israeli tomatoes.

Water was a different story. Zionists had long dreamed of channeling water to the country's dry south from the Jordan River's rainy season overflow. In the late 1950s, a project was begun to convey water from the Sea of Galilee to agricultural areas countrywide, but when Dayan took office, it was at a standstill. He strongly supported the project's revival, and in May 1964 the National Water Carrier, an integrated system of pipes, tunnels, reservoirs, canals, and pumps, was inaugurated. Jordan waters began to flow to the Negev, dramatically changing Israeli agriculture. Dayan could chalk up an accomplishment on par with his military feats.

Dayan's work at the Agriculture Ministry did not prevent him from participating in internal party and general politics. While Dayan was instrumental in helping Israel's deserts bloom, the Lavon Affair sidetracked the Mapai Party, much to the satisfaction of the parliamentary opposition, led by Menachem Begin's Herut Party. On January 31, 1961, following a motion of no-confidence brought by Herut and General Zionists, David Ben-Gurion was unable to form a new coalition and resigned as prime minister, causing the coalition government to collapse after the shortest Knesset term in Israel's history and prompting new elections for the Fifth Knesset. In general, Dayan supported Ben-Gurion's policies, but he believed Pinchas Lavon had been blameless for activating the Cairo spy ring and told Ben-Gurion so. He also disagreed with Ben-Gurion's insistence on resolving the matter through legal channels, considering it preferable to conclude the affair out of the public eye and contain the political damage.

Party infighting and strong public criticism tarnished Ben-Gurion's position. Kariel "Dosh" Gardosh, a noted cartoonist for *Ma'ariv*, drew a cartoon of Ben-Gurion smashing a statue of himself with a hammer. The message was clear: Ben-Gurion was being spurned by the party he had built. The old-time Mapai leadership drew closer to Ahdut Ha'Avodah (Labor Unity Party) on the left, the small party representing a good proportion of the kibbutz movement and headed by people who at one stage or another had clashed with Dayan. After the Mapai Party received more than one-third of the votes, however, Ben-Gurion formed a new coalition. When the new government assembled at the end of 1961, Yigal Allon, now a leader of Ahdut Ha'Avodah, was offered the Agriculture Ministry. Dayan was offered the Ministry of Housing, a more junior position, but he refused, insisting that he be given agriculture or nothing. Dayan retained his ministry.

During the final stretch of Ben-Gurion's premiership, his relationship with Dayan cooled. On May 25, 1963, just before Ben-Gurion retired from politics, he goaded Dayan during a cabinet meeting discussion about Israel's Defense College. Dayan reported to Neora Matalon that Ben-Gurion told the cabinet, "Generally, I would like to say to Moshe Dayan that seven years have already passed since he was in the army and many things have changed since then." Dayan told Matalon, "If it hadn't been Ben-Gurion, I would have said that what I've forgotten in those seven years, he never knew. But because it was Ben-Gurion—I said nothing."[17]

In 1963, contention in the Mapai Party spilled over into the entire political arena. The Lavon Affair had now become the Ben-Gurion Affair. Confronted in May 1963 by strengthened internal party opponents, David Ben-Gurion resigned, leaving Eshkol to form the new government. Like Ben-Gurion, Eshkol assumed the additional post of defense minister, blocking Dayan from this senior position. Mapai Party veterans and

Ahdut Ha'Avodah members combined forces to ensure that their opposition to Dayan would outweigh his soaring public popularity. A public opinion poll published on July 14, shortly after Eshkol took over, had shown that Dayan was the most popular leader after Ben-Gurion and far ahead of Eshkol and Golda Meir.[18] Initially, Dayan tried to fight his party opponents, but when it became clear that Ben-Gurion's resignation was final, Eshkol's position as prime minister was bolstered. There was an implicit alliance in his government against Dayan, both personally and politically, and the former IDF chief of staff no longer had a say in matters beyond the Agriculture Ministry. A political clique congregated around Eshkol that decided all matters of importance and excluded Dayan even from discussions on defense and military issues. Eshkol and his minister of finance, Pinchas Sapir, began to undermine Dayan's position within his own ministry. The Finance Ministry started setting the prices of agricultural produce and the party's daily newspaper, *Davar*, repeatedly attacked Dayan. Having little left to lose, Dayan became outspokenly critical of Eshkol's leadership, and he lasted only sixteen months in Eshkol's government. On November 3, 1964, he tendered his resignation. "My problem was not Ben-Gurion's absence from the premiership, but the oppressive atmosphere and hostility in which I found myself in Eshkol's government," Dayan later wrote. "I felt like the hero of another story. . . . Better to resign while I was still on my feet."[19]

Dayan remained a member of the Knesset, even though legislative work did not interest him. He began writing a book on the Sinai campaign, enlisting Neora Matalon's help. He also asked for additional governmental duties, however minor, and Eshkol put him in charge of a government fishing company active in Eilat and the Red Sea. The political scene, however, continued to be acrimonious. Ben-Gurion decided to form a new party, and on June 16, 1965, without consulting his parliamentary loyalists, announced that he would run as a candidate for the new party in the upcoming elections.

Though Dayan had opposed Ben-Gurion's resignation from the outset, he had reservations about turning a struggle over policy and principle into a personal vendetta against Eshkol. He also believed that Ben-Gurion could not muster a large enough party to affect the government's composition. While Ben-Gurion established Rafi, the Israel Workers List Party, Dayan delayed his decision on whether to join. Ben-Gurion's supporters knew that his leadership alone would not be enough for a new party, and they pressed Dayan to join. Dayan wavered, believing that a split from Mapai would be the wrong strategy to defeat it. "I don't share the mantra that they can't manage without us," Dayan told party activists at a conference. "I think they can manage . . . without me, without you, without us." He may have been hinting, "without Ben-Gurion" as well.[20]

The day after Ben-Gurion proclaimed the formation of his new party, Dayan announced that he was staying with Mapai. Some of his friends spoke of betrayal, and many thought that the war hero had shown himself to be no hero in politics. Avraham Schweitzer, a senior journalist known as a Dayan supporter, expressed his disappointment. "The public judges harshly someone who refuses to go to war and deserts his unit before battle," he wrote. "All the more so, a senior commander is judged harshly for announcing, on the day before confronting the enemy, that he is not prepared to risk the results and is therefore going home."[21]

Dayan admittedly sat on the fence for three months, countering criticism by saying, "I myself take a harsher view of those responsible for erecting the fence than of those who find themselves sitting on it." Ultimately, he joined Rafi. "I hesitated simply because I hesitated," he commented. "I was in no hurry to decide because I was unable to decide."[22] Dayan was also unwilling to submit to Ben-Gurion's capriciousness and did not want others to perceive him as the Old Man's gullible follower. But he had little choice: his path in Mapai was blocked. He aligned himself with those closer to his own political ideas.

The results of the Sixth Knesset elections were disappointing. Ben-Gurion's candidates garnered only ten seats, and the small party was excluded from Eshkol's new coalition government. Peres was appointed Rafi secretary while Dayan cut his political activity to a bare minimum. He felt as though he was stranded.

With his political post now settled, Dayan continued his extramarital affairs. "I knew of them all: the thin and the fat, the Frenchwoman and the student, the officer and the journalist," Yaël, who was to some extent his confidante, wrote disdainfully. She did not condemn him, she was merely shocked by the vulgarity of it all.[23] His liaisons occasionally found their way into the tabloids, and the affair of his university days caught up with him. The wife of his Nahalal friend did not get over his rejection and wrote a thinly veiled novel about the affair in which he was easily identified. The book was published in 1963 under the title *Hot Sands*, but made no waves. His weakness as a womanizer was so well known that the public was not overly bothered by the exposure of yet another affair.

Ruth, though, took the matter hard. "My world had fallen apart," she wrote. "Every day was a form of death, and the nights far worse. I seemed to be heading for disaster, and there was nothing I could do but endlessly bide my time. I felt as though I were being punished for my love."[24] The press repeatedly commented on Dayan's recklessness, writing that his behavior could not be glossed over. Apparently, however, it could. Yaël captured the public attitude toward Dayan's womanizing cynically but precisely: "The public eagerly swallowed up the gossip, which added to Father's colorful image as a folk hero.

Men envied him, women were curious, and admirers forgave him and found justification."[25]

Rachel, too, suffered from the public exposure of Dayan's escapades. At one stage, she decided to sever their relationship but was unable to stand firm for more than a few days. When the next scandal broke, she stood at his side. Dayan had a passing liaison with a young woman who claimed that he had proposed to her, and her mother threatened to sue unless he paid them a large sum. This time he yielded, though the affair had already made headlines. His lawyers advised him that a long trial would keep the affair alive, revealing additional embarrassing details. "I loved Moshe very much, and I felt sorry for him," Rachel acknowledged. "I learned to forgive and forget, never doubting his love for me."[26]

Dayan's excesses also spilled over into lawlessness. Caught driving at more than a hundred miles an hour, he told the police that with one eye, he could see only half the speed. The stories made headlines but hardly a dent in his popularity. Rather, they added a perverse dimension to his devil-may-care image.

In April 1966, Dayan accepted an offer from the *New York Times* to cover the Vietnam War as a correspondent. The Knesset and his own faction condemned his new role, fearing that his trip would be interpreted as Israeli support for U.S. actions in Vietnam. Dayan dismissed the criticism, claiming that he was interested in learning about the management of modern warfare. "My chief expertise is in the defense field," he said. "Just as an expert of diseased plants travels to see diseased plants and how they are treated, I would like to see and learn about this war." As for appearing to support it, he assured his colleagues that his rejection of that notion "will become clear upon my return."[27]

He spent two months in Vietnam meeting with both Vietnamese and U.S. military leaders, including General William

Westmoreland, commander of U.S. operations during the Tet Offensive. Once a soldier, always a soldier; he spent most of his time on the battlefield, embedded with Marine units on missions inside villages. Press photographs showed him trudging through waist-high mud, his eye patch visible through the jungle trees.

On one of the few occasions he visited Saigon, he was surprised to find his wife, Ruth. She had come to Bangkok for a world conference on traditional crafts and decided to visit Saigon as well. There, under the unusual circumstances, their old love blossomed, if only for a day. "That night, most surprisingly, we had a wonderful time," Ruth later wrote. "We ate at a Chinese restaurant and danced, something we hadn't done in a long time. That night, for the first time in years, Moshe opened his heart to me."[28]

When he returned from Vietnam, Dayan published a series of articles criticizing U.S. policy in the war and the Americans' faltering military performance. He had reached the conclusion that the United States could not win and would eventually give up. The articles were reprinted in various languages, earning him international fame, and on a subsequent trip to the United States, England, and France, he was invited to meet state leaders, senior military commanders, and journalists. Opponents of the war used his articles as ammunition. In Israel too, Dayan was once more seen as a world-renowned expert on military and defense affairs.

# 10

## The Six Day War

ON MAY 15, 1967, the nineteenth anniversary of Israel's independence, ominous news interrupted preparations for a festive parade in Jerusalem. In violation of the agreements ending the Sinai campaign ten years earlier, Egypt had flagrantly deployed troops in the Sinai Peninsula. The Israel Defense Forces began to call up reserves, and anxiety gripped the public. Should Egypt launch war, Israelis feared, Israel could suffer catastrophic consequences. Dayan was restless. He could not bear the thought of Israel fighting a war without him.

On May 20, he asked Prime Minister Eshkol for authorization to inspect the IDF units assembling in the South. Eshkol granted him permission, and on May 23 he was warmly welcomed at the command post in Beersheba. Eshkol knew that President Nasser had just ordered the Straits of Tiran closed to Israeli shipping, an action that Israel had repeatedly warned would be considered an act of war. Three IDF divisions were on alert in the Negev: the elite Armored Corps under the command of Gen. Israel Tal; another armored division led by Gen. Avraham Yoffe, who in the Sinai campaign had led his brigade to Sharm el-Sheikh; and the paratroopers and their celebrated but controversial commander Gen. Ariel Sharon.

Over the next seven days, Dayan toured all the Southern Command units. He met with commanders, spoke with soldiers, and for the first time kept his own diary, having neither a secretary nor a bureau chief. He knew most of the senior officers well, and they all knew and admired him. On the instructions of the IDF chief of General Staff, Gen. Yitzhak Rabin, the officers showed him their strategic plans, naturally expecting him to share his thoughts. Dayan was reluctant. "I came to see and to hear, not to express opinions," he said, but soon enough he was unable to withhold his reservations.

He slept in Beersheba, returning to Tel-Aviv intermittently to keep abreast of the political situation. One evening he was spotted on his way to a café and immediately surrounded by an enthusiastic crowd. "Moshe Dayan! Moshe Dayan!" The crowd's embrace was a local expression of the mounting public anxiety at the end of May, an anxiety that also permeated political ranks. Prime Minister Eshkol was viewed as hesitant and indecisive, and there was talk among the public, the press, and the leadership of replacing him as minister of defense. Dayan's name surfaced. As a member of Ben-Gurion's small opposition Rafi Party, he did not believe that he would receive the appointment and asked his brother-in-law Ezer Weizman, then head of GHQ Operations, to re-enlist him into the army.

Eshkol, under heavy pressure to include more people in the decision-making process, called Dayan in for a personal meeting and suggested he join the special ministerial committee on foreign and defense affairs. Dayan refused. He was prepared to make himself available for consultation whenever Eshkol or Rabin desired, but he saw no point in sitting on a committee of seven or nine ministers who did not set policy. He repeated his request to rejoin the IDF, asking to be appointed commander of the Egyptian front.

Eshkol grasped at the suggestion and instructed Rabin accordingly. Now, however, pressure to appoint Dayan minister of defense came from within Eshkol's own party. Key party women demonstrated in support of Dayan outside Mapai headquarters, but Eshkol dismissed them as the "merry wives of Windsor." But soon afterward, a member of the Knesset, Chaim Zadok, a prominent party leader loyal to Eshkol, threw his support behind Dayan during a stormy meeting. "Dayan is the minister of defense that the people most want," he declared. "The public living here in Israel today, the mobilized public . . . know Dayan as a commander, a statesman, the victor of Sinai. That is the important image at this moment."[1]

Eshkol surrendered to the calls, agreeing to a national-unity government with Dayan as minister of defense. The expanded cabinet first convened on the evening of June 1. With a major military showdown with Egypt and other Arab countries both assured and imminent, the Israeli government had no time for formalities: Dayan assumed the position with the Knesset endorsement to follow later. He was already familiar with the operational defense plans and most of the information available to the Intelligence Branch. That same day, King Hussein, who had recently allowed Iraqi troops to deploy in Jordan, flew to Egypt and signed a pact with President Nasser. He was escorted back to Amman by two Egyptian commando battalions and an Egyptian general who would soon take command of the eastern front. With Arab military interests against the State of Israel coalescing, it appeared as if Israel could no longer postpone making an attack.

The decisive deliberations took place on the morning of June 2. The ministerial committee and the IDF top brass, including division commanders, convened at "The Pit," the popular designation for the wartime bunker of the General Headquarters. Eshkol still favored delaying the operation for at least another week to permit the Americans time to exhaust all diplomatic efforts to resolve the crisis. In a cable from Washington, President Lyndon B. Johnson entreated Israel not to launch an attack, and in Paris, President Charles de Gaulle wrote firmly that the party to shoot first would be denounced.

The Pit air was fraught with tension. Eshkol argued that Israel stood to lose all international support and needed time to explain its position to the United States before taking irreversible steps. Yitzhak Rabin, however, pointed out that time was not on Israel's side. "I feel—more than feel—a military and political noose closing in on us," he said. "I don't think that an outside party will loosen it. I therefore think that the IDF should be permitted to act at once."[2] Rabin was not only voicing his assessment, he was also articulating the crux of the strained relations between the military officers and the prime minister, and their increasing lack of confidence in him. Dayan shrank from the acrid remarks, though he clearly supported their gist. According to Rabin, "We found support and reinforcement for our stance in the words of the new minister of defense, Moshe Dayan, who backed up our position at his first appearance in his new role."[3]

Later that day, Eshkol convened several ministers for further consultation. Not one believed that an IDF attack was avoidable. The Israeli Air Force (IAF), it was decided, would mobilize to destroy the Egyptian air force in one fell swoop. Now that Eshkol could be certain that a military conflict would ensue, he stood behind the war effort and called on the government to make a formal decision. "We have fully exhausted our diplomatic actions," he said. "It is no longer possible to wait. We must decide finally."[4]

Dayan did not wait for the government's approval. That same evening and into the next day, he closely reviewed the operational plans and offered his own suggestions on three points. First, the IDF would not conquer the Gaza Strip in the first stage, to avoid spilling unnecessary blood or having to divert troops to handle Palestinian refugees, whose numbers had doubled since 1948; second, the IDF would not go as far as the Suez Canal in order to avoid the international complications that would surely arise if Israel encroached there; and third, a major objective would be to open the Straits of Tiran by taking the coastal village of Sharm el-Sheikh, even if this could be done only at a later stage.

Dayan wished to concentrate all efforts on the Egyptian front. When the O.C. Northern Command David Elazar (Dado) suggested using the war as an opportunity to improve Israel's border on the Golan Heights, Dayan was opposed. The northern forces were not to act, he ordered, even if Syria shelled and bombed Israeli towns. Unless there was an outright troop attack, the IDF was to take no initiative. Escalating hostilities on the Syrian front could rouse the Soviet Union, which had close ties with Syria. This disagreement over the war in the North would soon have a dramatic sequel. Meanwhile, Dayan instructed the O.C. on the eastern front similarly: as long as Jordan's armored troops remained on the eastern side of the Jordan River, he was not to act.

The final decision to go to war was made at an extraordinary session of the special ministerial forum. All the ministers except two, who represented Mapam, a small party that always favored a conciliatory approach, voted for Dayan's proposal. They approved, in principle, launching the war and authorized the prime minister and defense minister to instruct the IDF to choose the time, place, and means as they saw fit. Dayan left the meeting, phoned Rabin, and advised him of the decision. War would begin the next morning.

As Zero Hour approached, maintaining the element of surprise against the Egyptian air force became more pressing.

News reports of the contacts between Israel and the United States, coupled with the government's decision on May 26 to continue to pursue diplomatic channels, lent credibility to Dayan's careful leaks about waiting. He exploited one chance given in an interview with journalist Winston Churchill, grandson and namesake of the celebrated British leader, who asked him whether war was imminent and whether he should remain in Israel to cover it, by assuring him that he could return to England without any qualms. Churchill did so. Dayan eased his conscience over the crude deception by noting that "if he is a true friend of Israel, as he says, it is proper that he help dupe the enemy."[5] At his first press conference as minister of defense, on June 3, he left a general impression of "no urgency." Egypt apparently fell for the ruse and the state of emergency declared in the country days earlier was canceled.

On the morning of June 5, Dayan ate breakfast at home with Ruth and then headed for the command post about an hour before the campaign's start. He asked Rachel to accompany him to a nearby café, but revealed nothing of what was about to happen. Afterward she was not overly upset that he had not told her that war was about to break out, though on her way back to her apartment at 7:45 A.M. she was surprised when the sirens sounded all over the country. By then, Dayan was already in the air force control room following events on the situation table, where miniature planes were being moved about with long rods. Some two hundred Israeli planes approached their targets, flying low over the Mediterranean in a communications blackout. "The air could be cut with a knife," Dayan recalled. After the bombing began, communication was restored. The surprise had been complete. The IAF destroyed 204 Egyptian planes within the first thirty minutes of the attack.[6] At the same time, the amassed ground forces near the border received the order to penetrate Sinai and attack. The hundreds of Israeli tank crews heard the command on their wireless sets: "Move! Move!"

During the six days that the war lasted, Dayan toured the fronts but was unable to spend long hours with the troops on the lines as he had done in the Sinai campaign. He was now bound by the intricacies of rank and duty and had to stay in constant touch with the prime minister and participate in cabinet meetings. He could influence the campaign only during brief visits to Pit headquarters before having to rush back to Tel Aviv or Jerusalem. Among the officers, his prestige from his days as CGS elevated his stature. He had, however, come to this campaign very late, after the command had already formed conceptions, plans, expectations, and hopes about the war's management. Command Headquarters was made up of a tight group of officers who had traveled a long road together. Despite his authority and personal status, Dayan struggled to direct them and implement the changes he thought necessary in the battle plans. He was also resented in his civic capacity. "My membership in the government was precarious," he later wrote. "The veteran members of government, especially of the ruling party, Mapai, saw me as an outsider foisted on them as a military and defense expert."[7]

His position was further complicated by the intervention of Yigal Allon, who was involved in the war planning, and by Rabin's free access to the prime minister, still smarting over his ousting as defense minister. Against this internal political backdrop, the military command operated with a certain freedom of action and license to ignore Dayan's instructions. He felt more isolated than ever, as if he were shouldering all the responsibility alone.

Dayan spent most of the first morning of the war in the air force control room, sitting on a raised bench behind Commander Moti Hod, who managed the campaign. "Though the war has only just begun, the opening is promising," Dayan noted later that afternoon. "The Egyptians have no air force. Not only is there no danger of bombing Israel's civilian population, but our ground forces are assured a decisive advantage; they have aerial assistance at their disposal, the Egyptians do not."[8] After the first morning of fighting, 286 of Egypt's 420 combat aircraft had been demolished.[9]

Israel had assured King Hussein that Jordan was not a target and asked him to stay out of the confrontation. But Jordan activated its artillery and small air force against Israel and dispatched a unit to capture the demilitarized zone around the U.N. headquarters in Jerusalem. Dayan still wanted all military attention concentrated on Sinai, but the Jordanian actions sparked their own reaction. Dormant dreams awakened in the hearts of IDF officers who had served in the 1948 war and regretted the missed opportunities in Jerusalem; the Old City had remained in Jordanian hands and off-limits to Israel since 1948, and many Israelis, Dayan included, had hoped that it would revert to Israel one day. The O.C. Central Command, General Uzi Narkiss, and some of the brigade commanders had fought on the Jerusalem front in 1948 and were avid for action there when Jordan entered the fray in 1967. Dayan and the GHQ were under constant pressure from the lower ranks to expand operations to Jerusalem and the entire west bank of the Jordan River, and Dayan tried to prevent commanders from devising their own battle plans. In response to Jordan's attack, he limited Israel's initial reaction to urgent locations: conquering Jenin in northern Samaria to stop Jordanian artillery fire at Israel's northern air bases and taking northern Jerusalem to connect with the besieged unit in the Israeli enclave on Mount Scopus. Dayan feared that bringing the fight to Jerusalem would incur unnecessary damage to holy sites in the city, including the Church of the Holy Sepulcher and the mosques on the Temple Mount.

From the first day of fighting it was clear that some of Dayan's instructions were being ignored. On the Sinai front, IDF engagement proceeded according to plan, although in the morning hours Egyptian cannon and mortar began shelling Israeli settlements on the Gaza border. With Rabin's approval, the O.C. Southern Command decided to attack the Egyptian-controlled Gaza Strip according to the original plan, but contrary to Dayan's instructions. By the time Dayan learned of the insubordination, the force was already on its way, and he could merely sanction the action. Though the IDF conquered Gaza, the steep—and tragic—price validated Dayan's instructions not to attack. The infantry encountered stiff resistance, and GHQ was forced to send paratroopers into the battle. The IDF captured the Strip on the third day, when the armored troops were already near the Suez Canal. Israel lost seventy soldiers.

As the various battles raged, Dayan was summoned to Jerusalem for his swearing-in ceremony in the Knesset. The main road was exposed to Jordanian fire and blocked by the armored brigade called in to relieve the Israeli-controlled sections of the city. He arrived via a roundabout route only to find the entire Knesset personnel in shelters because of the Jordanian shelling. He lost patience and left. The Knesset endorsed the new cabinet minister in his absence. Ruth, too, had found herself under bombardment in Jerusalem. She managed to reach the Knesset and accompanied Moshe back to the coast. "Mother was again a proud, loving witness to unfolding events," Yaël later wrote. "Father issued instructions and received reports while driving. On the road winding up to Jerusalem, the inky shadows of heavy tanks advanced in the dark."[10]

The GHQ under Rabin was frantically prosecuting the war. Dayan was present for all the cardinal decisions; he had an office in the Pit and occasionally dropped into the war room for updates. The campaign management demanded detailed, concerted coordination, operative decisions, and organizational handling, which he observed but left up to the GHQ. The fine line between purely military concerns and ministerial intercession was blurred.

On the second day of the war, developments accelerated. Dayan repeatedly urged that his troops take Sharm el-Sheikh as soon as possible. The U.N. Security Council had already begun discussing demanding a halt to the fighting. "[Dayan] phoned me and said rather impatiently: 'News is mounting of stepped-up Soviet diplomacy to end the war. What about Sharm el-Sheikh?'" Rabin later recalled. "'We will find the war ending and be deprived of our reason for launching it.'"[11]

Dayan also repeatedly blocked the opening of a third front, against Syria. The IDF there was merely to "brake and swallow": stand its ground and tolerate Syrian provocations.[12] In the morning, news came that paratroopers had broken through to Mount Scopus, and Dayan decided to go to Jerusalem. A small command group including Uzi Narkiss, Ezer Weizman, and Dayan went up to Mount Scopus and met the brigade commander near the deserted buildings of Hebrew University. The O.C. pressed Dayan to permit his troops to enter the Old City, but Dayan insisted on their first taking the Mount of Olives without, as he put it, "that whole Vatican."[13] At the afternoon meeting, many ministers, among them Begin and Allon, pushed to send IDF troops to the Old City at once. Dayan, backed by Eshkol, stood his ground. The entry into the Old City and capture of the holy sites was deferred to the next day.

On the third and largely decisive day of battle, word came that Egypt had ordered its troops to retreat from Sinai, but they were bogged down in combat with Israel's Armored Corps and could not withdraw. One Israeli armored team on the northern route from El Arish heading west rumbled close to the canal but stopped on Dayan's explicit instructions. The O.C. Southern Command questioned the order again and was firmly turned down. Shortly before noon, naval forces and paratroopers dropped from helicopters gained control of Sharm el-Sheikh without resistance. The IDF troops had won the race against the Security Council resolution, and Israel's control of the Straits of Tiran was now a reality that would have to be reckoned with. It would be fifteen years before the IDF withdrew, in the wake of Israel's peace treaty with Egypt.

That morning, Dayan gave instructions for troops to enter Jerusalem's walled Old City. From atop the Mount of Olives, Col. Motta Gur, the paratroop commander, issued a formal order, predictably not lacking in historic pathos. Gur broke through the Lions' Gate, one of eight gates into the Old City, crossed the compound of mosques on the Temple Mount, and from there descended to the Western Wall. Many of the paratroopers wept. Rabbi Shlomo Goren, the chief rabbi of the Military Rabbinate, blew the shofar. In the afternoon, Dayan strode through the Old City with General Rabin and General Narkiss. The group was photographed entering the Lions' Gate, and in keeping with Jewish tradition, Dayan inserted a note in a crack of the Western Wall, with three Hebrew words: *Lu yehi shalom* — "May there be peace." He also briefly addressed the soldiers and gathered journalists who printed his words in every Israeli newspaper the next day: "We have returned to our holiest site so as never to part with it again. To our Arab neighbors, Israel stretches out its hand in peace, and the members of other religions may rest assured that all their religious rights and freedoms will be fully protected. We did not come to conquer the holy sites of others or to restrict their religious rights, but to ensure the integrity of the city and to live there with others in brotherhood."[14] Publications worldwide reprinted the snapshot of Dayan, Rabin, and Narkiss walking together, wearing steel helmets and fatigues. It became one of the war's iconic images, enhancing the acclaim Dayan would soon reap.

Levi Eshkol, of course, also wished to get to the Wall. Told that there was still shooting and it was unsafe, he arrived in the evening and made a formal declaration. The next morning's papers carried the photo of Dayan at the Lions' Gate and his address at the Wall on the front page while Prime Minister Eshkol's words appeared on the inside pages. Eshkol's military secretary, Israel Lior, was furious. "Dayan stole the glory," Lior said, presumably venting Eshkol's frustration as well. "This could not be erased from the pages of history written in Jerusalem that day. There was no choice, Eshkol filled the role of a mere minor player here."[15]

On Thursday, June 8, the fourth day, heavy fighting continued with Egypt's retreating army in Sinai. In the afternoon, the troops along the Mediterranean captured eastern Kantara, a small town on the shores of the Suez Canal. The cover photo of the June 23 issue of *Life* magazine featured a young Israeli officer who had jumped into the water holding his gun pointed skyward with his left hand. Dayan still believed that the IDF troops should stop short of the canal and a defense line should be demarcated in the hilly passes some twelve and a half miles to the east. But battles have their own dynamics. While pursuing the last of the retreating Egyptians, IDF troops on all fronts reached the banks of the canal. Dayan did not order them to withdraw.

On the Jordanian front, the fighting had stopped on the third day. By that evening, IDF soldiers reached Jericho, and Israeli tanks crossed the Allenby Bridge over the Jordan River and captured positions on its eastern bank. Dayan instructed them to return, and making sure there was no misunderstanding of his objective of severing the western and eastern banks of the Jordan, he ordered the soldiers to blow up the bridge.

South of Jerusalem, IDF troops captured Bethlehem and Hebron, and Dayan set out for the historic cities on the same day. In Hebron, he went to the Tomb of the Patriarchs, where Abraham, Isaac, and Jacob are buried along with their wives, Sarah, Rebecca, and Leah. The site is holy to both Jews and

THE SIX DAY WAR

Muslims, because Abraham was the father to both Isaac, who perpetuated the Jewish religion, and Ishmael, the forefather of Muhammad. Since the erection of a mosque thirteen hundred years earlier, Jews had not been permitted to go past the seventh step leading to the tomb. Dayan wanted to have "Jews and Arabs praying and prostrating themselves together on the tombs of their common forefathers," and gave instructions to remove the Israeli flag that had been raised on the building. To Dayan's displeasure, after he left, Rabbi Goren brought a Torah scroll into one room and sanctified it as a synagogue. Dayan believed that it was sufficient to allow Jews to pray there and that making the site into a synagogue was unnecessary. But he did not revoke the rabbi's measure. It would not be the last time that he failed to impose his own views about the occupied territories, especially in Hebron.

At this stage the focus turned to Syria. It was now or never. The O.C. Northern Command, Dado Elazar, feared that the war would end before he could act on his main front—the Golan Heights, which many in the military establishment believed was a vital strategic high ground needed to defend northern Israel. He again urged Rabin to approve the long-planned attack, and northern farmers, called on to pressure the government, arrived in Jerusalem in the afternoon of June 8, met with the prime minister, and demanded immediate action.

Eshkol submitted to the pressure and voiced his full support. He summoned Rabin, Elazar, and Allon, excluding Dayan from the talks. In the evening, Eshkol convened the ministerial committee, a maneuver calculated to sway Dayan, who opposed taking the Golan. Defying even the semblance of standard procedure, the prime minister invited the settler delegates to the meeting. Dayan was furious. He reiterated his reasons for not attacking Syria.

"Yes, the Golan Heights are a high point, but airplanes fly higher," he argued.

He saw no justification for opening a third front. As it was, Israel would have a tough struggle to retain its gains after the war. There was no chance that Syria would accept Israel's conquest of the Golan, and Israel had no interest in adding its defense to the postwar pressures. The thought of further provoking Russia, Syria's main backer, would not bode well for Israel's foreign policy. "In the international jungle, Israel should not walk the path of elephants," Dayan remarked. "There are always other paths."[16]

Perhaps fueled by his anger, Dayan was adamant, and his statements were borderline heresy for a man who grew up in Nahalal. "It is true that the Syrians embitter the lives of our settlements on the northern border," he said. "But if the settlers are unable to stand it and the situation needs changing, it is better to move the farm buildings away from the border than to embroil Israel in a state of war with another Arab state."[17]

His listeners were stunned. Eshkol closed the meeting without a decision, and the matter was left to his and Dayan's discretion. At 3:20 A.M. on June 9, Syria announced that it was accepting the U.N. ceasefire order. When Dayan arrived at the command post at 6:00 and read the announcement, he knew it was Israel's last moment to act. He phoned Elazar and asked him whether he was ready to attack. Elazar said he was. "Attack! Attack!" Dayan instructed. He immediately advised the prime minister that he had changed his mind, but Rabin was upset that Dayan had gone straight to Elazar rather than through proper channels—namely himself, the IDF chief of General Staff.[18] "The unpredictable Moshe Dayan . . . surprised [us] once more," Rabin noted cynically.[19] Dayan's decision also irked Eshkol's office; the prime minister had been authorized to be part of the decision. But there was no point in opposing the order. Eshkol supporters believed that Dayan had acted as he did so that he could take all the credit. Israel Lior, still upset by Eshkol's missed photo opportunity in the Old City, observed that when the news was received, Eshkol spat out a single word: "Sneak!" "He immediately realized that Dayan was stealing the limelight on this front too," Lior said. "Again, it looked as if Eshkol were trying to hold back the army while Dayan, the hero of Israel, once more undertook to do the right thing, the patriotic thing."[20]

Dayan must have felt that he had not acted properly. Years later in his autobiography, he struck an apologetic note while justifying his actions. "I searched for the CGS, but he spent that night at home and was not at GHQ," he wrote. It should not, however, have been difficult to locate Rabin had Dayan considered doing so important enough. At the least, his actions attest to a typical impatience with bureaucracy. As for Eshkol, Dayan wrote: "I asked my secretary to contact the prime minister's military secretary to advise Eshkol of the instruction I had given, of my reasons, and to hear his reaction. I had no doubt that Eshkol wanted the operation with all his heart."[21] His rationale sounded more like an excuse. After all, the operation could have been delayed for a minute or two while he phoned Eshkol before issuing instructions. But Dayan was never alert to the finer points of dealing with people.

The fighting on the Golan Heights started at 11:30 A.M. Though there were several difficult battles, by the end of the day most of the Syrian units had disappeared. The next day, the IDF captured Kuneitra, the Golan's main town, and the troops ascended Mount Hermon, from which they could see the suburbs of Damascus. As Dayan feared, the Soviets severed diplomatic relations with Israel, but they took no steps beyond indignant declarations and anti-Israel activity in United Nations corridors.

On the first day of fighting on the Golan, Dayan toured the command post. What he learned there annoyed him, for he came to believe that Elazar had been disingenuous in reporting the situation. If he had not lied outright, he had at least

withheld important information. Dayan had considered bringing the campaign to an end and had asked Elazar whether an
additional division that had readied to attack the southern part
of the Golan Heights might be halted. Elazar had told him
that the troops were already on their way to the Golan and
could not be stopped. Dayan found out that the troops were
still holding and awaiting further orders to mobilize toward
the Golan.[22] "Not everything is smooth with the O.C.," Dayan
noted. "The information I receive is inaccurate. . . . I did not
say anything to him, though inwardly I was boiling, and even
more—saddened."[23] Dayan did not forget such feelings, and
they tainted his relationship with Elazar when the latter was
CGS during the Yom Kippur War.

On Saturday, June 10, as evening approached, Israel ceased
fire. The Six Day War had come to an end.

Although the IDF enjoyed a sweeping victory, disagreements among the military and political leaders left their marks.
Dayan, for his part, received tremendous publicity but was
widely accused of having stolen the acclaim from Rabin, who
had in fact prepared the army for victory and was responsible
for the military planning. Dayan had certainly played no part
in these efforts. Nevertheless, his appointment was a great
boost to public and military morale. Ezer Weizman summed
up Dayan's contribution in one sentence: "Dayan provided a
powerful drive for the readiness to fight."[24]

# II

—◆◆◆—

## *Occupation Policies*

DEFENSE MINISTER MOSHE DAYAN'S order to blow up
the Allenby, King Abdullah, and Damia bridges leading to Jordan after the IDF reached the Jordan River was a dramatic,
concrete move to demarcate what he thought should be Israel's
eastern line of defense. But within hours of cutting off the
crossings, he pondered a question with which he would grapple
for the rest of his life: How should Israel control the territory
captured west of the Jordan without imposing an alien rule on
the people living there? His first step toward answering this
question was to fix the bridges. When he visited the sites, he
learned that numerous Palestinians were fording the seasonally
shallow river on foot or by car, and trucks with farm produce
were crossing to markets in Jordan's large East Bank cities. On
the spot, he issued instructions to permit regulated Palestinian
passage, and placed a temporary bridge opposite Jericho and
another near Damia, below Nablus. Allowing Palestinians to

have contact with their Arab neighbors became a basic principle of Dayan's policy in the occupied territories. Many West Bank inhabitants had relatives who had moved to the East Bank or other Arab states. Additionally, many young people, lacking universities in the West Bank, pursued studies elsewhere in the Arab world. Now, in June, summer vacation was near, and thousands of students were streaming homeward. The eastward flow demanded little supervision, but westbound traffic was a potential opening for infiltration by guerrillas, necessitating checks and control. Dayan toiled to streamline and ease the crossings.

Israel faced another new problem, this one in regard to passage across the old Jewish-Arab Jerusalem border. After the city was captured, a curfew had been imposed on the Arab quarter in the east. But Israelis were impatient to visit the newly conquered area, especially the holy sites, whether for religious or historical reasons or out of just plain curiosity. The rest of the areas conquered remained "occupied territories," their fate to be decided in the future. East Jerusalem, however, was annexed to the municipal jurisdiction of Israeli Jerusalem by Knesset legislation. The handling of the city's problems and its Arab residents fell to Jerusalem's legendary mayor, Teddy Kollek, who dismantled the walls and fences without delay and called a meeting on June 8 to discuss the question of passage between areas of the city. Most of the representatives present feared Arab violence in protest of the annexation. Dayan, who had considered the matter important enough to attend the meeting, demanded that Arabs and Israelis both be accorded free two-way passage without permits. The bodies in charge of public order were vehemently opposed, but he insisted and won them over. The next morning, thousands of Israelis poured eastward to view the historic sites to which they had been denied access for nineteen years, while thousands of Arab residents flowed westward to feast their eyes on modern Jerusalem. "There is a festive air in the city," Kollek wrote Dayan the following day, "Kudos! You were right; all the Arabs are at Zion Square and all the Jews at the [Arab] bazaars."[1]

On June 18–19, a week after the war, the government discussed policy regarding the conquered territories. Dayan held that Judea and Samaria, along with the Gaza Strip, were "part of our land, to be settled, not abandoned." The border between Israel and Jordan had to be the Jordan River. But he did not think there was any urgency to the decision because the Arabs would not be prepared to sign peace treaties with Israel in the near future. The real question facing Israel, according to Dayan, would be "to find practical ways to improve our relations with the Arabs [within the occupied territories], even in the absence of peace."[2]

Dayan served as minister of defense for seven years and was the prime architect of policy in the occupied territories. Though a variety of issues there fell under the authority of other ministers, too, most did not personally deal with these issues. Initially, Prime Minister Eshkol attempted to assume management of the territories. He held consultations, created inter-ministerial forums, commissioned surveys, and even intervened in such specifics as road routes, licenses for waterworks, and approval of Jewish settlements. However, as his biographer wrote, "Reality was stronger: the fact that the military government ruled the occupied territories exclusively, combined with Dayan's profound interest and personal dedication in dealing with the inhabitants' day-to-day life, forged the realities on the ground. Ultimately, the defense minister managed the Palestinians living in the occupied territories."[3]

In time, Dayan came to symbolize understanding and empathy toward the Arabs. Nonetheless, he maintained an extremely hawkish view on Israel's continued control of the territories, repeating, like a mantra: "Israel must not return to

the border that is less than ten miles from coastal Netanya. . . .
In 1949 we had impossible borders, and we must not return to
them for they are worse than war, they spell permanent war."[4]
He embraced the new situation created by the Six Day War, his
rational arguments overlaying powerful emotions about withdrawing from areas that since his meandering trek as a youth
he had seen as an integral part of the Jewish homeland. In these
places the Bible came alive before his eyes. In a eulogy for the
1948 casualties of Jerusalem's Old City delivered on the occasion of their reburial on the Mount of Olives, he said, "We have
returned to the Mount, the cradle of our people, the patrimony
of our forefathers. The land of the Judges and the stronghold of
the Kingdom of David."[5] Of his newfound homeland he wrote,
"There was something special about Judea and Samaria. I could
never still the quiver in my heart at the local [biblical] names,
even when a site retained only ruins."[6]

He struggled to find or create a political solution that
would be in line with his emotional response and never abandoned the search for that elusive formula. During Dayan's last
years, the violence of Palestinian terror organizations was already rocking the country, and the whole world recognized that
the Palestinians were fighting for their own national liberation.
But Dayan kept trying to reconcile his conception of a Jewish
homeland with his understanding of the Palestinians' needs and
motives. He was able to lead Israel to peace with Egypt, but he
could not find the road to peace with the Palestinians. On the
contrary, his policies established political realities that would
impede future efforts to compromise with the Palestinians.

It is little wonder, then, that most of his declarations in
this period were obscure and contradictory. At a conference
of the IDF senior command in September 1967, he listed four
policy elements: to make the ceasefire lines permanent borders; to reach peace settlements with the Arabs through direct

negotiation; to prevent the rise of a bi-national state; to thwart the possibility of a future Arab majority in the occupied territories.[7]

Today it is hard to conceive of more unrealistic aims. But even then it was clear that turning the ceasefire lines into permanent borders would preclude all possibility of peace with the Arabs, and that retaining the territories would inevitably create a bi-national state, sustainable only by force. The desire to forestall an Arab majority in the territories at a time when not a single Jew lived there was a delusion.

As soon as the fighting died down, Dayan turned his attention to the problems he had inherited after the war. A week after the cannons went silent, he met with Arab mayors of the major cities of the West Bank and Gaza, whose cooperation he considered essential to building a new government apparatus. Most belonged to old, well-connected families that enjoyed the support of the Palestinian elite, and they became the mainstay of Dayan's policies.

One of his early steps was to invite to his home the Palestinian poet Fadwa Touqan. From a prestigious Nablus family, she was known for her strong voice expressing hatred and anger at Israel and the occupation. She arrived at his home on October 12, 1968, accompanied by her uncle, the mayor of Nablus, Qadri Touqan. Dayan's invitation to an established foe of Israel aroused the ire of Israel's right-wing establishment. He responded to their gripes on Israel Radio: "I read her poems and was impressed by her personal sincerity and nationalist spirit," he explained. "Fadwa Touqan is now the nationalist poet of the Palestinian Arab public, and I believe we should try to know what that public thinks, what they feel, what they will accept, and what they will fight; not only what their political leaders say."[8]

In mid-August 1967, he appointed Shlomo Gazit, the bureau chief from his early days as chief of the IDF General Staff, the Coordinator of Activities in the Occupied Territories. Gazit later noted three tenets of Dayan's policy: "an invisible government of occupation; normalization; a wise penal policy."[9]

On the idea of an invisible government of occupation, Dayan held that "we must make sure to minimize the points of friction between the two peoples. To do so, we must permit . . . local Arabs to run their own lives without having to see or talk to any Israeli officials so long as they do not break the law."[10] Dayan gave instructions to relocate IDF command posts from the cities to rural areas; to remove Israeli flags from Arab areas; and, where possible, to avoid army patrols in Palestinian population centers, relying on local officials and municipal government to run day-to-day life.

While Dayan was at the helm, he was able to maintain calm and prevent the sort of uprisings that erupted in the late 1980s. Yet it is clear today that a people cannot be occupied invisibly. His goals, including the "wise penal policy," were unrealistic. In the war on terrorists, he tried to avoid harming innocent civilians, which, in the long run, proved impossible. Most measures aimed to deter, a policy that could be directed only at the families of terrorists or the civilian population collectively.

Dayan not only opened the border to permit Arabs from the territories to visit Israel, he fostered Palestinian economic activity to raise their standard of living. Israel's labor market was open to Palestinian workers, West Bank farm produce was sold in Israeli markets and vice versa. He attempted to integrate economically two communities that were asymmetric in every way and inexorably made the conquered dependent on the conqueror. The economic activity and relative well-being in the territories did not dampen the nationalist sentiments of the Palestinians. Dayan seemed to have insight into short-term

processes but not the foresight required for long-term historical goals.

Following the Six Day War, various workers parties united
around Mapai to form a new organization known as the Labor
Party. The party included Ahdut Ha'Avodah, headed by Yigal
Allon and Israel Galili, and Rafi, led by Dayan and Peres. For
the first time since the early 1940s, Allon and Dayan, Yitzhak Sadeh's protégés from their days patrolling Hanita, found
themselves in the same party. Both were widely regarded as the
chief candidates for party leadership after the changing of the
guard—the generation of Eshkol, who passed away in February 1969, and of Golda Meir, his replacement. Both Allon and
Dayan aspired to chart Israeli policy on key issues. Allon could
count on the unreserved support of his party leaders, and Galili,
his mentor and friend, was Meir's faithful adviser. Dayan, the
lone wolf, drew power from the public, who regarded him as an
inspiring leader. During the years between the Six Day War and
the Yom Kippur War in 1973, Allon and Dayan clashed sharply
on most issues of state.

Soon after the Six Day War ended, in July 1967, Allon
submitted a document to Prime Minister Eshkol titled "The
Future of the Territories and Management of the Refugees."
Known as the Allon Plan, it proposed defining permanent borders as the basis for negotiating peace with Arab states. Israel,
according to the Allon Plan, would retain sovereignty over a
narrow strip along the Jordan River, over East Jerusalem and
its environs, and over the area around Rafah Junction in the
southern Gaza Strip. Dayan proposed a "functional partition,"
a division not of territory but of authority and administration.

A more concrete disagreement between Dayan and Allon
crystallized over the issue of Jewish settlement of the occupied
territories. Dayan had never valued the use of civilian settle-

ments to solve strategic problems. He envisioned controlling the territory by relocating army bases to the hilltop ridge. He was not, however, opposed to the settlement process, which he viewed as a guarantee of continued Israeli rule there. In principle, he agreed, it was inconceivable to keep Jews from living anywhere in the Land of Israel. He also did not think that Israel should withdraw from the Jordan River, Rafah, or Sharm el-Sheikh, though he was opposed to Jewish settlement in densely populated Arab areas.

The ultimate test case of the settlement policy came in Hebron, from which Jews had fled after the 1929 massacre. On April 2, 1968, less than a year after the war ended, some of the champions of a Greater Israel held a Passover seder at a rented hotel in an Arab neighborhood of Hebron, having agreed to leave the next day. Instead, Rabbi Moshe Levinger, one of the leaders of the new, religious-Zionist settlement camp, called for Jews to return to the "City of the Patriarchs" and settle. Allon provided them with equipment and paid them a highly publicized visit the day after they arrived. Although Dayan had sent greetings to the seder participants, he opposed their continued presence in Hebron, which he considered an unnecessary provocation to the Arabs. But he was in the hospital at the time,[11] and unable to intervene. By the time he returned to work, the settlers could no longer be dislodged.

The public regarded such episodes as a prelude to a contest between Dayan and Allon for the premiership down the road. Allon claimed that for every proposal he made, Dayan proposed the opposite.[12] Dayan responded by sending a message with General Joseph Geva, the director-general of Allon's Ministry of Immigrant Absorption, affirming that he did not aspire to be prime minister and therefore Allon should not feel threatened. Allon was not convinced. "Don't believe that sly fox," he told Geva.[13]

Dayan's liberal policy toward the Palestinians did not prevent him from applying tough, even cruel, measures against those who resorted to violence or abetted terrorists. By August 1967, the Palestinians had adopted a policy of terror: shooting Israelis and laying mines on roads, detonating bombs in Jewish cities. To punish and deter the terrorists, the IDF blew up homes, detained suspects or their relatives, shut down shops whose workers went on strike, and imposed curfews on Palestinian cities. "One of the painful, effective retaliation measures was the exile of political leaders and agitators responsible for organizing strikes, demonstrations, and other means of resistance," Shlomo Gazit wrote.[14]

Yasir Arafat, leader of Fatah, the main Palestinian guerrilla movement, founded in 1959, began setting up bases in Jordan and striking at Israeli targets across the border and around the world. The Jordan Valley became a hotbed of unrest. Militants from Jordan tried to ford the river at night to reach the hilltop ridge west of the river by dawn and blend in with the dense Palestinian population. Israel responded by installing a surveillance system along the river that included outposts, fences with electronic sensors, and roads that were covered with fresh earth every morning to monitor and detect footprints.

Defending Jewish communities in the Jordan Valley against mortar shells and missiles fired from across the river was a more challenging task. Dayan assigned cannons, tanks, and airplanes to the area and hoped to restrict IDF retaliation to military targets only. That hope clashed with reality, and the entire population on the Jordan's eastern banks suffered; the fertile region turned barren. Moreover, as Dayan defeated the terrorists on the battlefield, Arafat and his people gained in power and status.

Even military failures empowered the Palestinian Liberation Organization. On March 12, 1968, the IDF carried out a broad offensive against the village of Karameh, the main Palestinian base on the eastern slopes of the valley. It was the largest IDF operation since the Six Day War. Within hours, paratroopers conquered the village, killing some 150 militants and taking 130 captive. Yet the incident became a symbol of Palestinian resistance. In the eyes and lore of the Palestinians, the Battle of Karameh remained a victory. Abu Ayad, a senior Palestinian leader, described its effect on morale to Eric Rouleau, a French journalist: "The Palestinian masses were gripped by fervor. After decades of humiliation and persecution, they could hold their heads up thanks to the Karameh victory, which they saw as the start of their liberation. Thousands, tens of thousands of young and old wanted to join the Fatah movement. High-school pupils and students left school to join its ranks."[15]

Dayan learned of the Karameh fiasco in the hospital, where he lay injured after a brush with death. A day before the IDF operation, he had gone digging in Azor, a town near Tel Aviv, after a local boy named Arieh told him that bulldozers had uncovered a burial cave. Dayan hurried to the site, entered the chamber, and while poking around was completely buried under a cave-in. "This time, I really thought I was done for," he later recalled. "I saw the upper part of the sand hill that had given way falling and rolling down on me. I had time to think: this is the end. I could not move or flee or stop the enormous block that landed on my head."[16]

Dayan lost consciousness, and Arieh summoned neighbors, who dug him out and called for an ambulance. Dayan was badly hurt and bleeding all over his body, with two broken ribs and a torn vocal cord. He was hospitalized for more than three weeks, the upper part of his body in a cast, unable to speak. Physiotherapy treatments were agonizing, and he required a speech therapist before he could talk again. His family—Ruth, Yaël, Udi, and Assi—sat at his bedside every day. Rachel, his love, would arrive after lights-out. His appearance shocked her, and he had to reassure her daily that he would fully recover.[17]

For a long time after his discharge from the hospital, Dayan experienced tremendous pain, and his voice remained hoarse and weak. Yaël believed that he never fully recovered, that "this blow was the start of a process of declining health; from then until his death he was never completely healthy."[18]

He returned to work to find the Jordanian border heating up. The Palestinians were now operating from refugee camps in the hills, and though King Hussein endeavored to curb them, they enjoyed the backing of Syria, Egypt, and Iraq. Following a Palestinian assassination attempt on Hussein's life and the bombing of three airplanes hijacked from Europe en route to a Jordanian airport, tensions erupted. In September 1970, Hussein ordered his army to attack Palestinian strongholds; after several battles, the army won control of the camps. Known as "Black September," the attacks by the Jordanian army killed thousands of Palestinians and sent the rest into exile. Along with other guerrilla organizations, Arafat moved Fatah's headquarters to Lebanon, and the Jordanian front cooled. Life on both sides of the Jordan Valley returned to normal. Dayan regarded the episode as a political victory. However, it soon became clear that a military defeat, even as decisive as Black September, does not stop a liberation struggle. The various PLO factions regrouped at new bases in Lebanon.

Dayan faced his toughest test as minister of defense on the Egyptian front. Nasser never came to terms with Egypt's defeat in 1967, and the Soviets replenished the Egyptian and Syrian armies, vastly augmenting their weapon supplies. Soviet officers and technicians arrived in the Middle East en masse to train and prepare the Arab militaries for the next round of fighting. In the first year after the war, Israel's southern front remained largely quiet, for Nasser calculated that Egypt was not yet prepared for a renewed showdown. But on September 8, 1968, the front flared up when Egypt pummeled IDF posts along the Suez Canal with artillery shells. The IDF forces were inadequately protected and suffered heavy losses that day: ten dead and eighteen wounded. Daily incidents at the canal opened an active front that lasted for two years. The War of Attrition, as it came to be known, claimed heavy casualties on each side, but both the Israelis and Egyptians strengthened their resolve and refused to submit.

Dayan, assessing the situation in Suez, described a scene he came upon at an IDF post. "The place looked like a typhoon had hit it," he noted. "A shell with a delay device had penetrated the concrete layer of the main bunker's roof and exploded inside. There were twenty soldiers inside at the time; all were hurt."[19]

He concluded that the bunkers and posts along the Suez had to be reinforced immediately, though he did not believe that defensive measures alone would prevent the Egyptians from crossing the canal. He reverted to the aggressive policy he had employed during the 1950s. "The decisive question is: Can we implement a policy to show the Arabs that it is better for them to reach a peace settlement or at least a ceasefire because wars with us will cost them dearly and they will not achieve their goal?" he asked himself. "We must now strike back hard, not rely on fences and mines."[20]

The IDF installed heavy fortifications in a series of strongholds along the canal to better protect the soldiers on the waterline. These posts were known as the Bar-Lev Line, after Chaim Bar-Lev, who had replaced Rabin as the IDF chief of staff on December 31, 1967.

The Israeli public believed, incorrectly, that the line was meant to stymie attempts by the Egyptian army to cross the canal, much as France's Maginot Line along the German and French borders had been intended to do after World War I. In fact, the Bar-Lev Line's sole purpose was to protect the soldiers from artillery fire so that the IDF could maintain a presence on the banks of Suez. The fall of the Bar-Lev Line in the 1973 Yom Kippur War thus appeared to Israelis as the collapse of their first line of defense, though Dayan had never seen it as such. Yet once again, despite his experience and acumen, which may have led him to consider a more mobile defense system along the canal, as minister of defense in 1968 he did not interfere in GHQ military considerations, leaving the decision to the CGS.

Dayan acknowledged the need to reinforce the Bar-Lev Line, but the War of Attrition became a campaign of constant escalation. The IDF carried out complex commando raids that incorporated aircraft and tanks. In one such raid, on November 1, 1968, the IAF bombed the Qina Bridge, and paratroopers, dropped by helicopter, blew up the Naj Hammadi Bridge, both on the Nile. Aerial dogfights soon followed.

In the spring of 1969, the Egyptian army amplified its attacks. In March, it conducted 150 offenses, and in April 600. Despite suffering heavy losses, Egypt showed no inclination to stop. Nor did Dayan. He recommended expanding the fight by permitting the air force to strike deep inside Egypt. On January 6, 1970, the IAF attacked army and missile bases and radar installations not far from Cairo. Egyptian military morale appeared to plummet, and Nasser appealed to Moscow for help. The Soviets answered Nasser's call and outfitted Egypt with longer-range missiles and three additional cutting-edge flight squadrons. Soviet soldiers manned both the missile batteries and the aircraft, and on July 30, Soviet and Israeli pilots engaged directly. Israelis downed five Soviet aircraft. But the new actor in the war elicited concern. "The question is not which pilots are better, the Israeli or Russian, but how to do everything to avoid clashing with the USSR," Dayan told the proud Israeli pilots.[21]

By the spring of 1970 both the Israelis and the Egyptians seemed thoroughly exhausted. On April 10, Nasser publicly appealed to U.S. President Richard Nixon to intervene. On June

19, Secretary of State William Rogers launched an initiative directed at Israel, Egypt, and Jordan, demanding that they cease their fire and hold direct talks through Norwegian U.N. mediator Gunnar Jarring. In early August, the warring nations agreed. Firing stopped on both sides of the canal, but on the night after the ceasefire went into effect, Egypt, contrary to its commitment, moved missiles nearer the canal. Israel protested sharply, yet Golda Meir and Dayan refused to violate the ceasefire. The missile repositioning would seriously impede the Israeli Air Force in the next war, two years later.

On the ceasefire, Dayan wrote: "Both sides breathed in relief. The soldiers raised their heads above the dugouts. On both sides of the canal, they sat on sand ramps and exchanged words—not necessarily greetings and pleasantries, but that too was preferable to bullets and shells."[22]

In his memoirs, Dayan treated the War of Attrition as an Israeli victory. The IDF did manage to thwart Nasser's intention of wearing Israel down and forcing the IDF out of Sinai; and after long refusing to halt his fire, Nasser ultimately asked for American intercession. Still, today, Israel's part in the War of Attrition seems like a pyrrhic victory. Nasser apparently impressed on the international community that Israel's hold on Sinai was temporary and, if retained, in the long run would be intolerable. Without a political settlement, the ceasefire was bound to be fleeting: the countdown to the next war had already begun. Nasser's boldness in challenging Israel along the canal and the intermittent crossings raised military morale in Egypt. Indeed, despite the IDF superiority, Egyptian soldiers dared strike across the canal.

On September 28, a few weeks after the ceasefire took effect, Nasser died of a heart attack. He was replaced by his vice president, Anwar Sadat, who would utilize the experience of the War of Attrition to cross the canal—not merely with commando units, but with his entire army.

# 12

## Controversies

THE CEASEFIRE ON THE JORDANIAN and Egyptian fronts was largely maintained for the next three years, but the political stalemate worried Dayan. He believed that Israel should not retreat from the Jordan River, its natural eastern border, or from Sharm el-Sheikh, the Rafah Salient, and the Gaza Strip. Yet he knew that the Arab regimes, Egypt's in particular, would not accept the impasse, and sooner or later war would resume.

This expectation led him to seemingly contradictory conclusions. To preserve a de facto state of nonbelligerence, conditions for the Arabs must be tolerable: Palestinians needed to be allowed maximum autonomy in the West Bank and the Gaza Strip, and the IDF had to retreat from the Suez Canal, enabling Egypt to open it to international navigation and repair the towns that had been virtually destroyed in the War of Attrition. At the same time, he sought to consolidate Israel's control over the territories attained in the Six Day War by developing integrated utilities and large Jewish settlements so that the territories vital for Israel's security would remain Israeli after the Arabs eventually concluded that never-ending war with the Jewish state was not in their best interest. Between these two poles, he introduced initiatives in the early 1970s that were both conciliatory and politically hawkish.

On March 22, 1971, Dayan brought up his astonishing policy calculations at a discussion in "Golda's kitchen," a regular, informal gathering of ministers and advisers that was often held in the prime minister's own kitchen, where she would serve tea and biscuits. "To breach the solid wall, we should aim for an interim agreement," Dayan told the group. "Contrary to our position that so long as there is no peace treaty we will hold the current ceasefire lines, we should retreat from the Suez Canal as part of an imperfect agreement."[1]

Dayan had never wanted the IDF to sit on the banks of the Suez, and the War of Attrition further convinced him that Israel should not be the party blocking international passage through the canal. Now he sought to trade IDF withdrawal for a nonbelligerence agreement or at least a situation that would tie Egypt's hands.

The initiative failed, however, because the prime minister and most of the ministers were unwilling to draw back more than six miles, which Egypt found insufficient and would not even discuss. Meir had been influenced by General Bar-Lev and the GHQ, who claimed that Dayan's plan endangered the IDF. Further, she did not trust Egypt to honor an agreement. Dayan, believing that Israel's withdrawal and Egypt's renewal of shipping would greatly reduce the threat of war, proposed redeploying some eighteen miles farther east. He also suggested dismantling the Bar-Lev Line and treating the arrangements as lasting. He was under no illusion that Egypt would accept the new line as permanent, but he assumed that Sadat would agree to settle the final border through political negotiation rather than war.

Dayan's proposal was rejected, and he did not insist on it; the Egyptians, too, hardly welcomed the idea. It would take another war to vindicate Dayan, and while it is not the historian's task to muse about what might have been, one thing is certain: Meir's proposal to retreat only six miles and leave the area demilitarized was unacceptable to Sadat. Egypt readied for battle, and two years later, in the Yom Kippur War, dealt Israel a severe blow, compelling a withdrawal not to the lines Dayan had suggested but all the way back to the pre-1948 border.

In addition to staving off threats from Egypt, Dayan also struggled with Palestinian militant organizations. Israel's eastern border remained calm after King Hussein expelled the Palestinian militias from Jordan in 1970, but a new front opened in the north. Arafat's Fatah movement joined the PLO in 1968 and quickly took control. After being expelled from Jordan, the PLO continued to carry out attacks against Israel from combat bases in Palestinian refugee camps along the Mediterranean and in Beirut's suburbs in southern Lebanon. The group launched a campaign of global terrorism, including hijackings. In an attempt to force the Lebanese regime to rein in the terrorists, the IDF raided the Beirut airport on December 29, 1968, destroying fourteen planes belonging to Arab airlines.

Deterring Palestinian terrorists was a particularly vexing task in Lebanon, a country with no definable regime. Torn by ethnic factions for centuries, Lebanon had no central power capable of checking the Palestinian forces. Here Dayan's retaliation tactics were ineffective: the Palestinian militants in Lebanon incessantly barraged Israeli border towns and northern communities with katyusha rockets. Terrorists infiltrated Israel and ambushed a civilian bus, killing eight children and four adults, and wounding twenty-nine more people. Many of the PLO attackers reached Israel from the sea. IDF retaliation did not relieve the daily distress. Israeli attacks may have sowed destruction in Lebanese refugee camps and villages, but at the end of the day, the IDF soldiers returned to their bases and the Palestinians returned to terrorism. Dayan conceded that his reprisal strategy to deter the terrorists had failed.

"The tough policy of initiated reprisal didn't stop the terrorism from Lebanon," Dayan later admitted. "The Lebanese government, its army, leaders, and population—whether willingly or from weakness—grew resigned to the situation. They accepted a military force within the state independently operating and conducting policy. The IDF's hardest, boldest strikes . . . shocked the Lebanese, but did not induce them to expel the terrorists."[2]

In contrast to his flexibility over Israel's relations with Egypt and the Palestinians in the occupied territories, Dayan was firm in the early 1970s about the conditions Israel should establish for final-status negotiations with the Arabs. His views placed him at the extreme right on Israel's political spectrum. Though the national religious fervor of the Greater Israel movement, which advocated full annexation of the entire land west of the Jordan River, was alien to him, his love of the land continued to guide him. Believing that peace with the Arabs was impossible, he thought that Israel would always have to exist within "defensible borders"—with or without Arab consent. When Israel's War of Independence ended, the 1949 armistice line left Israel only ten miles wide at its most populous area and with the Egyptian-controlled Gaza and Syrian-controlled Golan Heights abutting its communities. The Jordanian-controlled West Bank land Israel gained in 1967 widened the country's narrow waist and according to many created defensible borders. As the 1969 summer elections approached, Dayan outlined his view of the ideal permanent borders for the State of Israel, and the Labor Party incorporated his draft into its platform. "Israel regards the Jordan River as its eastern defense border, non-crossable westward by foreign army forces," the chairman of the platform committee broadcast on the radio on August 3, 1969. "We will continue to control the Golan Heights and the Gaza Strip and our independent forces, controlling the straits in an area . . . territorially contiguous with Israel, will ensure freedom of shipping from Eilat southward." This position appeared in all of the Israeli newspapers the following morning.

Despite the Labor Party's reunification following the Six Day War, the various factions within the party occasionally convened in informal caucuses. Dayan's coterie increasingly emerged as the internal opposition, its political strength deriving primarily from his popularity. Veteran party leaders felt that he was constantly threatening to break away and perhaps join up with elements on the right. Given Golda Meir's struggle against Ben-Gurion and his followers in the early 1960s, and her vigorous opposition to Dayan's appointment as minister of defense during the Six Day War, Dayan was apprehensive about their relationship when she was elected prime minister. His fears were overblown. "Neither of us forgot the past," he stated, "but we both dealt with the present and thought of the future." Dayan respected Meir's integrity and the transparency of her work. "She had 'intimates'; I was not one of them. But on topics concerning my work, we were not divided."[3] Together they would endure the storm of the Yom Kippur War, and together they would be toppled by it, but Meir never tried to shift the blame to Dayan. The same cannot be said of Mapai's other old-timers or of Yigal Allon and Israel Galili, who stood among Meir's close advisers and spared no effort to undermine him.

Dayan's position hardened before the elections scheduled for the fall of 1973, and he demanded that the Labor Party adopt a clear policy on the occupied territories. He assembled several hundred supporters at a Tel Aviv convention, which the public understood as an undisguised threat to break away from the Labor Party. Even though he was a lone dissenting voice and most Labor leaders were hostile toward him, he was still able to influence policy. Galili, seeking to keep the Labor Party from collapsing, joined Dayan in formulating what became known as the Galili Document, though it was in fact Dayan's brainchild.

The document proposed a far-reaching program of Jewish settlement in the occupied territories, with a new town on the Golan and a rural center in the Jordan Valley. Dayan also added the dramatic proposal of constructing a deep-water port between Rafah and El Arish, to be called Yamit, in the Sinai Desert. The party secretariat approved the Galili Document on September 3, a month before the outbreak of the Yom Kippur War, which postponed the elections. By the time the party returned to draft a platform for the elections held three months later, circumstances had radically changed, and the Galili Document did not remain politically feasible. On the eve of the Yom Kippur War, Dayan's public image was of an extreme, intransigent right-winger. His assertion that having Sharm el-Sheikh without peace was better than having peace without Sharm el-Sheikh still resonated when war erupted.

During this period, there were two major developments in Dayan's personal life. After fifteen years of living with a husband who was in love with another woman, Ruth decided to divorce him. Moshe later wrote: "We were married for thirty-five years. . . . We had walked a long way together, but our married life was not successful. Especially the latter half. Neither incidents nor crises ran our marriage aground, but the reverse: the absence of a vital, emotional intimacy as well as growing inner alienation erected a barrier between us. . . . I suggested to Ruth that I leave and she remain in our home. But she refused; she said that she wished to make a fresh start and build herself another home."[4]

According to Yaël, her mother "never stopped loving Moshe but claimed that she loved the 'Moshe' who had been, not the man he had become. She was fed up with his avarice, indiscriminate womanizing, loss of idealism and megalomania." More than forty years after the divorce, Ruth refused to utter a single syllable of disapproval. She guarded his memory as sacred. Her memoirs begin with the sentence, "One can divorce a husband, but not a legend." As she described her feelings, "When I banged the iron gate shut and heard the clang of metal on metal for the last time, I thought: I'm free. Looking back through the grate and seeing the garden, I felt as if I were stepping out of a fairy tale that I had never wanted. I left behind my emotional loneliness that over the years had become unbearably oppressive—for both Moshe and myself."[5] Rachel moved into Moshe's home in Tzahala, near Tel Aviv, and they married on June 26, 1973, eighteen years after they had first met on the flight from Rome to Tel Aviv.

Ruth's departure put an end to the fragile family life. Yaël was close to her father and maintained cordial relations with Rachel, continuing to visit the house. But the sons, Udi and Assi, no longer considered it home. They had never had a warm relationship with their father. When they were small, he played with them occasionally, and took them on excursions around the country and on hunting trips. He apparently enjoyed their mischief and vivacity, and Ruth noted that he "was a good father, a bit conservative."[6] But as they grew older, he was away from home more, and they became increasingly estranged.

He seldom mentioned his sons in his memoirs, though he must have been proud of their military service. Udi joined a naval commando unit and Assi volunteered for the paratroopers, serving in Sinai during the Six Day War. Both chose their own paths in life. In the 1950s, Udi took over the family farm at Nahalal and developed his talent as an iron sculptor. Assi became a film star and made a brilliant career for himself as an actor, scriptwriter, and director. Moshe was hardly involved and only rarely revealed a soft spot for them.

When he was injured in the cave-in, both sons joined Ruth at his bedside, and Udi brought him home from hospital, as Moshe described:

> After managing to get out of the car, I had him help me walk briefly around the garden. These were my first steps, and I hung onto him with one hand and held a cane with the other. I felt a total weakness, no strength in my limbs, and aches and pains inside my plaster prison. Udi watched me—and saw a broken man, blind in one eye, scarcely able to shuffle, virtually paralyzed, and literally speechless. Was this his father? He told me much later, after I had fully recovered, that in the garden that day he had thought I would remain like that for the rest of my life, permanently crippled, mute, an invalid, and he had struggled to choke back tears.[7]

During the Yom Kippur War, Dayan met Assi in Sharm el-Sheikh, where he was serving in the reserves. Moshe did not describe his emotions on this occasion but merely noted that Assi had updated him on the action in the area.

When Ruth shut the iron gates behind her for the last time, even these frayed threads tore. Dayan had a new family.

The other personal development concerned Dayan the archaeological miscreant. His most prized archaeological treasure—and the epitome of his misconduct—was a collection of unique anthropoid sarcophagi found in the early 1970s in the Gaza Strip near the town of Deir el-Balah. In the fall of 1967, Professor Trude Dothan, a specialist in Canaanite and Philistine civilizations, noticed that necklaces, ornaments, pottery, and beads from the thirteenth and fourteenth centuries

B.C.E. had begun to appear in antiquity shops in Jerusalem's Old City. Her curiosity was heightened when an unknown collector brought her a piece of broken pottery in the form of a human face, apparently part of a sarcophagus. She was convinced that the source of the mask was on the coast, somewhere in Gaza. Deciding to trace it, she turned to the minister of defense. "Dayan had an extraordinary nose for ancient finds," she recounted. "He had already learned a lot and knew a lot. We archaeologists used to joke among ourselves that he saw better with one eye than we did with two. Dayan swore to me that he knew nothing about the find, but promised to find out through his contacts and inform me when he knew something."[8]

Dayan had long been in contact with a Bedouin by the name of Hammad from the area of Deir el-Balah, and he soon learned that Hammad himself was the source of the rare anthropoid. Three months later, Dothan was allowed to visit the area under the protection of a military guard Dayan arranged, but found nothing. While waiting for the chance to make the visit she surveyed the finds that had appeared on the market and with private dealers, and her search led her back to Dayan. He, in the interim, had collected some twenty anthropoids from Deir el-Balah and built a special structure for them in his courtyard. She could hardly believe her eyes. By now, he had also become a dealer, buying the anthropoids with money, not the coffee and sugar he had bartered for finds twenty-five years earlier, and his collection was worth millions. Legally, anyone could buy antiquities on the free market. Indeed, he had not dug up the finds at Deir el-Balah himself—Hammad had done it for him—but clearly he had used his office to obtain the treasures.

His commissioned digs also failed to follow standard scientific procedure and unwittingly destroyed evidence vital for research. He was quite a deft pottery restorer and spent hours gluing shards together in his courtyard, but he made mistakes.

On one of her visits, Dothan found him stirring a pot on a small stove, concocting a new type of glue. He told her proudly that no one would be able to separate the pieces he stuck together. And indeed, when his collection made its way to the Israel Museum after his death, the restorers had a hard time trying to repair some of his mistakes.

# 13

## *Yom Kippur*

DESPITE REPEATED TERRORIST ACTS by Palestinian guerrilla organizations from 1970 to 1973, a general sense of security pervaded Israel, especially among senior IDF staff. The IDF assumed that Egypt would not go to war so long as its air force was unable to launch a massive attack on Israel's air bases. The IDF also calculated that the Egyptian army could not cross the Suez to endanger Israeli control of Sinai and that the IDF could repel any such attempt within days. If Dayan did not altogether share his colleagues' assumptions, he did not question them either. But he was well aware that the political stalemate was unacceptable to the Arabs and that another war was unavoidable. He cautioned the public and the officers against complacency, but in all his public appearances, he transmitted a sense of security. His status was at its peak. Dayan was "Mr. Security," and he imparted the perception of safety to the people.

Meanwhile, Anwar Sadat regularly declared that the Day of

Judgment was near and seemed to be backing up his words by stockpiling the generous supply of weapons he received from the Soviets. He ordered canal-side facilities installed. IDF soldiers assumed these were defensive, but they were, in fact, suitable for offense too.

In early summer 1973, Israel received a number of high-level warnings from trusted sources that an Egyptian attack was imminent. The IDF mobilized its reserves and placed its troops on alert. But Egypt did not attack. When similar warnings resurfaced at the end of September, the head of IDF intelligence was convinced that the maneuvers would fizzle out. The common calculations concerning the probability of war breaking out remained low.

Dayan, as usual, read the intelligence reports, preferring the raw to the filtered material. However, as minister of defense, he had no staff or mechanism to offer alternative analyses and had to rely on the opinion of Military Intelligence. He based his warnings on intuition and asked the CGS to re-examine the intelligence assessments and report back to him. The CGS complied and agreed with the Intelligence personnel.[1]

In late September, Dayan toured the North and backed the O.C.'s demand for additional tanks and artillery. His greatest anxiety focused on the situation on the Golan Heights. Unlike Sinai, where the IDF had room to maneuver, on the Golan the Syrians could easily infiltrate Israel and reach the Jordan River in an initial sortie, endangering not only Israeli communities in the Golan but Israeli cities in pre-1967 areas. In early October, both frontline observations and reliable espionage reported advanced preparations among the Arab countries for war.

On October 5, the situation peaked. At 2:40 A.M., news leaked that the Soviets were evacuating their officers' families from Damascus and Cairo. Furthermore, a senior Mossad agent requested an urgent meeting about the impending war, and the head of the agency flew off to Europe to meet the agent. To be safe, the IDF placed the standing army on highest alert. Operating on the assumption that there would be a further warning, the reserves were not yet called up. At sundown, Jewish people in Israel and around the world would usher in Yom Kippur, Judaism's holiest day, a twenty-five-hour holiday that even many nonbelievers observe by attending synagogue.

On Saturday, October 6, at 4 A.M., the head of Mossad advised the government and the IDF that, according to his source, Egypt would attack Israel at 6 P.M. Senior government and security personnel, headed by Golda Meir and Dayan, kicked into high gear, a state in which they would remain for the duration of the three weeks of war.

As it turned out, the Mossad chief's source was Ashraf Marwan, Nasser's son-in-law. His intelligence tip was slightly off: the Egyptians launched their attack at 2 P.M., taking Israel by surprise. War erupted. David Elazar, the man Dayan had suspected of withholding information during the Six Day War, was serving as CGS. Dayan would have preferred someone else in the position, but Elazar's appointment had been pushed through by Yigal Allon, who knew him from the Palmach, and Dayan respected Meir's decision. Over the course of the war, a number of disagreements broke out between the two military icons. Elazar, with free access to the prime minister, often went against Dayan's judgment. Deputy Prime Minister Allon and acting Minister of Information Galili had great influence with Meir and attended most of her meetings with Dayan; it frequently seemed as though Elazar had discussed matters with them beforehand. Dayan was conscious of his precarious situation and generally left his disagreements with Elazar to be decided by Meir. Though not fond of or close to Dayan, she respected him and appreciated his intelligence and advice, even if she did not always back him.

The first disagreement occurred on October 6, when war was clearly becoming a reality. Elazar wanted to mobilize the entire air force, two armored divisions, and various auxiliary units (roughly two hundred thousand people) immediately and launch a preemptive strike against Egyptian and Syrian forces. Dayan feared that extensive mobilization, and especially a preemptive strike, would make Israel appear to be the aggressor. He considered it vital to retain the trust of Israel's close ally the United States, which had recently signed a détente agreement with the Soviet Union, an important diplomatic move orchestrated by Secretary of State Henry Kissinger. In this international climate, it would be difficult for the United States to support Israel if it instigated a conflagration that could light the Middle East powder keg. Dayan therefore wanted to mobilize only those units that the CGS deemed critical to shield Israel from the first blow. Short of a preemptive strike, Elazar wanted to mobilize enough troops for a counterattack after the enemy was forced back. Neither Dayan nor Elazar at this stage had any doubt that the IDF would foil the assault easily.

The two mobilization options landed in Meir's lap at 8:00 that morning in the presence of Allon, Galili, and General Bar-Lev, who was now minister of industry and trade. Meir accepted Elazar's position on mobilizing the reserves and Dayan's on ruling out a preemptive strike. Only hours later, Egypt started the war. Once the sirens sounded, the reserves could be fully mobilized by public radio and the controversy lost its significance.

In Israel's public memory, the Yom Kippur War went down as *ha'Mehdal*[2] — The Blunder — primarily because Egypt and Syria's bold actions in opening the war took the Israeli security establishment by surprise. Although the blunder mostly resulted from poor intelligence assessments, it was not the primary cause of IDF casualties and operational quagmires, both of which were a result of the leaders' subsequent mishandling of the war. In this regard, the tragedy was less reminiscent of Pearl

Harbor than of the defeat of the French knights of Agincourt in 1415, when the hail of longbow arrows shot by British peasants taught the knights that the battlefield had changed beyond recognition. Even if Israel had understood that war was imminent and mobilized all the reserves two or three days beforehand, the IDF would still have faced the problems it confronted in the first days of fighting. Had the IDF been more alert and prepared, it is unlikely that it could have stopped Egypt from crossing the canal and entrenching on its east bank.

Dayan shared the prevalent IDF view that Israel's aerial superiority, canal fortifications, and permanently stationed tanks near the canal would stop Egypt from making significant advances on the ground. Moreover, the canal crossing could probably be halted at the waterline; if, in the worst-case scenario, Egyptian soldiers managed to take the east bank, fast-mobilizing armored reserves could still oust them. But the synthesis of an entirely new set of circumstances and superior weaponry took the IDF by surprise. This revolutionary combination included effective cover of the battlefield by an array of anti-aircraft missiles, which prevented Israel's air force from assisting the army in the first three days; more than a thousand field guns launching massive shelling along the entire front; and the slick use of modern, efficient anti-tank weapons. The IDF had known that Egypt possessed these weapons, but no one in Israel had conceived of their lethal effect on Israeli armor. Thousands of Egyptian Sagger and RPG missiles pounded Israeli tank positions. Most devastatingly, IDF planners failed to grasp how the battlefield would look when a hundred thousand Egyptian soldiers crossed the canal simultaneously at some fifteen different points and attacked the IDF on a broad front.

In the first forty-eight hours, Israel's air force lost close to 10 percent of its aircraft, an armored division on the front line lost more than half of its tanks, and the Bar-Lev Line collapsed. No one had foreseen such a thrashing. For three days the IDF continued to engage the Egyptians on the basis of out-dated military conceptions. An attempt to counterattack Egyptian advanced forces failed. Only then did the GHQ pull itself together and start to construct a plan of action to meet the new circumstances.

Dayan, too, had not anticipated the dramatic changes on the battlefield, but he was quicker than others to absorb them, and this perspicacity led to his second disagreement with the chief of staff. By the end of Yom Kippur—the first day of fighting—Dayan apparently realized, after flying to visit the command post on the southern front, that the battlefield was radically different from what Israel had imagined. Elazar remained optimistic, even zealously so. In an interview on Israel Radio on October 8 he promised that "the IDF would soon break Egyptian bones."[3] Dayan, in contrast, spoke pessimistically, articulating anxiety about Israel's future. Most IDF commanders agreed with the chief of staff's assessment that as soon as the armored reserves moved into action, the situation would change. Dayan's Cassandra-like warnings in those hours gave the impression to his officers that he had broken down, and rumors circulated that he was panicking. Dayan's dark sentiments swiftly spread, filling senior commanders with gloom and near despair.

Dayan was certainly in the grip of anxiety. He later acknowledged in his memoirs that on Sunday morning, October 7, he believed that the existence of the State of Israel was in peril. "I do not remember ever [feeling] such worry and anxiety in the past," Dayan wrote, aware of his own share in the IDF misjudgments, a responsibility that presumably compounded his dejection. But were his extreme reactions as irrational as many thought?[4]

That morning, Dayan was particularly concerned about

the situation on the Golan Heights, where Syrian tanks had breached the front lines at two points and reached the cliffs above the Sea of Galilee. He set out for the field, and when he got there the O.C. at the command post described a far worse situation than Dayan had feared. One of two armored brigades that had been fighting since the previous afternoon had been crushed. No troops remained on the southern Golan to halt the Syrian advance.

During an early-morning phone call, Dayan ordered General Benny Peled, the air force commander, to call in aircraft to stop the Syrians on the southern Golan. The air force commander later recounted that Dayan had said, "The Third Commonwealth is in danger."[5] (The Third Commonwealth refers to the Jewish peoples' third sovereign control of the Land of Israel, established with statehood in 1948.) Dayan was undoubtedly dispirited by what he heard at the Northern Command that morning. A few hours later, on his visit to the Southern Command, he reached a professional nadir upon witnessing the collapse of the Bar-Lev Line, the considerable loss of men and equipment, and the incapacity of Israeli tanks to execute the defense plans. He concluded that there was no chance, for the time being, of dislodging the Egyptians from the East Bank of the Suez, and worse still, he feared that Egyptian tanks would break through into Sinai. He recommended consolidating a defense line farther back, perhaps on the mountain passes eighteen miles to the east. Though two reserve tank divisions under two of the IDF's top commanders, Ariel Sharon and Avraham Adan, were assembling en route to the front, Dayan worried that by the time they arrived and organized, the whole front would already have collapsed. "This is now a war for the Land of Israel," he told Elazar on his return from the South. "In my heart, what I fear most is that the State of Israel will ultimately survive but without sufficient armament to defend itself. It does not matter where the line will be. We will not have enough tanks and planes or trained people. It will simply be impossible to defend the Land of Israel."[6]

At 3 P.M., Dayan met with Golda Meir, as usual along with Allon and Galili, and his assessment diverged from the chief of staff's. "We have to concede the canal line," Dayan told the prime minister. "At this moment there is no need for a counteroffensive."[7] Elazar recommended that the IDF attempt to remove the Egyptians with the help of the two fresh tank divisions that had just reached the field. The meeting concluded with the decision that Elazar would go south to consult with the field commander about a possible counteroffensive the following day. Dayan did not oppose the decision and told Elazar, "If you conclude [that an offensive is possible], go for it." Once again, Dayan switched his stance in the face of internal opposition; he did not fight for his beliefs. Dayan felt that the cabinet and commanders no longer trusted his opinion. "It seemed to me that they were convinced that there was a weakness not in our military capability but in my character, that I had lost my confidence and my evaluation was therefore wrong, too pessimistic."[8]

On Tuesday, October 8, the Southern Command tried to follow Elazar's plan and sent the two tank divisions forward. The attack failed, and the IDF suffered heavy losses in human life, tanks, and aircraft. In the evening, when Elazar reached the command post on the Egyptian front, he observed the carnage and entirely reversed his strategy. There would be no counteroffensive; instead, IDF troops would take defensive positions. Dayan's early opposition to a counteroffensive was validated, but he had largely lost his authority in the officers' eyes.

On October 9, the situation in the Golan Heights was also grim, with the IDF suffering heavy loss of life and tanks. Unlike in the South, however, the Armored Corps had managed to crush a fair number of Syrian tanks and at numerous points to repulse the enemy. For the first time in the war, Defense Minister Dayan and Chief of Staff Elazar agreed on a military strategy. They decided to concentrate all efforts on the northern front over the following days. Elazar also backed Dayan's position on the southern front without reservation, aiming to contain the enemy troops in the Sinai by preparing a line of defense farther back, in the mountain passes to the east.

Dayan believed it was time to inform the Israeli public of the realities on the battlefield. The IDF could not withhold this information, certainly not from frontline soldiers. In the absence of reliable information, exaggerated rumors were spreading, official announcements were terse, and Colonel Pinchas Lahav, the IDF spokesperson, had lost his credibility. "The people should be advised of the true situation on the fronts; [we must] be straight with them, not feed them heroic tales and illusions of a swift, glorious victory,"[9] Dayan told his spokesman, Naphtali Lavie.

Dayan convened the daily-press editors on Wednesday, October 10, at 5 P.M. His statements left his audience utterly shocked. Many of them attributed his gloomy portrayal as further proof that his mental state had deteriorated because he was unable to reconcile his pessimistic descriptions with the CGS's rosy promises of the previous evening. "There is great danger that a small state of less than three million people will be left powerless," he said plainly. "There should be no insistence on holding or capturing a specific line if it can cause a serious depletion of forces. To hell with the Bitter Lake and the non-Bitter Lake, the State of Israel comes first and foremost. We need tanks, airplanes, and decent lines of defense."[10]

His words were apparently too blunt and grave for the journalists to absorb. *Davar* editor Hannah Zemer burst into tears. *Ha'aretz* editor Gershom Schocken termed Dayan's words an "earthquake," protesting against the gloom that the minister of defense was presenting to the public. That evening, Dayan was supposed to appear on state television, but after several editors intervened, Meir canceled his appearance for fear of "deepening public depression." Dayan did not insist. He would not appear before the public with glib words that whitewashed the grim situation. The Israeli public, however, already believed that he had lost his nerve, and that image was reinforced as rumors proliferated.[11]

Dayan's prophecies of doom did not materialize. Despite the IDF's decision to abort the counteroffensive, the Egyptians did not broaden their hold east of the canal and in retrospect seemed to have pursued limited gains. If they had been bold enough to continue their momentum and had introduced their armored reserves into the campaign on the first days of the war, Dayan's dark predictions would have sounded less far-fetched. Dayan, for his read on the situation, was derided for the negative image he had projected at the war's start.

Every day of the war, Dayan went to a frontline command post. Some said he disturbed the officers at work, others thought he was running away from his job at GHQ, and some even claimed that he was looking to die on the battlefield. There is little doubt that he felt more comfortable with the officers on the front than amid the tension permeating the rooms where cabinet ministers and GHQ senior officers met.

Yet there on the battlefield he felt the constraints of his position as minister of defense. With his military experience, it was only natural that he would express his opinion both about what to do and how to do it, but in doing so he overstepped the political boundary dividing his strategic role and the operational role of the IDF officers; he even offered tactical advice. He could not issue direct orders to the lower ranks when touring the different commands—they repeatedly referred him to the CGS in accordance with protocol. But he continued to state his views on clear military issues, though he learned to qualify them as "ministerial advice," which they were not obliged to obey. Their orders came only from their superiors within the army hierarchy.

Unable to withhold his tactical input on the battlefield, Dayan was not oblivious off the battlefield to the growing public criticism of his management of the war. On October 12, he told Golda Meir that if she believed someone else could manage the war better, he would "submit [his] resignation at once." He added that he was not speaking from loss of confidence; on the contrary, he believed that "no one in Israel could do the job better than me, and I am ready and willing to continue in the post. Moreover, I really, really would not like to abandon ship in the middle." Meir replied that the idea of replacing him had never crossed her mind. "She trusted me completely and regarded herself as sharing the responsibility as far as the war was concerned," Dayan recounted.[12]

In the days following the failed counterattack in Sinai, two Egyptian army units controlled a strip of land east of the Suez Canal, and the IDF, anticipating a surge, planned to ambush them with tanks in the hills. Meanwhile, attention focused on the northern front. Within days, three IDF armored divisions penetrated Syria, reaching a position twenty-five miles from Damascus. The western suburbs of the Syrian capital were now in range of Israeli cannons. This forward position foiled Syria's threat to Israeli territory, and Dayan's mood changed drastically. Though concerned about the war's final outcome, he stopped worrying about the IDF's ability to hold out. He and Elazar hoped to neutralize Syria and force the Syrians from the campaign. But despite the trouncing of its army, Syria did not leave the fight. With the help of Iraqi and Jordanian troops, Syria continued to keep the IDF busy on the northern front, though it no longer posed a serious danger.

With Syria in check, focus returned to the southern front.

There were growing signs on the international stage of an impending U.N.-imposed ceasefire. It appeared that the Egyptian hold east of the canal could not be loosened, and Israel's only option was to capture territory west of the canal as a postwar bargaining chip. Most of the officers, led by Ariel Sharon, suggested crossing the canal on the seam between the two Egyptian units north of Bitter Lake, a saltwater lake near the canal. Dayan approved the plan.

On October 13 and 14, as expected, Egyptian armored troops attempted to push eastward and incurred heavy losses, opening the way for the IDF to cross the canal westward. Sharon led the bold campaign, and Dayan believed that Sharon could accomplish the IDF's goals. His mission began on the night of October 16–17. A paratroop brigade crossed the canal in rubber boats, capturing a bridgehead on the western side. But Egyptian forces summoned to the area from the north and south blocked the crossing point. Heavy fighting raged for four days. Nevertheless, the IDF managed to transfer three armored divisions across the canal and gain control of a broad strip west of Bitter Lake. During the afternoon of October 22, an advance unit reached the Suez-Cairo highway, where a signpost marked the distance to Egypt's capital: 101 kilometers (63 miles).

As the IDF continued its multifront battle, Israel's political leaders were holding intensive talks with the United States in an effort to expedite the delivery of arms promised by President Nixon to replace the equipment lost in combat. Golda Meir managed the contacts through Israel's ambassador in Washington, Simcha Dinitz, whose contact, Secretary of State Kissinger, was caught in a web of conflicting interests and motives, trying to prevent Israel's defeat while placating the Arab states, which had imposed a general embargo on oil supplies to the West. Kissinger was playing an intricate game of realpolitik that did not always end in Israel's favor.[13]

Dayan followed the political gains and losses from afar. For him, fate was being decided around the temporary bridges across the Suez and the swath of land that was widening as the IDF deployed farther and farther west of the canal. Everything now depended on the soldiers in the line of fire, and that was exactly where he wanted to be.

As the IDF pushed across the canal and talks of a ceasefire grew louder, political considerations took on added weight. The military brass grappled with the problem of deciding where the IDF should stop its advance, knowing full well that the answer depended on the pace of military operations. Dayan increasingly—and embarrassingly—interfered in the officers' discussions. Both the O.C. Southern Command and the CGS complained that his actions caused confusion on the front lines.

In the afternoon of October 17, Dayan joined Sharon's command car and crossed the canal westward. The entire area was under fire, and Sharon suggested that Dayan transfer to an armored half-track. Dayan refused, wanting to experience the combat firsthand, and insisted on roving about by jeep or on foot. The farmer from Nahalal admired the diligence of the Egyptian peasants who cultivated that desert area into a verdant oasis. He saw fruits ripening, peanuts spread out to dry on the sand within fenced-off properties, and juice dribbling from red dates. Most of the farmers had fled in fear of the war with only a brave handful still on their farms.

In the evening, Dayan returned to the Pit and participated in Elazar's discussions with the senior command. It is apparent from the records that his personal sheen had dulled, his "ministerial advice" rendered ineffectual. He may have run about on the battlefields, but it was Elazar who managed the war and ruled the military hierarchy.

On October 19, Kissinger left for Moscow to formulate a framework to end the war. A ceasefire was expected within days, and Dayan convened the senior GHQ to raise the question of where the IDF should stop. This was his turf: an issue made up of both political and strategic elements. The battles west of the canal were not easy but the potential gains were significant. The westward advance toward Cairo posed a severe threat to the Egyptian army. More important still was the opportunity to besiege Egypt's forces from the rear. Years later, Arie Brown, Dayan's adjutant, who accompanied him on all his tours, repeatedly mentioned in his account of the war the pressure Dayan exerted on division commanders to extend their control of the territory along the canal. Dayan considered it vital to tighten the siege around the Egyptian Third Army entrenched in the south, east of Bitter Lake.[14]

When the U.N. Security Council declared a ceasefire to take effect on Monday, October 22, at 7:30 P.M., the Soviet Union and United States jointly insisted that Israel halt hostilities. But the deadline passed and the fighting persisted. On Tuesday, Dayan convened a broad forum of GHQ officers at his office to discuss the implications of the ceasefire. Unlike the previous discussion, this one focused on the future of relations with the Egyptians after the war. Dayan knew that leaving the IDF west of the canal for any length of time would not be an option. He returned to an idea he had previously formulated in 1971: a separation of forces, in which both sides would draw back, and Israeli forces would withdraw completely from the banks of the Suez Canal. This would allow Egypt to reopen the canal to international navigation, breathe new life into canal towns, and create a de facto peace in the region.

At the same time that Dayan and the officers were debating future arrangements, Israeli troops were advancing into Egypt, despite Sadat's demand that they retreat to the positions held on the evening of October 22. Repeated attempts by Egypt to repulse the IDF gave Israel a chance to surround Egypt's Third

Army over the next forty-eight hours. The ceasefire finally went into effect on October 24 at 7 P.M.

The ceasefire did not end the crisis that had developed between Jerusalem and Washington on the last day of the war. The IDF maintained its siege on the Egyptian Third Army. Backed by both the United States and the Soviet Union, Egypt demanded the right to supply provisions to the troops across the canal and in the town of Suez. Israel had its own demands of Egypt: to release the Israeli prisoners of war and to lift the blockade on Israel-bound ships at the Straits of Bab el-Mandeb, between Yemen and the Horn of Africa. The United States demanded that Israel immediately open the road from Cairo to a convoy of a hundred food and aid trucks for the Third Army, but Dayan insisted on reciprocity, which led to an international crisis. The Soviets feared the Third Army's collapse, which, more than anything, would symbolize their protégé's defeat. They announced their intention of stationing Soviet troops on Egyptian soil. Washington, of course, opposed the appearance of Soviet troops in the Middle East. Nixon placed the U.S. forces stationed in Europe on alert and ordered the Sixth Fleet to sail for the eastern Mediterranean. On a call to the Kremlin on the red phone, he made it clear that Washington would not accept the intervention of Soviet troops in the conflict. Nor did he mince his words to Golda Meir. He demanded that Israel allow the convoy through without delay. On October 26, Israel yielded and allowed the convoy to pass. The siege of the Third Army was lifted, and though the IDF was permitted to check the contents of the supply vehicles, it could not block their passage.

In retrospect, it seems that Kissinger believed that it would be possible to advance a policy of stability and peace in the Middle East only if the war ended in a stalemate. He understood that the war had left an opening for a basic change in Egypt's international standing and, on a short visit to Cairo, presumably enjoyed the friendly welcome he received in Egypt's capital as the U.S. secretary of state. The tension between Israel and America gradually subsided, and Kissinger played a key role in the contacts that eventually led to the IDF's withdrawal from positions west of the Suez Canal.

# 14

## *In the Crucible*

IN GOLDA MEIR'S MEMOIRS, she pegged Henry Kissinger as the most forceful personality of the Yom Kippur War. "The main figure turned out to be not President Sadat nor President Assad nor King Faisel nor Ms. Meir," she wrote, "it was U.S. Secretary of State Henry Kissinger, whose efforts for the sake of regional peace can only be defined as superhuman."[1] Certainly, in the final stages of the war and the months following, Kissinger was the prime mover in the political and military theaters. Dayan had known Kissinger for years and entertained mixed feelings about him. He had great respect for Kissinger's talents but still greater fear of his position within the world's major superpower, which could press and reward, influence and promise. During the war, Dayan had met briefly with Kissinger when the secretary of state stopped off in Jerusalem on his way back from Moscow, and he gained the impression that Kissinger would robustly facilitate negotiations with the Arabs. However, he feared that improved U.S.-Arab relations and the lifting of the oil embargo imposed by the Organization of Arab Petroleum Exporting Countries in response to President Nixon's delivery of military hardware to Israel during the war would be achieved at Israel's expense.[2] Dayan's intuition was correct.

After the guns fell silent in late October 1973, Dayan returned to center stage, primarily in the political and diplomatic arena. But with his departure from the Ministry of Defense slated for June 1974, he still had defense responsibilities to assume. Though daily contact with the U.S. administration was left to Ambassador Simcha Dinitz, with the close involvement of Prime Minister Meir, Dayan was engaged in the discussions, which revolved around the IDF's withdrawal and redeployment farther east in Egypt. Dayan had suggested this redeployment, though now it signified Israel's acknowledgment of the advantage gained by Egypt in the Yom Kippur War. Subsequently, both banks of the canal would remain sovereign Egyptian territory and President Sadat's depleted forces would be stationed on lines Israel had held for the previous seven years. Egypt understandably viewed the war as an achievement, both because of its bold launch and because of the terms of its conclusion.

Dayan now argued for his prewar position, claiming that the resumption of international navigation through the Suez Canal and the rehabilitation of its surrounding towns would foster a state of nonbelligerence. In early December, he set out for a United Jewish Appeal convention in New York, but he spent most of his time in talks with the Nixon administration, particularly with Kissinger. With Meir's permission, Dayan presented his personal ideas on the separation of forces. Without committing the prime minister, he put out feelers aimed at the Egyptians and at his home audience to convince Israelis of the plan's viability. Kissinger was not enthusiastic but requested another meeting. Over the following days, while bargaining with the Egyptians, he adopted Dayan's proposal of a separation of forces, even relying on maps Dayan had supplied at their first meeting.

On December 21, 1973, an international conference convened in Geneva under U.S. and Soviet auspices. Dayan did not attend. As per protocol, the foreign minister, Abba Eban, headed the Israeli delegation. The gathering presented additional opportunities for both sides to deliver impassioned declarations, but the practical documents and maps in Kissinger's briefcase affirmed Dayan's pivotal role once again.

On December 31, Israel held the elections that had been postponed by war. Although Golda Meir's Labor Party lost five seats, it still emerged as the largest electoral party, and President Ephraim Katzir granted Meir the mandate to form a coalition government. That same day Meir sent Dayan off for talks with Kissinger, clearly intending to reappoint him minister of defense. On January 4, Dayan formally presented his Egypt plan as government approved to Kissinger in Washington, and this time the secretary of state listened attentively.

Large, uncompromising areas of disagreement continued to divide Egypt and Israel, however, and in January 1974 Kissinger began to shuttle back and forth between Jerusalem and Cairo. Dayan seemed to be his old self again, persuading his colleagues and, if necessary, circumventing them and cutting corners. Sometimes he would yield on minor matters in order to gain essential points. During an informal visit of the U.S. delegation to his home, he spread a map on his bed, took a pencil, and without consulting his colleagues redrew the redeployment lines. No one questioned his authority.[3]

On January 18, 1974, the separation of forces agreement was finalized and signed by IDF Chief of General Staff Elazar and Egypt's CGS Mohamed Abdel Ghani El-Gamasy, as befit a military agreement. It stated that "in Egyptian and Israeli eyes it would not be a peace treaty. It was only a first step towards a full, just and lasting peace."[4] Five years would pass before this hope would be realized, and Dayan would no longer be a representative of the Labor Party but a minister in the right-of-center Likud government, no longer minister of defense but foreign minister; and it would come only after much frustration, tribulation, and travail.

In the aftermath of the Yom Kippur War, the Israeli public focused on trying to understand how Israel had been taken by surprise at the outbreak of the war and why the military had performed so poorly in the first few days. Barbs were hurled in various directions, but most were aimed at Dayan. In the public's eyes, the glorified hero in all of Israel's previous wars, the ultimate military icon who in the preceding eight years had enjoyed worldwide acclaim, had failed. He was widely seen as a fallen god and given most of the blame.

The first volley came on October 24 from within the prime minister's cabinet. Yaakov-Shimshon Shapira, the opinionated minister of justice, demanded that Meir dismiss Dayan. But Meir once more assured Dayan that he had her full trust and she wanted him to continue as minister of defense. She did, however, bow to the growing public pressure and established a commission of inquiry headed by Supreme Court Justice Shimon Agranat. The commission, a prestigious and impeccable group, comprised two former IDF chiefs of staff, Yigael Yadin and Chaim Laskov, another judge, and the state comptroller.

The commission's mandate was limited to the period before the war through its first three days, which worked against IDF officers, particularly CGS Elazar, whose early mistakes would be scrutinized while his excellent subsequent management of the war would be excluded. The commission also reviewed Dayan's performance and that of other ministers, but regarded its authority as confined to examining "the practical responsibility for commission or omission of deeds in which one was personally involved."[5] Commission members considered it beyond their scope to express an opinion on ministerial responsibility, agreeing that the decision of whether a minister should resign was a political rather than a legal issue. It was this same issue, however, that served as the impetus for the protest movement demanding Dayan's dismissal, regardless of the extent of his personal involvement.

In November 1973, some 150 Israeli prisoners returned from Egyptian captivity and started talking about their experiences and their commanders' shortcomings in the first days of the war. The families of the more than twenty-five hundred IDF soldiers killed and seven thousand wounded needed little to spark their pain and bitterness into protests. When Meir formed her new government with Dayan still in place as defense minister, public rage reignited. Freshly discharged military reservists organized protest groups.

On February 3, 1974, Motti Ashkenazi, a young officer, sat down opposite the prime minister's office in Jerusalem holding several signs. One read, "I demand ministerial accountability!" and another, more bluntly, "Dayan—resign!" Ashkenazi's most personal sign stated, "From Budapest—in protest!"[6] The meaning of that sign became clear only days later when it was discovered that Ashkenazi had been a company captain of a reserve brigade on the Bar-Lev Line before the war. He had commanded a solitary post, code-named "Budapest," which was attacked and surrounded at the war's outbreak. Although he was wounded, his post held out. Ashkenazi harbored deep misgivings about the conduct of the war and decided to focus his protest against Dayan.

As February wore on, Ashkenazi's demonstrations gained more supporters. The press reported daily on the swelling numbers, and Ashkenazi became the icon of the protest movement. Dayan agreed to meet with him and later described their conversation as "virtually a monologue" as Ashkenazi condemned a host of figures for a host of reasons. Most vociferously, he reiterated his demand that Dayan immediately resign. Questioning Ashkenazi's rationale for the demand, Dayan received an impassioned response. "When my soldiers sat crouched in the bunkers of the Budapest post and asked why we were not being rescued, I said to them: 'Count on Moshe Dayan. He won't abandon us,'" Ashkenazi told him. "'You were god to us, Dayan. Now you are not responsible for the political situation that led Egypt to war, you are not responsible for the IDF's unpreparedness and inferior equipment, you are not responsible for the Intelligence blunder, you are not responsible for the strategic planning of the counteroffensive. In short, you are not responsible for anything. God has abandoned responsibility.'"[7]

On March 23, various groups organized a mass rally attended by twenty-five thousand people—a considerable turnout for Israel in the 1970s. Dayan was not apathetic. Following a cabinet meeting one day, as he passed the demonstrators a young woman cried out, "Murderer!" "I felt as though I had been stabbed in the heart," he later recounted. Dayan found significance in the composition of the protesters: mainly young soldiers and bereaved parents. This dynamic gave the movement an uncommon public and emotional weight. "One could not remain indifferent," he wrote. "In any case, *I* was certainly affected."[8]

On April 1, the Agranat Commission published a preliminary report that identified guilty parties and recommended measures against them. General Eliahu Ze'ira, head of the Intelligence Branch, and another three senior Intelligence officers were ousted. O.C. Southern Command Shmuel Gonen was suspended pending the commission's completion of its work. CGS Elazar received the harshest blow. The commission found him personally responsible for events on the eve of the war and recommended that he resign from the military.[9]

The commission did refer to the defense minister but limited its criticism to "personal responsibility"—matters in which

Dayan was personally involved. The group decided not to deal with the matter of "ministerial responsibility." "According to the criteria of reasonable conduct required from the incumbent of the office of Defense Minister, the minister was not obliged to order additional or other means of caution than those recommended to him by the IDF's GHQ," the commission concluded.[10]

The report's publication intensified the cries for Dayan's removal. Many saw Elazar's dismissal as unjust and Dayan's exoneration as chicanery that discredited the public standing of the commission. Israelis were not interested in details but in the issue the commission had not explored—ministerial accountability. The public sensed that the commission lacked backbone.

Meir's own Labor Party ratcheted up pressure on the prime minister to dismiss Dayan, claiming that his presence threatened party integrity. She did not feel capable of continuing in her current role and informed the party leadership on April 10 that she was unable to bear the responsibility of the premiership. "Five years are enough," Meir said; "the burden is too heavy."[11] Under Israeli law, when a prime minister resigns, the cabinet must also resign but remain as a caretaker government until a new coalition is established. It took Yitzhak Rabin, the new candidate for prime minister, nearly two months to form a coalition. On June 4, Meir and Dayan went home.

In the month before leaving the Defense Ministry, Dayan faced one last frustrating and tragic experience. Palestinian terror organizations had stepped up their violence, adopting a new tactic of taking schools hostage, hoping to free their comrades imprisoned in Israeli jails. On May 15, a group from Lebanon attacked a school across Israel's northern border in the small town of Ma'alot-Tarshiha. They held some hundred pupils and teachers hostage and demanded the release of twenty of their own jailed members. Against Dayan's better judgment, the government decided to meet their demands. But there were delays caused by disagreement over the exchange arrangements. The terrorists had issued an ultimatum for 6 P.M., threatening to blow up the building with the hostages inside, and time was running out. CGS Motta Gur ordered the IDF soldiers surrounding the building to break in. Though three terrorists were killed, the operation did not go well: twenty-one students died and sixty-eight were wounded.

Only weeks away from leaving office, Dayan was unable to influence events. The new CGS headed the rescue attempts and was unreceptive to Dayan's suggestions. Dayan was at the scene but could do nothing. When he approached the building, he could make out the faces of the children and terrorists through the window. "I crawled to a house, a few dozen meters from the school building," he recalled. "The frightened children peered out of every window in hope: now, now, the soldiers will break through and save us. The terrorists, young and mustached, paced back and forth, their machine guns in hand and ready, if attacked, to shoot the children dead."

Several times, terrorists spotted Dayan in his position. One even aimed his gun at the minister of defense, but a girl positioned behind the terrorist motioned to Dayan to withdraw. He did so but not before seeing how sad and tired her eyes were, "like children look before they fall asleep." He was consumed with frustration—and exhausted. He was no longer the omnipotent Israeli hero. The sight that greeted him inside the school when he entered behind the soldiers did not make things any easier. He recognized the girl who had motioned to him, wounded. She opened her eyes momentarily, recognized him and burst into tears. "It was terrible. Terrible."[12]

On June 4, Rabin's new government was sworn in. Dayan described his first day out of office: "After seven years in the

Defense Ministry I was an ordinary citizen again. The phone didn't ring at night and I didn't rush off to the office in the morning."[13] Instead, he sought archaeological recreation at the upright walls of the Beersheba riverbed, a destination familiar to him from previous visits. That winter's abundant rainfall promised new finds, and at a bend in the wadi he spotted a cave opening. He tied a rope to the fender of his car, lowered himself to the cave, and crawled inside, where he discovered traces of cave dwellers dating back six thousand years.

"In this cave, a family lived two thousand years before our Patriarch, Abraham," he later wrote. "They couldn't read or write. Sometimes, they drew on rocks. They decorated their pottery with red lines—dark, warm red. This was their home, here they lived, wandering back and forth through the Negev and Sinai. Knowing every wadi, every hill. This was their country, their homeland. They must have loved it. When attacked, they fought for it and for their lives. Now I've crawled into their home. I'm sitting near the hearth. The fire is out now, but I don't need to close my eyes to revive it. To see the hissing embers and the woman stooped over them, setting a pot on the fire for her family. My family."[14] He was speaking about a family that had lived in the country thousands of years before him. Even Abraham was no longer important, just the hills and valleys of this land for which he, too, was prepared to give his life.

Dayan served as a member of the Knesset for the next three years, but he devoted little time to the position. He seemed to have reached the end of his political career and settled in to writing his memoirs. He recruited Neora Matalon and Re'aya Aloni, his former secretary at the Defense Ministry, to help him produce his autobiography, *Milestones*, an undertaking that took about a year and a half to complete. Matalon collated the plentiful material from the IDF Archive, the safety-deposit box he had kept with Ben-Gurion's approval at the Bank of Israel, and a concealed drawer at home. According to Matalon, Dayan made sure to write about two episodes personally: his share in the victory of the Six Day War and his role in the failure of the Yom Kippur War. The other chapters he merely edited, adding reflections and occasionally semi-lyrical passages.

He met with Matalon and Aloni every day to review their drafts and discuss ongoing work. "The Moshe who now sat opposite us was a sad man," Matalon wrote of these editorial meetings. "His physical presence had shrunk compared with the figure I remembered as CGS or Minister of Agriculture." When the work was complete, and Dayan placed the final pages before his former assistants, there was a sense of relief but also of regret. "This billy-goat will yield no more milk," he told them.[15]

But he was wrong. After a short break, he started writing *Living with the Bible*, this time without editorial assistance. For this book, he required no archives or sources, merely the antiquities he had amassed, his personal memories, and, of course, the Bible. The book is a rove among biblical episodes, Land of Israel scenery, and personal memory. In rich, simple, modern Hebrew he reintroduces the reader to the biblical heroes, patriarchs, judges, and kings of the Jewish people. Emerging from the prose is his lifelong interpretation of the concept of "homeland." To him, the Land of Israel remained the land of the Bible from the mountains of Gilead and Moab to the Great Sea. His perception of the homeland was never marred by the presence of other peoples and religions in this space. It included Arab peasants and Bedouin nomads, who were also part of his home. The book's closing words expose the depths of his life's experience. He writes of how, as minister of defense, he roamed the territory with officers, discussing military and political matters. In the evening, however, when he flew home by helicopter, all rational considerations melted away. "Below, one land was visible. With no division between Jews and Arabs, one land strewn with towns and villages, fields and gardens. A land bordered in the east by the Jordan River, in the west by the Great Sea. In the North, it was crowned by the snow-capped Mount Hermon; in the South the arid desert closed in on it. The Land of Israel."[16]

"He was at peace with himself, attaining a measure of serenity previously missing," Rachel Dayan said, describing the period from 1974 to 1977 when writing books consumed much of her husband's energy. "He spent a lot of time at home and apart from writing, worked on his archaeology collection. He sat in the garden for hours, gluing shards together."

Once, when she suggested going out to a film, he refused. She knew that when he was married to Ruth, they had gone to films on Saturday nights with neighbors. Rachel asked him why he would not go. "Now I have no reason to go out," he replied. "I find it pleasant here."[17]

The three years of Dayan's absence from the political summit were stormy, both politically and militarily. Yitzhak Rabin, the IDF chief of staff during the Six Day War, was now prime minister; Yigal Allon was foreign minister and deputy prime minister; and Shimon Peres was serving as minister of defense. After another round of shuttling between Cairo and Jerusalem, Henry Kissinger was able to broker another interim Israeli-Egyptian agreement in September 1975: the IDF withdrew farther and were now east of the mountain passes. Egypt's rehabilitation of the canal towns and the reopening of the Suez Canal to international and Israeli navigation reinforced, as Dayan had expected, the sense that Egypt preferred calm to war.

The struggle against Palestinian terrorism continued apace and found one of its most dramatic victories in the astonishing rescue at Entebbe airport in Uganda of more than a hundred Israeli passengers and crew members aboard an Air France plane hijacked by German and Palestinian terrorists. In 1974, a movement of young religious Jews arose in Israel that urged settlement of the occupied territories. Gush Emunim (The Bloc of the Faithful) began building settlements in Arab areas without official permission. At the end of 1976, a government crisis erupted after a ceremony welcoming the arrival of new fighter planes from the United States was held on the Sabbath. The religious party, a member of the government coalition, cast a vote of No Confidence in the coalition, leading to Rabin's resignation. Elections were set for May 17, 1977.

Dayan played no part in any of these events. Peres visited him and occasionally sent Naphtali Lavie, the Ministry of Defense spokesman, to update him on developments.[18] Peres also ensured that Dayan would again hold a respectable position on the party candidate list for the upcoming elections. Ultimately, however, Dayan remained estranged and alienated. Israeli politics galloped ahead without him.

# 15

## *"Shall the Sword Devour Forever?"*

As the 1977 candidate lists were being drawn up, Dayan's former brother-in-law Ezer Weizman suggested to Dayan that he join the right-wing Likud Party, part of the Knesset opposition since 1948. The disgraced former defense minister did not dismiss the idea but demanded a commitment from the Likud leader, Menachem Begin, that he would not annex the occupied territories if he had an opportunity to make peace with the Arabs. Dayan thought that peace was possible and did not wish to jeopardize its prospects. He and Begin held secret meetings, exchanging formulations on Israel's policies in the occupied territories and the prospects of peace with Arab states, and they neared an agreement with each other. But they could not reach it in time. A few minutes before the deadline to submit candidate lists, Dayan signed a form that made him once more a Labor Party candidate.[1]

Nonetheless, after Likud won the election, Begin suggested

that Dayan join the government as foreign minister, though before he could do so Begin had to convince his skeptical Likud colleagues. "Dayan enjoys international renown, and statesmen all over the world defer to him," Begin reasoned. "His reputation is similar among Diaspora Jewry, and he is respected in Arab states. My call to him trumps party calculations. Israel faces a hard time and should enlist its best minds and efforts to protect our national interests."[2]

Dayan, however, remained indecisive. "I was plagued by the worst doubts I had ever known," he admitted. "Would I find a common language with Menachem Begin and his cabinet ministers—even on those political issues where I was closer to Begin than to the then leadership of the Labor Party?" But he knew that to influence possible peace measures, he had to be in the cabinet.[3]

Consulting Rachel, he sensed that she would have liked him to reject the offer, to avoid facing any more controversy. Ultimately, though, she left the decision to him. "If they'll just let me," he said, "I will achieve peace with Egypt."[4] Dayan disagreed with Begin about the future of the occupied territories, but they reached common ground. As Dayan described their position: "The Land of Israel is our ancient homeland, and it is inconceivable that upon Israel's rebirth and return to Zion, Jews be barred from settling Judea and Samaria, becoming foreigners in that land. We may be exiled from it by force but we cannot cut ourselves off from it voluntarily."[5]

Although their areas of agreement were not enough to avert Dayan's eventual resignation three years later, at that time the Palestinian question was not the top item on the new government's agenda. Dayan for some time had believed that President Sadat was interested in peace with Israel, and he wished to be part of shaping Israel's future policy with regard to Egypt. Maybe he was also trying to atone for the fiasco of the Yom Kippur War. Dayan accepted Begin's offer and on June 23, 1977, was sworn in as foreign minister in the Likud government. He brought Naphtali Lavie from the Ministry of Defense to take charge of Foreign Ministry public relations, and Elyakim Rubinstein, a talented young attorney, to serve as his bureau chief. These two would accompany him on most of his diplomatic trips, documenting his work as foreign minister.[6]

In the early weeks, Dayan concentrated on finding a mediator who could have direct dealings with Egypt. World leaders were only too pleased to meet with the man still considered the most brilliant, fascinating man in Israel, and in a ten-day period that summer Dayan met with India's prime minister Moraji Desai, the shah of Iran, and Jordan's King Hussein, who had been in covert contact with Israeli leaders for some time. But little came of these meetings.

The only mission that produced real results was Dayan's trip to Morocco on September 4. Israel and Morocco did not have formal diplomatic relations, and Dayan flew to Rabat disguised in a beatnik wig and black mustache. Israel sought King Hassan II's intercession with Egypt, aiming for an eventual peace treaty. Hassan promised to help, and on September 16, en route to the United States for a meeting with the new president, Jimmy Carter, Dayan slipped away during a stopover in Brussels, drove to Paris by roundabout routes, boarded a Moroccan airplane to Rabat, and met with the Egyptian envoy, Hassan el-Tohami. Dayan's impression was that Egypt wanted peace, and the two men agreed to exchange document drafts as a basis for further talks, planning to reconvene in Morocco within two weeks. But dramatic events interrupted their momentum.

Dayan reported the developments to Prime Minister Begin and proceeded to New York. Following the Yom Kippur War, the Geneva Conference of 1973 had engendered a diplomatic formula for Israel-Arab conciliation that stipulated peace talks under U.S. and Soviet auspices. Dayan assumed when he took over as foreign minister that the U.S. bid to reconvene the

Geneva Conference was on the table. Dayan disagreed with the Geneva blueprint because he opposed Soviet participation. He preferred direct talks between Israel and Egypt with the United States mediating but not dictating terms unilaterally. When he arrived in the United States on September 18, however, he learned that the Americans were assiduously working on a declaration of principles to form the basis of the revived Geneva Conference formula.

While in New York and Washington, he met twice with President Carter and Vice President Walter Mondale, and several times with Secretary of State Cyrus Vance and his aides. His first meeting with Carter was unpleasant. Carter, and especially Mondale—apparently playing "bad cop"—freely condemned Israel as intransigent, sabotaging U.S. efforts to reconvene the Geneva Conference. Dayan lost his patience, but kept silent. "There was palpable tension between the two sides of the oblong table," noted Naphtali Lavie, who was present at the meetings. "Dayan did not hide his resentment at the substance and tone of the conversation. The contribution of Mondale, who stood at Carter's side and irritated Dayan with snide remarks, was most unfavorable. Dayan showed his anger by ignoring him whenever he spoke from across the table."[7]

Recognizing his disgust, Dayan's hosts became embarrassed. Carter tried to soften his words and invited Dayan for another talk to clear the atmosphere. But the United States planned to issue a joint statement of principles with the Soviets, and this added to the tension. Dayan rejected the proposed draft. "We are not party to this statement, and you did not ask us or attempt to consult with us, though we are directly affected," he said. "You would do better to give it up and not restore the Soviets to the arena."[8]

The official reason for Dayan's trip was to address the U.N. General Assembly, but he remained in America for four weeks, speaking to Jewish communities from coast to coast and holding numerous meetings with the media and Congress. He did not mask his displeasure with the White House's Middle East policies, and his condemnation was not lost on the Carter administration. Articles critical of Carter and supportive of Dayan's position appeared in newspapers all over the United States. The leaders of the American Jewish organizations and communities were not idle either. In four days, the White House received more than seven thousand telegrams and a thousand phone calls protesting U.S. policy.

The pressure was effective, and Carter asked for another meeting before Dayan left New York. Dayan's impatience was growing. He treated the president respectfully, but when Carter reiterated that Israel could rely on him, Dayan delivered a stirring emotional response. "Mr. President, I may have only one eye, but I can clearly see the dangers posed to our existence as a people if we accept your advice," he said, referring to Carter's proposed joint statement with the Soviets which included consideration of the Palestinians' aspirations and, he felt, preempted the fostering of bilateral negotiations with the Arab states. "Personally, I am no coward, but as a son of the Jewish people I have good cause to be worried. In our own time, disaster already befell us, and there are those among us who experienced it firsthand. As long as it is in our power, we will spare our people another tragedy."[9]

Following further clarification, Dayan and Vance formulated a new press statement for the United States to issue jointly with Israel instead of the Soviet Union, establishing a new framework for the pursuit of Middle East peace. Though it was 2 A.M. in New York, Dayan insisted that they first send the watered-down and generalized statement, which was much closer to the government's initial positions, to Begin for approval, and Israel adopted it as the working paper for negotiations. Dayan considered this an achievement and an important component for pursuing the peace process.

Cairo, too, was evidently concerned about Carter's wish to revive the Geneva Conference formula, especially his intention of including the Soviets in the process. President Sadat decided that the best plan would be to reach an understanding with Israel before they arrived at the conference. Without consulting any of his colleagues, he boldly announced to Egypt's parliament on November 9 that he was prepared to set out for Jerusalem to address the Knesset concerning his vision for peace between their nations. After some hesitation, Begin rose to the challenge and issued a formal invitation for Sadat to appear. The dramatic event confirmed Dayan's assumption that Sadat was interested in peace, but he understood that in exchange for this unprecedented step, Sadat would expect Israel to withdraw from all the territories occupied in 1967. And in that expectation, Israel would clearly disappoint him.

Israelis welcomed Sadat with open arms, though Dayan found little to allay his concerns when he drove with Egyptian Foreign Minister Boutros Boutros-Ghali from the airport to Jerusalem.[10] Boutros-Ghali made it clear that Egypt would not consider a peace agreement with Israel that did not include a resolution of the problem of Palestinian self-governance.[11]

The next day, November 20, Sadat addressed the Knesset, saying much that Dayan had expected: the Palestinian problem was the heart of the conflict, and Palestinians had to have their own state. Nonetheless, he was applauded by his listeners, by the Israeli public, and by the world press. The mutual hope that Sadat and Begin pledged—"No more war!"—became a prayer for the nation.

Still, Sadat was disappointed by the results of his visit; it lasted less than twenty-four hours, and the diplomatic ceremonies left no time for real discussion. The sole tangible accomplishment was an agreement in principle to continue the contacts, a continuation to the process that was reached without imposition by foreign powers. During the visit Defense

Minister Ezer Weizman captivated Sadat with his humor and colorful anecdotes. Dayan, in comparison, was tense, his face often sour. His relations with Egypt's president were proper but cool.

The first attempt at practical negotiation took place two weeks later, when Dayan and Tohami met again in Morocco, at King Hassan's exotic palace in Marrakech. But Tohami did not seem to have the authority to negotiate; he could only read from a handwritten document he had brought from Cairo. The document further highlighted the differences between Egypt and Israel. Dayan believed that Sadat wanted peace but did not know how to achieve it. He concluded that if there were to be any hope for progress, the Americans had to become involved and throw their weight behind the process.

On December 25, Begin, Dayan, Weizman, and a large entourage of aides and advisers arrived in Ismailia on the banks of the Suez Canal to meet with Sadat. Dayan, dispirited, observed that Egypt's reception of the Israeli delegation was cool and lacking in ceremonial features: no honor guard, no flags or anthems, no signs of welcome. Dayan focused on the stark contrast to the warmth Israel had shown Sadat a month earlier.

Not surprisingly, the talks did not go well. The attempt to formulate a joint declaration of principles failed. Instead, two committees were established: one for military, the other for political and civilian issues. Dayan, irritated by the fruitless talks, wandered out to the balcony overlooking the canal, where the Bar-Lev Line had once stood, and was overcome with bitter memories of the Yom Kippur War. He gazed at the area he had crossed and decided that Israel faced a brutal choice: "To make heavy concessions or not make peace with Egypt."[12]

Weizman headed the military committee appointed in Ismailia and set up a permanent legation of IDF officers in Cairo. The Egyptians liked Weizman's light-hearted manner and made him feel at home.[13] The political committee, however, soon faltered. On January 15, 1978, Egypt's new foreign minister, Muhammad Ibrahim Kamal, headed a delegation to Jerusalem comprised of professional diplomats who had been influenced by the general feeling in the Arab world. They hardened their position, and the talks were fruitless and acerbic; the visit ended with the two sides breaking off negotiations.

The rift lasted half a year. Begin and Dayan visited Washington, Mondale and Vance visited Jerusalem and Cairo, but none of them was able to revive the process. Palestinian terrorists posed an additional obstacle. On April 11, a particularly brutal attack struck to the heart of Israel. Eleven Palestinian guerrillas landed on a deserted beach between Haifa and Tel Aviv and hijacked a bus to Tel Aviv. The bus was stopped on the outskirts of the city, and most of the terrorists were killed, but they managed to set fire to the bus first, massacring thirty-five passengers. "The peace process that in any case has been hanging between life and death is now dying in the flames of the burning bus," Weizman lamented.[14]

Israel decided on a major reprisal, the largest since the Yom Kippur War. The IDF captured an extensive area in Lebanon, south of the Litani River, and held it for a few days. The soldiers destroyed Palestinian strongholds and returned home.

It took the Americans half a year to reach Dayan's initial conclusion that the declaration of principles must be abandoned and the two parties should directly discuss the contentious issues in detail. On July 17, the United States invited both sides to a conference at a castle near Leeds, England. Dayan was charmed by the ambiance, filled with "ballads and knights, towers, large halls with years of moss in the cracks and hoary walls, abounding with splendor and power."[15] During the discussions, the sticking point remained Egypt's demand that the talks focus on the Palestinian problem. Dayan, heading the Israeli delegation, thought it possible to reach an agreement on bilateral issues affecting only Israel and Egypt based on re-linquishing the Sinai for the sake of peace, but on the Palestinian issue he could not see Begin's government agreeing to the IDF's withdrawal from the West Bank and Gaza, or recognizing the Palestinians' right to self-determination. It gradually became clear that the only way forward was to agree that Israel would withdraw from Sinai and to postpone discussion of the West Bank and Gaza, in the meantime giving some form of autonomy to the Palestinians there.

Dayan forced the issue and confronted the Egyptian delegation with a choice: the representatives could discuss the future of Sinai or fruitlessly continue to reiterate their position on the Palestinian issue. As Dayan phrased it to his team, "The Egyptians will not give up the bird they already have in hand."[16] To help Egypt move toward peace without settling the Palestinian issue, Dayan submitted to Vance, as his "personal opinion," a document containing an agreement to discuss the issue of sovereignty for the Palestinian population after a five-year period of autonomy.

When he returned to Israel, Dayan reported to Begin on the talks and the personal document he had submitted to Vance. Begin was displeased about the document, protesting that Dayan had not consulted him. For Dayan, the freedom to negotiate as he had done was a matter of principle: he did not mind if the government or the prime minister rejected his views as long as they were considered. "I do not think I am able to manage the negotiations if I am not allowed to voice thoughts and make suggestions while stressing that these are my own personal opinions and the government might not accept them," he told Begin. He made no threats, but it was obvious to both men that he would not back down. If Begin denied Dayan the freedom he sought, he would have to find himself a different foreign minister.[17]

Dayan was employing the same tactics he had used with

Ben-Gurion and Meir, offering his personal views without committing the prime minister at an early stage of the discussion. Begin, too, apparently understood that this was the best method to untangle the negotiations mess. The next day, Dayan was surprised to hear Begin recommend that the cabinet endorse Dayan's document to Vance.

The Leeds proceedings and Dayan's document encouraged the Americans to push ahead. It became clear that only Sadat and Begin could exhibit the flexibility required for the negotiations to succeed. In early August, Carter invited both leaders to a summit scheduled for early September at Camp David, Maryland, the U.S. president's summer resort.

The summit convened on September 5 and lasted thirteen days. Each side arrived with a dozen advisers and aides. Along with Begin, Israel's team included Weizman and Dayan, who described the meetings as "the most decisive, difficult, and unpleasant part of the peace negotiations with Egypt. Reaching an accommodation involved personal and ideological crises for both sides, abandoning traditional conceptions and adopting new positions."[18] The delegations' internal discussions were therefore no less important than the bilateral talks.

Camp David's sports facilities, films, billiard tables, and bars were available to the delegates, but Dayan did not indulge himself. Instead, he took daily walks on the ring road in the compound, seeking the solitude and reflection he needed most to allow his mind to relax.

The opening meetings were highly frustrating, each side obviously having to yield more in response to the United States than in response to the other. As the summit progressed, the Americans held separate talks with each side in an attempt to bridge the gaps. The United States ultimately urged Israel to agree to withdraw from Sinai to the pre-1948 border, dismantle the settlements around Rafah and Sharm el-Sheikh, and relinquish the airfields it had built. The Palestinian question was deferred in return for Israel's recognition of the Palestinians' "legitimate rights"; the Palestinians were also to have five years of autonomy in the West Bank and Gaza, at the end of which the two sides would discuss a permanent settlement. The details of this autonomy were to be worked out as soon as a peace treaty was signed.

The Americans greased the process with promises to each side. They agreed, for example, to finance the establishment of Israeli airfields in the Negev to replace those in Sinai, and to support Egypt's position on the Palestinian question, including the future of Jerusalem. This last commitment nearly derailed the conference. Carter, apparently respecting Dayan's integrity and creative thinking, occasionally met with him privately, asking that he make every effort to bridge the remaining gaps. When the issue of Jerusalem came up, the talks reached a boiling point. Dayan delivered a heated soliloquy about Jerusalem's significance to the Jewish people, expressing fervid opposition to Arab sovereignty there, while Carter insisted that he could not renege on his promise to Sadat. Finally, amendments were introduced into Carter's memorandum, and both Sadat and Begin agreed to attach their own memoranda on Jerusalem's future.

A fresh disagreement erupted shortly before the summit wound down on September 16. Egypt, with the Americans in agreement, demanded that Israel stop expanding its settlements in the occupied territories during the five-year implementation of the peace treaty. Begin was prepared to call a temporary halt of three months. The discussion ended inconclusively after midnight with a misunderstanding of Begin's exact undertaking with regards to the temporary freeze on additional settlements. This would mar future relations between Begin and Carter.

Shadowed by this misunderstanding, the agreement was signed in the White House on September 17. Outdoors in Washington, a storm brewed, while indoors great excitement

surrounded the historic occasion. The three-way handshake of
Carter, Sadat, and Begin immortalized the moment and sym-
bolized the dawn of a new era. Late that night, as the Israelis
celebrated at their hotel, Dayan stayed in his room to reflect
on the momentous occasion. He recorded in his diary: "This
evening was one of the greatest moments of my life. I have
traveled a long way since the peace negotiations with King Abdullah, the Sinai Campaign, the Six Day War, and Yom Kippur War. I was gratified to be one of its architects. Though
weary, I couldn't fall asleep. I longed for home. . . . In Israel,
I would have celebrated as I liked. A meal in the kitchen with
Rachel. . . . I wanted to be with myself, with Rachel, and with
the history of Israel down the generations."[19]

The Camp David Accords merely provided a framework for
a peace treaty; a formal treaty would still have to be negotiated.
The process, filled with pitfalls and crises, took six months.
When the delegations returned to Washington to begin the
peace negotiations, Dayan headed the Israeli delegation along
with Weizman. This stage of the process became known as
the Blair House Conference, after the presidential guesthouse
located diagonally across from the White House. The Americans remained involved, offering encouragement, compromise,
and pressure. The talks opened on October 12, 1978, one day
after Yom Kippur and a full five years after the war that had led
to the peace process.

In addition to the differences with Egypt and the United
States, the Israeli delegation also differed internally on Jerusalem. As the two countries drew closer to the final wording,
Begin recalled Dayan and Weizman to Jerusalem for a cabinet
discussion, as their critics believed they had made unnecessary
concessions. Dayan increasingly felt that Begin's camp did not
trust him, yet Begin knew he had no choice but to approve
the formulations brought from Washington. He persuaded

the cabinet to authorize Dayan and Weizman to complete the negotiations, but by the time they returned to Washington, on October 26, clouds had gathered. On November 1, Begin arrived in the United States en route to a state visit in Canada. He spent two days in New York and met officially with Vance and unofficially with Carter, whose suggestions were not to Dayan's liking.

Dayan, increasingly, felt isolated within the fray. Before returning to Israel, he jotted down a note in his diary about biblical heroes who had suffered lonely deaths: King Saul, who had fallen on his sword in the war against the Philistines; Samson, who had sought love among Philistine women and was friendless among his own people. He ended this sad, begrudging entry with the odd remark: "Why is Samson drawn to fire? Such was the man, and the Bible does not find him wanting."[20]

The stalemate continued. Washington offended Jerusalem by hinting that the Israelis were to blame for the deadlock. "We felt we were the victim of a double standard and even being misled," Dayan vented in his diary. "While Washington firmly refused to agree to Israel's demands to amend the formulated agreement, claiming that the removal of a single stone would topple the entire edifice, it consented to a good deal more than that to placate Egypt's government."[21]

Not surprisingly, key members of Begin's party began to clamor against Dayan's management of the negotiations, and Begin now seemed to share these views. Dayan's status had plainly eroded, and he felt his authority slipping away. On February 21, the Americans convened another conference at Camp David at the ministerial level. Egyptian Prime Minister Mustafa Khalil represented Egypt, and Dayan represented Israel. But now the asymmetry was reversed: Khalil was authorized to conclude matters, and Dayan was not.

The second Camp David conference was cool, brief, and fruitless. The weather was bitterly cold, with snow and heavy fog obscuring an infrequent sun that appeared equally cold and distant. As inclement winds blew from both Jerusalem and the White House, the two sides seemed farther apart than ever, and continuing the talks appeared pointless. Dayan was peeved and angry, worried and apprehensive. The peace he considered vital to Israel's security remained elusive.

Hereafter, Carter would be in direct touch with Prime Minister Begin, the only Israeli he deemed actually able to deliver a peace accord. He invited Begin and Khalil to another summit, in Washington, and Dayan remained at home. After intensive talks with Carter, Begin recommended that the delegation approve the formulations, which appeared to Dayan to be no different from those he had achieved in the past. Though slighted, he supported the recommendation in the cabinet. "Even if the new formulations are essentially no different from the previous ones, that is no reason to thwart the agreement," he noted sourly in his diary.[22]

A few days later, Carter set out for Cairo and Jerusalem to finalize the agreement and obtain Sadat's approval for wordings to which Begin had agreed. There were last-minute hitches. Egypt insisted on changing a few words and reiterating other demands: to station communications officers in Gaza and sell Sinai oil to Israel only via an American company. These were symbolic, not substantive, matters, which made them harder to resolve.

Carter arrived in Israel on March 10, 1979, and the next evening a crisis loomed when the Israelis rejected the latest Egyptian amendments. Carter was annoyed and announced that he would return to Washington the following day. Yet to return to Washington without an agreement would have meant a loss of face for Carter. To prevent this from happening, Dayan proposed a number of new formulations, to which Carter and Begin both agreed. Dayan felt that he had saved the day. Back in his hotel room, he permitted himself to boast to Rachel: "I resolved the crisis."[23]

Sadat chose to have the official signing in Washington. The public ceremony took place on March 26 at 2 P.M. on the White House lawn. It was another stirring moment, and the photograph of the three-way handshake of Begin, Sadat, and Carter, all looking happy, became the second most important document of accomplishment in the history of the Arab-Israeli conflict.

Outside, a handful of Palestinians demonstrated against the agreement. At the time their protest seemed negligible, even pathetic. But hindsight suggests that this minor demonstration was hinting at the failure of the peace treaty to solve the crux of the conflict: the national question of Palestinian Arabs.

# 16

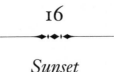

## *Sunset*

AT THE END OF APRIL 1979, Moshe and Rachel Dayan set out on a jaunt through Southeast Asia. He had not been well for the better part of a year. He felt weakened and found physical work, even his cherished archaeology, a strain. His body seemed to be shrinking. During their trip, Dayan set aside time to puff and pant in the oppressive heat between strides up steep paths leading to Buddhist shrines. On his return to Israel, his physician administered a complete checkup and found colon cancer. The doctor scheduled surgery for May 24. Dayan became absorbed by the prospect of death. "I've been psychologically ready to part with life for years, to shut my eyes and be gathered unto my forefathers," he told his physician. "Death is the perfect end beyond which there is nothing and I'm prepared for it at any time."[1] He was worried that he would need treatment and be incapacitated after the operation, but fortunately the operation went well. The day after surgery, he rose, shaved, and wandered about the ward. Although they scolded him, the physicians were pleased with his quick recovery. A week later, he returned to his office and routine affairs.

According to Rachel, however, he never fully regained his strength.[2] His heart muscles were apparently worn out. He suffered from various ailments and looked old for his age: gray, tired, dragging his feet. Moreover, he was losing the sight in his one eye and had difficulty reading. He was also aware that he had reached the end of his tenure in Begin's government. A few weeks after Israel and Egypt signed the peace treaty, the two sides began discussing Palestinian autonomy, as stipulated. Dayan believed it possible to reach arrangements of coexistence that would be acceptable to the Palestinians in the occupied territories, but to head the negotiations Begin appointed Minister of the Interior Joseph Burg, a member of the National Religious Party, which advocated hawkish positions and extensive settlement throughout the Land of Israel. Dayan refused to join the team if he could not steer it and waited months to see how the negotiations proceeded. After four months he realized that there was no real chance of progress on the Begin-Burg path, and he resigned from the government.

Dayan submitted his letter of resignation to the prime minister on October 2, 1979, succinctly stating his reasons for leaving in their final conversation. "The things that interest me, I'm not involved in, and those I'm involved in don't interest me," he told Begin. "I didn't join the government to meet ambassadors and attend cocktail parties."[3] Begin did not try to stop him, and he may have even been relieved. On October 23, Dayan left the cabinet table and took his seat as a one-man faction in the Knesset's back row, next to Likud extremists who had quit the party in protest over the peace treaty with Egypt. Though the company did not appeal to him, he was happy to sit near the exit: it was the end of his political career. After his

"betrayal" of Labor three years earlier, he could not justify returning to his old seat and given his differences of opinion with
Likud, there was no room for him among them either. Under
the assumption that these were his last days in the Knesset, he
typically decided to use what energy he had left to write a book
on the peace talks and his role in them over the previous two
years.[4]

Rachel remembered the period fondly. "For all the suffering, I remember the last two years with longing," she reflected,
years later. "Moshe became a real family man, often playing
with my grandchildren from my first marriage. He composed
limericks and rolled around with them in the garden and on the
carpet. He truly was a different person then, but he was already
weary and ill."[5]

Yaël remembered that time differently. She described her
father's last twenty-four months as "pathetic years of dying."
Granting her dying father little compassion, she elaborated:
"The man who all his life had been a constant fighter, who had
been destined for tests and challenges, had scaled heights and
shown his best when cruelly faced by the hardest demands . . .
had the fight go out of him in the two years of his dying," she
wrote. "He was coddled in kindness and swaddled in comfort.
He was loved and obeyed, pampered, cared for and diapered
until he withered like a desert flower from overwatering and the
removal of a beating sun."[6]

Yaël, clearly, did not like her father's new lifestyle. She describes conversations with him in his garden when instead of
discussing public affairs or moral issues, as they had done in the
past, he spoke of electricity bills, the rise in taxes, and inflation.
"His stinginess had always been a subject of family jokes," she
recalled. "Now, money became almost an obsession. At a time
when he needed it less than ever." Royalties from his books,
along with his salary, allowed him a higher level of comfort

than he had enjoyed earlier, and Rachel noted that he spent hefty sums on antiquities.

Occasionally, when Rachel was not present, he would attempt to justify his bourgeois lifestyle. "He tried to excuse his shallow, expensive personal grooming as an esthetic value," Yaël wrote. She could not reconcile this "new lifestyle packed with shallow perks" to her mother's simple ways. "Mother was poor and a spendthrift, generous, sometimes excessively so, whereas Father in his latter years was rich and a penny-pincher—a combination I found hard to accept."[7]

Dayan did not want to quit the public arena completely. He continued the fight outside of the government for accommodation with the Palestinians. He belonged to the Public Forum for Political and Social Questions initiated by a relatively new Likud member, Zalman Shoval, in the summer of 1977, when the controversy over Begin's appointment of Dayan as foreign minister had been at its peak. The forum, open to the public, convened every few months with various guest speakers, but Dayan commanded the most interest. After his resignation from the government, it became his chief podium, and he continued to make headlines.

Initially nonpartisan, the forum was regarded in political circles as a constant threat lest it develop into a party under Dayan. But this was not Dayan's aim, and he had long stated that Israel did not need another political party. And although he had various opportunities at the rostrum, he elaborated his position on the Palestinians mainly at the forum.[8] The year demarcated for discussing Palestinian autonomy was drawing to a close, and Dayan was worried about repercussions that would affect the peace treaty with Egypt. He suggested imposing unilateral autonomy on the Palestinians, and on December 24, 1980, his one-man Knesset faction put forth a proposal to discuss "self-management" in the territories: annulling the military government and transferring the management of civilian affairs to Palestinian mayors. He thought coexistence was possible even without official Palestinian consent.

Drawing fire from both the right and left, his plan contained three caveats that rendered it meaningless: there would be no Palestinian state; the IDF would remain in the territories; and Israel would negotiate with Jordan, not the PLO. He saw the PLO as a mere nuisance forcing Israel to use bullying tactics.[9] He also reiterated his support for Jewish settlement in the territories. "Nowhere in the Land of Israel is extraterritorial to us," he declared, and he held that autonomy related to people, not territory: Israel would remain the governmental authority.[10] The proposal was voted down by a solid majority of the attending members of the Knesset.

Looking back thirty years later, we can recognize that his proposal was naïve and detached from reality: in 1980, the Palestinian national movement was already a consolidated, active entity with considerable international standing. As long as he was still able to read, Dayan often scanned the Bible or literature on Land of Israel antiquities or the works of Jewish national poets. But his knowledge and understanding of historical processes and the international realities that took shape after World War II left much to be desired. For all his acuity and intuition, his political thinking remained basically provincial. He claimed that his plan amounted to a recognition of the existence of the Palestinian people but not of their right to self-determination. This position was already outdated under U.S. President Woodrow Wilson's initiatives at the end of World War I.

High inflation, internal friction, a handful of criminal scandals in governmental circles, and the resignation of several ministers moved Prime Minister Begin to advance the elections for the tenth Knesset. According to the cycle, the elections were supposed to occur in November, but Begin called for early elections to be held on June 30, 1981. Dayan, despite repeated denials of any intention of converting the Public Forum for Political and Social Questions into a political party and run for office, yielded to his colleagues' entreaties and established a new party, the National Renewal Movement, better known as Telem, its Hebrew acronym. "It was very sad," Rachel said, describing her husband's efforts. "He was ill and weary. I tried to shield him from it, but they pressed and he couldn't resist."[11]

The initial polls showed a Dayan-led party garnering quite a few seats. He let himself believe that as the head of even a small party, he might impose his ideas on unilateral Palestinian autonomy on the next coalition. Ill and weak, he nonetheless campaigned throughout the country with Rachel at his side. But he was no longer the star he once was. "It was pitiful," Rachel recalled; "I was with him everywhere, but the public didn't show up."[12]

On election night, Moshe, Rachel, and a handful of loyal supporters at the party office watched the television polls. Telem won two seats. Any hope of tipping the scales in the next coalition disappeared. The supporters gradually dispersed, full of disappointment and despair. A Dayan biographer, Ehud Ben-Ezer, described the scene televised that night. "Telem Party headquarters began emptying out, and the final frame imprinted on the viewers' minds . . . was of Moshe sitting virtually alone at the center of the table beside Rachel," Ben-Ezer wrote. "Then, he too rose to leave, looking terrible—thin, skeletal, drab, wan as if sentenced to death."[13]

Dayan's health deteriorated swiftly after the elections. On October 6, Muslim extremists assassinated President Sadat, and Dayan was asked to address the tragedy on live television. It was his last public appearance. "Only skin and bones remained of the mythic sabra," a young journalist noted.[14] Gad Yaakobi, Dayan's close friend from his days at the Agriculture Ministry, hurried to see him and was stunned to find his home completely dark. Dayan appeared, feeling his way along the wall to reach the door. When Yaakobi asked why he did not turn on the light, Dayan replied, "I hardly notice the difference between light and dark. I've virtually lost my sight. I can barely make out your image, a sort of hazy dot. I'm blind, I know this scourge won't continue much longer."[15]

On Thursday, October 15, Dayan felt strong chest pains and was taken into intensive care. At 8 P.M. he lost consciousness, and all attempts to revive him were unsuccessful. "It is the end," his personal physician told Yaël and Rachel, who were waiting outside his room. They entered and stayed beside him, holding the lifeless hands of the father and husband. He was sixty-six years old.

At Dayan's state funeral, six former IDF chiefs of staff served as pallbearers. Throngs of people, ordinary citizens and powerful politicians, loyalists and opponents, turned out. Moshe Dayan was buried in the cemetery on Givat Shimron, next to his parents, brother, and sister. As he had requested, there was no eulogy. Heaps of flowers covered his grave, dug into the fertile soil of Nahalal.

# 17

## *Legacy*

MORE THAN THIRTY YEARS AFTER HIS DEATH, Moshe Dayan remains a controversial figure. Many remember him with admiration; others bristle at the mere mention of his name. Numerous streets and institutions in Israel pay tribute to him, yet new criticisms continue to arise. Over the years, literary portrayals and the media have cultivated a stereotype of Dayan, always depicted with his iconic black eye patch. That stereotype, for better or worse, represents him as a fearless warrior and nonconformist, impervious in his opinions, inclinations, and passions to external influence or social convention. The public saw him as a lone wolf, guided only by his inner compass.

In the 1950s, he was undeniably the leading figure in Israel's defense establishment. During this period, the Arabs, refusing to come to terms with their defeat in 1948, and rising young forces in the Middle East led by Gamal Abdul Nasser, worked in the hope that the Jews would ultimately be beaten. Peace was not part of their agenda. At this stage, all Israel could do was secure itself in the face of Arab threats. It was Moshe Dayan who molded Israel's self-defense capability.

The opportunity for peace did not come until after the Six Day War in June 1967. The IDF's trouncing of the Arab armies undermined the Arabs' hopes of vanquishing Israel, whose territorial gains, it was thought, could perhaps be bartered for rapprochement. In this period, Dayan was unable to understand how the world had changed. In charge of the occupied territories, he pursued a soft policy. He did not grasp that he was up against not only a people in need of a decent living and personal well-being, but one in need of a collective identity and dignity. Dayan's support for Jewish settlements in the occupied territories—and denial of the Palestinians' right to self-determination—placed him in the heart of Israel's rejectionist camp. Even in his final days in Israeli politics, while fighting for unilateral autonomy, he stressed that autonomy was only for the people, not the territory. This illusory dichotomy epitomizes the myopia of one who prided himself on political realism.

The differentiation between people and territory was embedded in Dayan from youth. His empathy for the Arab inhabitants enabled him to see things from their perspective but did not diminish his determination to safeguard the land for the Zionist enterprise. His affection for the young Bedouin Wahsh, who had helped him and his father plow and reap, did not preclude the conflict over Israeli-owned Nahalal land that the Bedouins and their forefathers had long used. His understanding of the motives of Ro'i Rothberg's murderers, who shot and mutilated the young commander near the Gaza border, did not stop him from exhorting Jews to take up arms to defend their land. His invitation to Palestinian poet Fadwa Touqan and his efforts to ease the daily lives of Palestinian civilians in the occupied territories after the Six Day War did not soften his tough measures against Palestinian nationalist activists. His concept of homeland applied to all the territory of the Land of Israel from the Jordan River to the Mediterranean Sea, including the Arab inhabitants living there—a profound contradiction he was unable to reconcile.

Moshe Dayan undoubtedly played a vital role in the peace treaty with Egypt. At moments of crisis, it was he who found the saving formula. Moreover, he was pivotal in helping Begin overcome his ideological prejudices in order to make necessary, painful concessions. Yet for all its importance, the treaty with Egypt did not settle the core issues of the conflict between Jews and Arabs. And for this failure, Dayan cannot be exonerated.

On a personal level, his public image wildly contrasted with his co-workers' perception of him. Beyond his immediate circle, he shut people out. He chose to be a loner—in his father's fields, in the tiny annex his parents built for him at home, and on his treasure hunts. He had no patience for social niceties and chitchat, and he had no close friends. He alienated people; some thought him cold, manipulative, an opportunist, and even heartless—an image compounded by his brazen archaeological misconduct, sexual promiscuity, and violation of conventional norms. Yet his co-workers also saw the other, softer Dayan: his love of poetry, occasional sentimentality, humor, playfulness, and warmth. And his impeccable integrity. He was certainly capable of manipulation—but not of pose, bathos, or falsehood.

At a few points in Dayan's career, many Israelis expected him to become prime minister, but he remained close to the top and preferred to operate in the shadow of an older, senior authoritarian figure like David Ben-Gurion, Golda Meir, or Menachem Begin. He never sought the ultimate responsibility. The psychoanalyst Avner Falk attributed this characteristic to his strong attachment to his mother.[1] Dayan, when asked about it, said that he was unable to perform the many boring and tedious tasks the prime minister's role demands. It seems that he was unwilling to make the compromises and sacrifices of his personal freedom that were necessary to reach the top. Even had he wanted the premiership, however, Dayan was unlikely to have gotten it because he turned too many members of the Israeli political elite against him, enraging them with his out-spoken and nonconformist attitudes.

However he is ultimately judged, even his worst critics must concede that Moshe Dayan remains one of the most fascinating and compelling figures to have appeared on Israel's stage.

Dayan possessed brilliant intuition and often had a grasp of a situation, understanding the solutions necessary to solve the problem better than most of his colleagues. Often among the dissenting opinions, his view was overruled, but he did not try to force it on others. He yielded to the will of his superiors but always remained true to himself and to the values he held dearest all his life: his love of the land and devotion to Zionism. In his own words, Dayan claimed he only knew how to "plow to build the homeland and hold a sword to defend the earth."[2]

All interviews were conducted by the author in Hebrew. Archival material and quotations from newspapers are in Hebrew unless otherwise indicated. All translations from the Hebrew are the author's unless otherwise indicated.

## Chapter 1: Wild Grass

1. The description is based on the memoirs of Shmuel Dayan in his *On the Banks of the Jordan and the Sea of Galilee* (Al Gdot Yarden ve-Kinneret) (Tel Aviv, n.d.), pp. 172–73 (Hebrew).

2. Ibid., pp. 28–29.

3. Moshe Dayan, *Milestones: An Autobiography* (Avnei Derekh: Autobiographia) (Jerusalem, 1976), p. 21 (Hebrew). The book was also published in English, but the translation does not always reflect the original, and I have translated the passages quoted in this book from the Hebrew source.

4. Ibid., p. 18.

5. Devorah Dayan, *In Joy and in Sorrow* (Be-Osher u-be-Yagon) (Tel-Aviv, 1957), p. 7 (Hebrew).

6. M. Dayan, *Milestones*, p. 19.

7. Ibid., p. 23.

8. The description of the attack on Deganya Bet and the burning shack appears in S. Dayan, *Banks*, pp. 260–62.

9. Literally, a seat of residence. A moshav by the name of Ein Ganim was actually founded near the veteran *moshava* (village) of Petah Tikva in 1908. It was based on small auxiliary farms to supplement worker incomes. In the 1930s, Ein Ganim was swallowed up by Petah Tikva's municipal boundaries. As a result, Nahalal is commonly regarded as the country's first moshav and remains an agricultural settlement to this day.

10. Shmuel Dayan, *Nahalalim: A Forty-Year Story* (Nahalalim: Sippur Arbba'im Shana) (Tel Aviv, 1961), pp. 80–83 (Hebrew).

11. The letter is reprinted in full ibid., p. 61.

12. M. Dayan, *Milestones*, p. 29.

13. The description is based on Shabtai Teveth, *Moshe Dayan* (Tel Aviv, 1971), p. 63 (Hebrew).

14. Moshe Dayan, *Living with the Bible* (Lihiot Im ha Tanach) (Jerusalem, 1978), p. 15 (Hebrew).

15. M. Dayan, *Milestones*, p. 29. The incident is also mentioned in S. Dayan, *Nahalalim*, p. 69.

16. Teveth, *Moshe Dayan*, p. 97.

17. Ibid., p. 99.

18. Ibid., p. 110.

## Chapter 2: On the Path of Command

1. Shabtai Teveth, *Moshe Dayan* (Tel Aviv, 1971), p. 139 (Hebrew).

2. Ruth Dayan and Helga Dudman, *And Maybe . . . The Story of Ruth Dayan* (Ve Ouly Sipura shell Ruth Dayan) (Jerusalem, 1973), p. 28 (Hebrew). The book was also published in English, but I have translated the passages quoted in this book from the Hebrew source.

3. Teveth, *Moshe Dayan*, p. 144.
4. Dayan and Dudman, *And Maybe . . .*, p. 31.
5. Ibid.; Teveth, *Moshe Dayan*, p. 149.
6. Moshe Dayan, *Milestones: An Autobiography* (Avnei Derekh: Autobiographia) (Jerusalem, 1976), p. 35 (Hebrew).
7. Cited in Ora Armani, *Friend and Confidant: Talks with Sini* (Haver ve-Ish Sod: Sihot im Sini) (Tel Aviv, 2008), p. 105 (Hebrew).
8. Teveth, *Moshe Dayan*, p. 171.
9. Ruth Dayan to Moshe Dayan, cited in the collection of letters Moshe Dayan wrote to Ruth during his imprisonment, *My Ruthie* (Ruti Sheli) (Lod, 2001), p. 34.
10. Moshe Dayan to Ruth Dayan, ibid., p. 33.
11. M. Dayan, *Milestones*, p. 45.
12. Moshe Dayan to Ruth Dayan, *My Ruthie*, p. 79.
13. Moshe Dayan, "With the Invaders to Syria," in Z. Gilead, ed., *A Clandestine Shield: Operations of the Jewish-Palestinian Underground during the Second World War* (Magen ba Seter: MePeulot ha' Mahteret ha Eretz-Israelit be' Milhemet ha Olam ha Shnia) (Tel Aviv, 1949), p. 140 (Hebrew).
14. Testimony of Zalman Mart, Israel Defense Forces Archive [hereafter IDF Archive], Tel Ha Shomer, Israel.
15. M. Dayan, "With the Invaders to Syria," p. 144.
16. Dayan and Dudman, *And Maybe . . .*, p. 108.
17. Army form W3118 RAF, Division 6057/File 1, IDF Archive. This form is in English.

## Chapter 3: Back to Military Work

1. Moshe Dayan, *Milestones: An Autobiography* (Avnei Derekh: Autobiographia) (Jerusalem, 1976), p. 52 (Hebrew).
2. Ruth Dayan and Helga Dudman, *And Maybe . . . The Story of Ruth Dayan* (Ve Ouly Sipura shell Ruth Dayan) (Jerusalem, 1973), p. 109 (Hebrew).
3. Shabtai Teveth, *Moshe Dayan* (Tel Aviv, 1971), p. 217 (Hebrew).

4. Dayan and Dudman, *And Maybe* . . . , p. 114

5. Menachem Begin, *The Revolt* (Ha-Mered) (Tel Aviv, 1954), p. 391 (Hebrew).

6. *Mapai* is an acronym for the Workers of Eretz Israel Party.

7. Dayan and Dudman, *And Maybe* . . . , p. 118.

8. M. Dayan, *Milestones*, p. 56.

9. Ibid., p. 57.

10. Ibid., p. 61.

11. The IDF did not yet have officer ranks but Yigal Allon was soon to be appointed one of four commanders of the main fronts, with the shoulder insignia of major-general.

12. M. Dayan, *Milestones*, p. 64.

13. Ibid.

14. Moshe Dayan, "The Commando Battalion Attacks Lod [Gdud ha-Commando Oleh al Lod]," *Ma'arakhot* 62–63 (July 1950), p. 37 (Hebrew).

15. M. Dayan, *Milestones*, p. 79.

16. Interview with Ruth Dayan, June 2009.

17. M. Dayan, *Milestones*, p. 88.

18. Ibid.

19. Minutes, Delegates Conference, July 23, 1950, File 2463/2, Israel State Archive, Jerusalem.

20. The document is included in the chief of General Staff Bureau logbook for January 27, 1958, IDF Archive, Tel Ha Shomer, Israel.

## Chapter 4: To the Top

1. Moshe Dayan, *Milestones: An Autobiography* (Avnei Derekh: Autobiographia) (Jerusalem, 1976), p. 98.

2. Moshe Dayan, *Living with the Bible* (Lihiot Im ha Tanach) (Jerusalem, 1978), p. 9 (Hebrew).

3. See, for instance, File 1034/425/1965, IDF Archive, Tel Ha Shomer, Israel.

4. After her marriage, she changed her surname to Barnoach; here she is referred to as Neora Matalon or Neora.

5. Neora Matalon-Barnoach, *A Good Spot on the Side* (Makom Tov ba-Tzad) (Tel Aviv, 2009), p. 21 (Hebrew).

6. Shabtai Teveth, *Moshe Dayan* (Tel Aviv, 1971), p. 376 (Hebrew).

7. Moshe Dayan, "Military Activity in Peacetime [Pe'ilut Tzva'it bi-Y'mei Shalom]," *Ba'Mahaneh* (September 5, 1955).

8. Dayan's article appeared with modifications in the soldiers' weekly *Ba'Mahaneh*, in the monthly review for IDF officers, and in the professional organ *Ma'arakhot* (Campaigns). An English version appeared in the U.S. journal *Foreign Affairs*. The quote in the text is from the Hebrew monthly review of August 1955, pp. 8-11.

9. Moshe Dayan, *Milestones: An Autobiography* (Avnei Derekh: Autobiographia) (Jerusalem, 1976), p. 114 (Hebrew).

10. For a good review of Arab infiltration during 1949-53, see Benny Morris, *Israeli Border Wars, 1949-1956: Arab Infiltration, Israeli Retaliation, and the Countdown to the Suez War* (Oxford, 1993), pp. 200-226.

11. Yaël Dayan, *My Father, His Daughter* (Tel Aviv, 1985), p. 99 (Hebrew). The book was also published in English, but I have translated the passages quoted in this book from the Hebrew source.

12. Moshe Sharett, *Personal Diary* (Yoman Ishi) (Tel Aviv, 1978), vol. 1, p. 29, entry for October 12, 1953 (Hebrew).

13. The two memoirs were *Milestones* and his first book, *Diary of the Sinai Campaign* (Yoman Ma'arekhet Sinai) (Tel Aviv, 1965).

14. Sharett, *Personal Diary*, vol. 6, p. 840.

## Chapter 5: Gathering Clouds

1. Moshe Dayan, *Milestones: An Autobiography* (Avnei Derekh: Autobiographia) (Jerusalem, 1976), p. 143 (Hebrew).

2. Ibid., p. 122.

3. Transcript of Dayan's lecture at a conference of senior commanders, January 15, 1956, author's personal files; also available in the IDF Archive, Tel Ha Shomer, Israel.

4. See the chief of General Staff's review at the GHQ meeting of April 18, 1955, IDF Archive.

5. M. Dayan, *Milestones*, p. 151.

6. Minutes of meeting of September 30, 1955, Protocol File, Ben-Gurion Archive, Ben-Gurion Center, Sde Boker, Israel.

7. Interview with Ruth Dayan, June 2009.

8. The telegram is cited in M. Dayan, *Milestones*, p. 154. Ben-Gurion was popularly known as the "Old Man."

9. M. Dayan, *Milestones*, p. 566.

10. Interview with Rachel Dayan, January 26, 2009, Tel Aviv.

11. Chief of General Staff Bureau logbook [hereafter CGS Bureau logbook], November 5, 1955, IDF Archive, Tel Ha Shomer, Israel.

12. Ibid., November 13, 1955; also quoted in M. Dayan, *Milestones*, p. 164.

13. M. Dayan, *Milestones*, p. 165.

14. Minutes of the meeting of the Senior Forum, November 17, 1955, IDF Archive.

15. Moshe Sharett, *Personal Diary* (Yoman Ishi) (Tel Aviv, 1978), vol. 4, p. 1307, entry for December 12, 1955.

16. Telegram from Moshe Sharett to Director General of the Ministry of Foreign Affairs, File 2455/4, Israel State Archive, Jerusalem.

17. Minutes of the meeting of the Senior Forum, December 15, 1955, IDF Archive.

18. Minutes of the meeting of the Senior Forum, January 5, 1956, IDF Archive.

19. Minutes of Ben-Gurion's speech to the High Command, Ben-Gurion Archive, Ben-Gurion Center, Sde Boker, Israel. Part of Ben-Gurion's speech is cited in M. Dayan, *Milestones*, pp. 174–75.

## Chapter 6: On the Edge of the International Storm

1. Moshe Dayan, "Facts to Assess the Situation of 1956" (Hebrew), mimeographed document handed out to senior IDF officers. A copy is in the author's possession.

2. Minutes of conference of senior military staff, March 8, 1956, IDF Archive, Tel Ha Shomer, Israel.

3. CGS Bureau logbook, April 4, 1956, IDF Archive.

4. The eulogy is printed in Moshe Dayan, *Milestones: An Autobiography* (Avnei Derekh: Autobiographia) (Jerusalem, 1976), p. 191 (Hebrew).

5. Shimon Peres, *David's Slingshot: The Secrets of Israel's Armament* (Kela David: Sodot Ha-Hitatzmut shel Israel) (Jerusalem, 1970), p. 42 (Hebrew).

6. Maurice Challe later served as military commander in Algiers and took part in the mutiny of generals against de Gaulle. He was imprisoned but released at the end of his life because of a terminal illness.

7. M. Dayan, *Milestones*, p. 207.

8. Minutes of meeting of Ben-Gurion, Dayan, and Shimon Peres, June 27, 1956, Ben-Gurion Archive, Ben-Gurion Center, Sde Boker, Israel.

9. Minutes of meeting of Ben-Gurion, Dayan, and Shimon Peres, July 10, 1956, Ben-Gurion Archive.

10. Ben-Gurion Diaries, entry of August 2, 1956, Ben-Gurion Archive.

11. Shabtai Teveth, *Moshe Dayan* (Tel Aviv, 1971), p. 454 (Hebrew).

12. M. Dayan, *Milestones*, p. 377.

13. CGS Bureau logbook, September 12, 1956.

14. M. Dayan, *Milestones*, p. 229.

15. Ibid., p. 228.

16. Ibid., p. 230.

17. Ibid., p. 235.

18. Ibid., pp. 243-44.

## Chapter 7: On the Front Line

1. Moshe Dayan, *Diary of the Sinai Campaign* (Yoman Maarekhet Sinai) (Tel Aviv, 1956), pp. 40-41 (Hebrew).

2. Anthony Eden, *Full Circle: The Memoirs of the Rt. Hon. Anthony Eden* (London, 1960), p. 512.

3. Quoted from an unpublished essay written in Hebrew by Shimon Peres a few days after the event. I would like to thank Peres for placing the document at my disposal.

4. Moshe Dayan, *Milestones: An Autobiography* (Avnei Derekh: Autobiographia) (Jerusalem, 1976), p. 253 (Hebrew).

5. Ibid.

6. The description of events at the Sèvres conference rests on my detailed minutes, entered into the CGS Bureau logbook for October 21-24, 1956, IDF Archive, Tel Ha Shomer, Israel.

7. M. Dayan, *Milestones*, p. 257.

8. CGS Bureau logbook, October 24, 1956.

9. Ben-Gurion Diaries, entry of October 23, 1956, Ben-Gurion Archive, Ben-Gurion Center, Sde Boker, Israel.

10. CGS Bureau logbook, October 25, 1956.

11. M. Dayan, *Milestones*, p. 288.

12. Ibid., p. 296.

13. Ibid., p. 311.

14. Ibid., p. 316.

15. Ibid., p. 278. This assertion was widely publicized and had several versions. Thus, for example, his daughter, Yaël, wrote: "Better to restrain a wild horse than to goad a stubborn mule" (Yaël Dayan, *My Father, His Daughter* [Tel Aviv, 1985], p. 98 [Hebrew]).

16. Mordechai Bar-On, *A Man of the Last Century* (Ben Ha'Mea She'Avra) (Jerusalem, 2011), p. 227.

17. Moshe Dayan, introduction to Nathan Alterman, *The Silver Platter: Selected Poems* (Magash ha-Kessef: Mivhar Shirim) (Tel Aviv, 1973), pp. 6-7 (Hebrew).

## Chapter 8: The End of the Military Career

1. Yaël Dayan, *My Father, His Daughter* (Tel Aviv, 1985), p. 129 (Hebrew).

2. Ruth Dayan and Helga Dudman, *And Maybe . . . The Story of Ruth Dayan* (Ve Ouly Sipura shell Ruth Dayan) (Jerusalem, 1973), p. 178 (Hebrew).

3. Interview with Rachel Dayan, January 28, 2009.

4. Dayan and Dudman, *And Maybe* . . . , p. 187.

5. Ibid., p. 189.

6. Interview with Rachel Dayan, January 28, 2009.

7. The letter is quoted in full in Y. Dayan, *My Father, His Daughter,* pp. 141–43.

8. Knesset session of November 7, 1956, *Knesset Records* (Divrei ha-Knesset) (Jerusalem), vol. 22, pp. 197–200 (Hebrew).

9. The quotation and description are taken from Dayan's report to Ben-Gurion at their meeting of December 21, 1957, which is cited in full in Moshe Dayan, *Milestones: An Autobiography* (Avnei Derekh: Autobiographia) (Jerusalem, 1976), pp. 365–72 (Hebrew).

10. CGS Bureau logbook, January 15, 1957, IDF Archive, Tel Ha Shomer, Israel.

11. Minutes of Ben-Gurion's talk with the generals are summarized in the CGS Bureau logbook, March 1, 1957, and cited in *Milestones,* p. 334.

12. CGS Bureau logbook, March 4, 1957.

13. Minutes of meeting of Ben-Gurion, Dayan, and Shimon Peres, March 15, 1957, Ben-Gurion Archive, Ben-Gurion Center, Sde Boker, Israel.

14. CGS Bureau logbook, March 5, 1957.

15. Minutes of meeting of Ben-Gurion, Dayan, and Peres, March 15, 1957.

16. CGS Bureau logbook, March 13, 1957.

17. M. Dayan, *Milestones,* p. 341.

18. Minutes of the GHQ meeting, March 10, 1957, IDF Archive.

19. M. Dayan, *Milestones,* p. 359.

20. Meir Amit, *Head On: A Personal View of Great Events and Other Affairs* (Rosh be-Rosh: Mabat Ishi al Eruim Gdolim u-Parashot Aherot) (Even Yehuda, 1999), pp. 87–88 (Hebrew).

21. The letter is quoted in full in M. Dayan, *Milestones,* pp. 375–76.

## Chapter 9: Government and Other Battles

1. Yaël Dayan, *My Father, His Daughter* (Tel Aviv, 1985), p. 102 (Hebrew).

2. Ibid., p. 103.

3. Interview with Rachel Dayan, January 28, 2009.

4. Shabtai Teveth, *Moshe Dayan* (Tel Aviv, 1971), p. 486 (Hebrew).

5. *Maariv*, May 26, 1958 (Hebrew).

6. Minutes of the Beit Berl Ideological Forum, June 7, 1958, Mapai Party Archive, Beit Berl, Tzofit, Israel.

7. *Maariv*, November 23, 1958 (Hebrew).

8. *Ha'aretz*, December 28, 1958.

9. *Davar*, December 31, 1958.

10. Neora Matalon-Barnoach, *A Good Spot on the Side* (Makom Tov ba-Tzad) (Tel Aviv, 2009), p. 75 (Hebrew).

11. Teveth, *Moshe Dayan*, p. 503.

12. Matalon-Barnoach, *Good Spot*, p. 76.

13. Teveth, *Moshe Dayan*, p. 505.

14. Moshe Dayan, *Milestones: An Autobiography* (Avnei Derekh: Autobiographia) (Jerusalem, 1976), p. 377 (Hebrew).

15. Interview with Leah Morris, February 20, 2009.

16. Knesset session of November 16, 1960, *Knesset Records* (Divrei ha-Knesset) (Jerusalem, 1961), vol. 30, pp. 245 (Hebrew).

17. Matalon-Barnoach, *Good Spot*, p. 104.

18. See, e.g., *Maariv*, July 14, 1963.

19. M. Dayan, *Milestones*, p. 388.

20. Minutes to Avihail conference, June 28, 1965, Avihail, Israel, published as a pamphlet.

21. *Ha'aretz*, June 29, 1965.

22. Teveth, *Moshe Dayan*, pp. 545–46.

23. Y. Dayan, *My Father, His Daughter*, pp. 112–13.

24. Ruth Dayan and Helga Dudman, *And Maybe . . . The Story of Ruth Dayan* (Ve Ouly Sipura shell Ruth Dayan) (Jerusalem, 1973), p. 193 (Hebrew).

25. Y. Dayan, *My Father, His Daughter*, p. 113.

26. Interview with Rachel Dayan, January 28, 2009.

27. Ibid.

28. Dayan and Dudman, *And Maybe . . .* , p. 175.

## Chapter 10: The Six Day War

1. Quoted in Arie Brown, *Personal Seal: Moshe Dayan in the Six Day War and After* (Hotam Ishi: Moshe Dayan be-Milhemet Sheshet ha-Yamim ve-Ahareha) (Tel Aviv, 1997), p. 16 (Hebrew). Brown was Dayan's military secretary.

2. Minutes of GHQ meeting, June 1, 1967, IDF Archive, Tel Ha Shomer, Israel.

3. Yitzhak Rabin, *Service Book* (Pinkas Sherut) (Tel Aviv, 1979), p. 181 (Hebrew).

4. Eitan Haber, *Today a War Will Erupt: The Memoirs of Brigadier General Israel Lior, the Military Secretary of Prime Ministers Levi Eshkol and Golda Meir* (Hayom Tifretz Milhama: Zikhronot Tat-Aluf Israel Lior, Ha' Mazkir Ha, Tsvais shel Rashei Ha'Memshala Levi Eshkol ve Golda Meir) (Jerusalem, 1987), pp. 212–13 (Hebrew). Colonel Israel Lior was Eshkol's military secretary.

5. Moshe Dayan, *Milestones: An Autobiography* (Avnei Derekh: Autobiographia) (Jerusalem, 1976), p. 423.

6. Michael B. Oren, *Six Days of War: June 1967 and the Making of the Modern Middle East* (New York, 2002).

7. M. Dayan, *Milestones*, p. 426.

8. Ibid., p. 433.

9. Oren, *Six Days*, p. 176.

10. Yaël Dayan, *My Father, His Daughter* (Tel Aviv, 1985), p. 133 (Hebrew).

11. Rabin, *Service Book*, p. 191.

12. Quoted from the minutes by Shimon Golan in *War on Three Fronts* (Milhama be-Shalosh Hazitot) (Tel Aviv, 2007), p. 236 (Hebrew).

13. Brown, *Personal Seal*, p. 64.

14. Dayan's words appeared in all the Israeli newspapers of Thursday, June 8, 1967.

15. Haber, *Today a War Will Erupt*, p. 234.
16. Y. Erez and I. Kfir, *Conversations with Moshe Dayan* (Sihot im Moshe Dayan) (Givatayim, 1981), p. 50 (Hebrew).
17. M. Dayan, *Milestones*, p. 475.
18. Brown, *Personal Seal*, p. 88.
19. Rabin, *Service Book*, p. 199.
20. Haber, *Today a War Will Erupt*, p. 251.
21. M. Dayan, *Milestones*, p. 475.
22. The chronology is recounted in Brown, *Personal Seal*, p. 95.
23. M. Dayan, *Milestones*, p. 480.
24. Ezer Weizman, *Yours Is the Sky, Yours the Land* (Lekha Shamayim, Lekha Aretz) (Tel Aviv, 1975), p. 265 (Hebrew).

## Chapter 11: Occupation Policies

1. Moshe Dayan, *Milestones: An Autobiography* (Avnei Derekh: Autobiographia) (Jerusalem, 1976), p. 494 (Hebrew). Zion Square was the main square in the western city.
2. Ibid., pp. 492–93.
3. Yossi Goldstein, *Eshkol: A Biography* (Levi Eshkol—Biographia) (Jerusalem, 2003), p. 586 (Hebrew).
4. Dayan first said this in a speech in Tel Aviv on November 30, 1967. He cites the speech in Moshe Dayan, *A New Map, Different Relations* (Mapa Hadasha—Yahasim Aherim) (Tel Aviv, 1969), p. 17 (Hebrew).
5. Ibid., p. 173.
6. M. Dayan, *Milestones*, p. 495.
7. Arie Brown, *Personal Seal: Moshe Dayan in the Six Day War and After* (Hotam Ishi: Moshe Dayan be-Milhemet Sheshet ha-Yamim ve-Ahareha) (Tel Aviv, 1997), p. 112 (Hebrew).
8. The radio broadcast was on December 28, 1968, and it is quoted in Dayan, *New Map*, p. 135.
9. Shlomo Gazit, *Trapped: Thirty Years of Israeli Policy in the Territories* (Peta'im ba-Malkodet: 30 Shnot Midiniyut Israel ba-Shtahim) (Tel Aviv, 1999), p. 61 (Hebrew).

10. Ibid., p. 62.

11. See below.

12. Tom Segev, *1967: And the Land Changed Its Face* (1967: Ve'ha'arets Shinta at Paneiha) (Jerusalem, 2005), p. 412 (Hebrew).

13. Conversation with Joseph Geva, April 3, 2007.

14. Gazit, *Trapped*, p. 67.

15. Abu Ayad, *Without a Homeland: Talks with Eric Rouleau* (Lelo Moledet: Sihot im Eric Rouleau) (Jerusalem, 1979), p. 98 (Hebrew).

16. M. Dayan, *Milestones*, p. 532.

17. Interview with Rachel Dayan, January 28, 2009.

18. Yaël Dayan, *My Father, His Daughter* (Tel Aviv, 1985), p. 146.

19. M. Dayan, *Milestones*, p. 513.

20. Ibid., p. 514.

21. Ibid., p. 518.

22. Ibid., p. 522.

## Chapter 12: Controversies

1. Moshe Dayan, *Milestones: An Autobiography* (Avnei Derekh: Autobiographia) (Jerusalem, 1976), p. 526 (Hebrew).

2. Ibid., p. 548.

3. Ibid., p. 551.

4. Ibid., p. 566.

5. Yaël Dayan, *My Father, His Daugher* (Tel Aviv, 1985), p. 151; Ruth Dayan and Helga Dudman, *And Maybe . . . The Story of Ruth Dayan* (Ve Ouly Sipura shell Ruth Dayan) (Jerusalem, 1973), pp. 7, 11 (Hebrew).

6. Interview with Ruth Dayan, June 2009.

7. M. Dayan, *Milestones*, p. 534.

8. Interview with Trude Dothan, April 4, 2009.

## Chapter 13: Yom Kippur

1. Arie Brown, *Moshe Dayan in the Yom Kippur War* (Moshe Dayan be-Milhemet Yom ha-Kippurim) (Tel-Aviv, 1997), pp.

28-29 (Hebrew). Lt. Col. Arie Brown was Dayan's military adjutant and managed his personal diary.

2. The Hebrew word *mehdal* was a new term that soon came to symbolize the criticism leveled at the leadership for its blunders in the Yom Kippur War.

3. The radio broadcast was also reported in all the major newspapers the next day.

4. Moshe Dayan, *Milestones: An Autobiography* (Avnei Derekh: Autobiographia) (Jerusalem, 1976), p. 598 (Hebrew).

5. The testimony of the air force commander in this regard appears reliable: Dayan himself confirmed it in an interview toward the end of his life. See Yaakov Erez, *Talks with Moshe Dayan* (Sihot im Moshe Dayan) (Tel Aviv, 1981) (Hebrew).

6. Brown, *Dayan in the Yom Kippur War*, p. 98.

7. Ibid., p. 101.

8. M. Dayan, *Milestones*, p. 600.

9. Naphtali Lavie was a senior journalist who on July 1, 1970, answered Dayan's call to serve as the spokesman of the minister's bureau and filled the position until Dayan's resignation as minister of defense. The quotation is from Lavie's memoirs, *A Nation Like a Lion* (Am ke-Lavie) (Or-Yehuda, 1994), p. 278 (Hebrew).

10. Brown, *Dayan in the Yom Kippur War*, p. 141.

11. Brown, *Dayan in the Yom Kippur War*.

12. M. Dayan, *Milestones*, p. 620. Meir, in her memoirs, recounts that Dayan had offered to resign on the first day of the war. She adds that she had never regretted spurning the offer. See Golda Meir, *My Life* (Hayai) (Tel Aviv, 1975), p. 312 (Hebrew).

13. For a detailed description of Kissinger's maneuvering, see Matti Golan, *The Secret Conversations of Henry Kissinger* (Ha-Sihot ha-Sodiot shel Henry Kissinger) (Jerusalem, 1976) (Hebrew). The book was also published in English, but I have translated the passages quoted in this book from the Hebrew source.

14. Brown, *Dayan in the Yom Kippur War*.

## Chapter 14: In the Crucible

1. Golda Meir, *My Life* (Hayai) (Tel Aviv, 1975), p. 321 (Hebrew).

2. Moshe Dayan, *Milestones: An Autobiography* (Avnei Derekh: Autobiographia) (Jerusalem, 1976), p. 663 (Hebrew).

3. These details appear in Matti Golan, *The Secret Conversations of Henry Kissinger* (Ha-Sihot ha-Sodiot shel Henry Kissinger), pp. 163 and 169 (Hebrew).

4. *Ha'aretz*, January 19, 1974. The document was written in English and appeared in English in the newspaper.

5. *The Agranat Commission Preliminary Report* (Jerusalem, 1974) (Hebrew).

6. The texts of the signs are cited in Motti Ashkenazi, *War Will Break Out This Evening at Six* (Ha-Erev be-Shesh Tifrotz Milhama) (Tel Aviv, 2003), p. 151 (Hebrew).

7. Ibid., p. 173. Dayan's reaction is in *Milestones*, p. 729.

8. M. Dayan, *Milestones*, p. 727.

9. *The Agranat Commission Preliminary Report*, pp. 34-43.

10. Ibid., pp. 45-49.

11. Meir, *My Life*, p. 332.

12. M. Dayan, *Milestones*, pp. 721-22.

13. Ibid., p. 737.

14. Ibid., pp. 737-38.

15. Neora Matalon-Barnoach, *A Good Spot on the Side* (Makom Tov ba-Tzad) (Tel Aviv, 2009), p. 228. *Milestones* was published in 1976 by a distinguished Israeli publishing house.

16. Moshe Dayan, *Living with the Bible* (Lihiot Im ha Tanacho) (Jerusalem, 1978), p. 202 (Hebrew).

17. Interview with Rachel Dayan, June 29, 2009.

18. Naphtali Lavie, *A Nation Like a Lion* (Am ke-Lavie) (Or-Yehuda, 1994), p. 306 (Hebrew).

## Chapter 15: "Shall the Sword Devour Forever?"

1. The description is from Ezer Weizman, *The War for Peace—Personal Observations* (Ha-Krav al ha-Shalom—Tazpit Ishit) (Jerusalem, 1981), p. 90 (Hebrew).

2. Arye Naor, *Begin as Ruler* (Begin ba-Shilton) (Tel Aviv, 1993), pp. 49–50 (Hebrew). Naor was Begin's cabinet secretary.

3. Moshe Dayan, *Shall the Sword Devour Forever? Peace Talks—Personal Impressions* (Ha-la-Netzah Tokhal Herev? Sihot Shalom—Reshamim Ishiim) (Jerusalem, 1981), p. 18 (Hebrew).

4. Interview with Rachel Dayan, June 29, 2009.

5. M. Dayan, *Shall the Sword?* p. 26.

6. Naphtali Lavie kept a logbook, which he cites in his memoir *A Nation Like a Lion* (Am ke-Lavie) (Or-Yehuda, 1994) (Hebrew). Rubinstein published a memoir about this period, *Roads of Peace* (Darkhei Shalom) (Tel Aviv, 1992) (Hebrew).

7. Lavie, *Nation Like a Lion*, p. 324.

8. Ibid., pp. 329–30.

9. Ibid., p. 334. While speaking, he pointed at Lavie, who was a survivor of the Holocaust.

10. Egypt's foreign minister, Ismail Fahmi, had resigned in protest over Sadat's visit to Jerusalem and was temporarily replaced by his deputy, Boutros-Ghali.

11. Elyakim Rubinstein was in the vehicle and describes the conversation in *Roads of Peace*, p. 50.

12. M. Dayan, *Shall the Sword?* p. 96.

13. On the liaison office in Cairo, see the book by his strategic affairs adviser, who headed the operation: Avraham Tamir, *Peace-Loving Soldier* (Hayal Shoher Shalom) (Tel Aviv, 1988) (Hebrew).

14. Weizman's remarks appeared in *Yedioth Ahronoth*, April 12, 1978.

15. M. Dayan, *Shall the Sword?* pp. 119–20.

16. Lavie, *Nation Like a Lion*, p. 362.

17. M. Dayan, *Shall the Sword?* pp. 124–25.

18. Ibid., p. 132.

19. Ibid., p. 158.

20. Ibid., p. 201.
21. Ibid., p. 204.
22. Ibid., p. 217.
23. Ibid., p. 223.

## Chapter 16: Sunset

1. Moshe Dayan, *Shall the Sword Devour Forever? Peace Talks—Personal Impressions* (Ha-la-Netzah Tokhal Herev? Sihot Shalom—Reshamim Ishiim) (Jerusalem, 1981), p. 233 (Hebrew).
2. Interview with Rachel Dayan, June 29, 2009.
3. Cited in Nathan Yanai, ed., *Moshe Dayan on the Peace Process and the Future of Israel* (Moshe Dayan al Tahalikh ha-Shalom ve-Atida shel Yisrael) (Tel Aviv, 1988), pp. 157–58 (Hebrew).
4. The book, *Shall the Sword Devour Forever?*, was published in the summer of 1981, a few weeks before Dayan's death.
5. Interview with Rachel Dayan, June 29, 2009.
6. Yaël Dayan, *My Father, His Daughter* (Tel Aviv, 1985), p. 180 (Hebrew).
7. Ibid., p. 185.
8. His positions are cited in full in Yanai, *Dayan on the Peace Process:* see the Seventh Conference, May 26, 1979, pp. 151–54; the Eighth Conference, November 10, 1979, pp. 163–77; and particularly the Ninth Conference, May 17, 1980, pp. 185–96.
9. Knesset session of December 24, 1980, *Knesset Records* (Divrei ha-Knesset) (Jerusalem, 1981), vol. 90, pp. 975–76 (Hebrew).
10. Yanai, *Dayan on the Peace Process,* pp. 152–53.
11. Interview with Rachel Dayan, June 29, 2009.
12. Ibid.
13. Ehud Ben-Ezer, *Courage: The Story of Moshe Dayan* (Ometz: Sipuro shel Moshe Dayan) (Tel Aviv, 1997), p. 321 (Hebrew).
14. Ibid., p. 324.
15. Ibid.

## Chapter 17: Legacy

1. Avner Falk, *Moshe Dayan, the Man and the Legend: A Psychological Biography* (Moshe Dayan, Ha'Ish ve Ha'agada: Biographia Pshycho'analitit) (Jerusalem, 1986) (Hebrew).

2. These words are from a Hebrew poem he wrote to his children and Rachel not long before his death. Rachel Dayan gave the author a copy of the poem.

# INDEX

INDEX

Sinai campaign (1956) (continued)
ment violations (1967) and, 125–26;
French munitions and, 78; successful conclusion of, 96, 101
Sinai Desert, 160
Sinai Peninsula, 42; Egyptian-Israeli
peace process and, 201, 202; Egyptian troop deployment (1967) in,
126; Israeli occupation of, viii, 67,
97, 130–36, 154, 165; Israeli withdrawal (1956) from, 104–5; U.N.
Emergency Force in, 101, 102, 106,
107
Six Day War (1967), 125–40, 159, 161,
164, 216; ceasefire lines and, 144,
145; conquered territories of (see
occupied territories); Dayan's acclaim from, 135, 136, 140; Dayan's
autobiography on, 190; Egyptian
defeat in, 140, 147, 151; Egyptian
provocation of, 125–26; end of, 140,
147; iconic image of, 135; as Israeli
surprise, 129–31; Israel's major objective in, 129; Israel's victory, viii,
ix; Rabin's military importance to,
140; Syrian front advocates, 129, 134,
137–38; territorial expansion from,
viii, 141–54, 155–56; U.N. ceasefire
and, 138
Sixth Fleet (U.S.), 179
Smilansky, Yizhar (nom de plume), 114
Southern Command (Israel Defense
Forces), 42–45, 93, 97; Six Day War
and, 126, 133, 134–35; Yom Kippur
War and, 172, 175–76, 177, 186
Soviet Union, 97, 139, 164, 183; Egyptian arms aid and, 62–63, 151, 153,
166; Egyptian-Israeli peace process and, 195, 196, 197, 198; Syrian
ties with, 129, 138, 139, 151, 166; U.S.
détente with, 168; Yom Kippur War
and, 178, 179
Stern Gang. See Israel Freedom
Fighters
Suez Canal, viii, 95, 96, 129, 165, 182,
199; Bar-Lev Line and, 152–53, 156–
57, 169–70, 171, 185, 199; blockage

of Israeli passage through, 54, 60;
Egyptian missiles repositioning at,
154; international passage through,
155, 156, 178, 182, 191; Israeli mili-
tary approach to, 133, 136; Israeli
withdrawal from, 155, 156, 178, 180;
Nasser nationalization of, 79–80, 87;
Yom Kippur War and, 154, 169, 171,
172, 175, 176, 177, 178
Suez crisis (1956), 79–80, 82–84,
86–98; Israeli Sinai strategy and, 92;
Sèvres summit and, 87–89, 90, 91,
92. See also Sinai campaign
Suez Gulf, 96, 202
Syria, 22, 23, 46, 67–68, 151; Israeli
War of Independence and, 31–32; Six
Day War and, viii, 129, 134, 137–40;
Soviet ties with, 129, 138, 139, 151,
166; Yom Kippur War and, 166, 171,
172–73, 175. See also Golan Heights

Tal, Abdullah al-, 37–38
Tal, Israel, 126
Tel Aviv, 12, 16, 33, 34, 38, 59, 74, 111,
200
Telem Party, 211
Temple Mount, 40, 132, 135
Tet Offensive (1968), 124
Teveth, Shabtai, ix–x
Tiran, Straits of, 65, 125, 129, 135
Tohami, Hassan el-, 195, 199
Tokan, Qadri, 145
tomato farming, 117–18
Tomb of the Patriarchs (Hebron),
136–37
Touqan, Fadwa, 145, 216
Tsemah, 4, 5, 31, 32

United Jewish Appeal, 182
United Nations, 37, 39, 43, 51, 139;
Dayan address to, 196; Egyptian-
Israeli ceasefire, 62; Egyptian-
Israeli tensions and, 72, 73, 76; Jerusalem
headquarters of, 36, 37, 132; Jewish
independent state and, 31, 32, 40;
partition of Palestine by, 30; Sinai
ceasefire, 96, 101, 102, 104; Sinai

*Groucho Marx*, by Lee Siegel

*J. Robert Oppenheimer,* by David Rieff

*Marcel Proust*, by Benjamin Taylor

*Rashi*, by Jack Miles

*Mark Rothko*, by Annie Cohen-Solal

*Ludwig Wittgenstein*, by Anthony Gottlieb